THE
NORTH NORFOLK
COAST

Steam, fields and sea: the North Norfolk Railway.

THE

NORTH NORFOLK
COAST

F<small>RANK</small> M<small>EERES</small>

Phillimore

2010
Published by
PHILLIMORE & CO. LTD,
Andover, Hampshire, England

© Frank Meeres, 2010

ISBN 978 1 86077 626 7

This book is dedicated to the memory of my half-brother,
Harold Fox,
of Leicester University (1945-2007),
il miglior fabbro.

He knew and loved those landscapes between sea and shore,
where 'ends the land suddenly beyond a beach
Of shapes and shingle. Here is unforced existence:
Facing the sun, untalkative, out of reach'

(Philip Larkin, from 'Here')

Printed and bound in Malta.
Manufacturing managed by
Jellyfish Print Solutions Ltd

Contents

List of Illustrations

ONE

The Prehistoric Landscape

THE LANDSCAPE of the north Norfolk coast, 'this indeterminate and empty / quarter, this mesh of sanding and marsh and creek', seems peaceful enough to any observer, but this is just one moment in a dramatic process of change that has gone on for more than 600 million years – and is still going on. At times the area has been high land, at other times many yards beneath the sea, changes that are reflected in what we see today. East Anglia ultimately rests on a platform of very ancient rocks, which shelve steeply to the north, from about 875 yards below present ground level at North Creake to 1,093 yards beneath Blakeney Point. These rocks reflect a very different landscape: 'far from being the lowland of England at this time (between 325 and 280 million years ago) East Anglia was part of the Highlands'.[1]

The best place to see later developments is to stand on the beach at Hunstanton and look back at the cliffs: they form a 'sandwich', with a layer of brown stone at the bottom, a thin red layer above it, and a thick white layer at the top. Here we can see more than one hundred million years of history. All the rocks in the Hunstanton cliffs were formed at times when the area was beneath the sea. The earliest, and therefore the lowest, in the cliff, arose in the Lower Cretaceous period: the sea at that time spread over the northern part of East Anglia and laid down deposits of sand which solidified to form carstone, the brown stone making the bottom piece of bread of the Hunstanton sandwich. In later centuries, about one hundred million years ago, the sea covered the whole area, leaving the deposits that make up the 'jam' of the sandwich – a one-yard-thick layer of reddish limestone.

Over the next 35 million years, there was a rise in sea level of some one hundred yards. The plankton type that lived in the sea left skeletal remains which sank to the seabed, gradually solidifying to form chalk. This was an unbelievably slow process – the sediment accumulated at a rate of just 0.2 inches every thousand years, but over millions of years the chalk layer became 440 yards thick, although it has since eroded. This chalk is the upper slice of the Hunstanton sandwich. It slopes away to the east, where it has since been overlaid by later deposits. In the sea were larger sponge-like creatures, whose remains also fell to the bottom and eventually formed

1   *Hunstanton beach – rock pools and the famous striped cliffs.*

2   *Erosion of the cliffs at Hunstanton.*

very hard nodules of rock within the chalk: these are flints.

Some 65 million years ago, there were great changes throughout the world: this is when dinosaurs became extinct and mammals replaced reptiles as the predominant life-form on earth. The chalk-making sea receded and Norfolk enjoyed a semi-tropical climate for the last time – so far, at least! Deposits such as those of the Cromer Forest Bed formation, which is exposed at intervals along the coast of Norfolk and Suffolk, between Weybourne and Kessingland, show rich collections of marine molluscs and plant life not unlike those of present-day Norfolk, but also many no longer found – elephant, rhinoceros, hippopotamus, bear and elk. This must have been a very different environment then, and one that lasted for many millions of years.

North Norfolk's first famous inhabitant is not a man but the West Runton elephant, a mammoth found at the base of the cliffs in 1990 after seas had eroded the cliff, around 600,000 to 700,000 years after it had died: a male, 13 feet

3   *An early inhabitant: the West Runton elephant.*

high at the shoulder, about 40 years old and weighing about eleven tons. Apart from the very largest of the dinosaurs, this is the largest animal ever to have lived on land. The Runton example is the most complete elephant skeleton ever found as well as the largest. It is probable that he died after becoming caught in a shallow swampy river channel: his carcass was scavenged by hyenas whose teeth marks can be seen on some of the bones. He was found within the Cromer Forest Bed. There is an information board at West Runton showing the elephant, and he also features in the Cromer Museum.

THE ICE AGES

Very important later developments have also shaped this coast, creating a large number of fascinating and varied landscape features, many now havens for wildlife. A series of ice ages over the last 300,000 years produced huge glaciers that pushed debris in front of them. There have been three of these, each one reaching just a little less far than the one before, so that some features caused by each wave of ice can still be seen along this coast. In between were periods of much warmer temperatures, known as inter-glacials.

The first Ice Age, the Anglian, was about three hundred thousand years ago. The ice sheet advanced south and west from Scandinavia, pushing in front of it rocks from that region and chalk and flint from the floor of the North Sea. These glacial deposits now make up the cliffs of north-east Norfolk, from Weybourne to Mundesley. Incorporated into them, from Sidestrand to East Runton, are great rafts of chalk, lifted tens of yards above their natural level by the power of this great glacier. This deposit of material at the southern limit of a glacier used to be called a terminal moraine, but is now more usually called a push moraine, a more accurate term as the ice pushed up the already existing strata as well as depositing the material that it carried with it. Beyond the moraine are outwash plains (known as sandurs), produced by the melt-water from the glacier, which deposited gravels as it flowed southwards; the plains are made of sands with layers of coarse gravels inclining gently southwards. The easternmost plain ends with steep slopes overlooking the Gunton Beck near Roughton, and the western one overlooks the Scarrow Beck near Gresham. A later phase of this glaciation pushed from the north and west, spreading chalky deposits over most of the county. These sands are now covered by later boulder clay, except in some of the deeper valleys where the latter has been washed away. Otherwise, the ridge of the Hunstanton scarp is the only part of the north coast region that is free of glacial-drift soils.

As the earth became warmer, the ice melted and sea levels rose, altering the borders between land and sea. The second wave of glaciation occurred about 130,000 years ago. The glaciers again just reached what is now the Norfolk coast. They produced features which, although not as dramatic as the cliffs of the first glaciation, are characteristic of the area. First are the gravel outwash plains of Kelling and Salthouse. The Kelling gravel spread begins at Muckleburgh Hill and Telegraph Hill, extends southwards at a low gradient through Holt and ends at Hunworth, with its eastern margin overlooking the upper Glaven Valley in Edgefield Heath – subsequent erosion has left Muckleburgh Hill as an isolated hill, or 'outlier'. The Salthouse sandur extends from Bard Hill as far as the valley known as The Hangs. The outwash that created these plains escaped southwards through a gap in the Cromer Ridge at Briston.

At about the same elevation as the Salthouse sandur, 65 yards above sea level, are detached patches of gravel lying on both sides of the Glaven. These form a second feature, the 'kames' of the Glaven valley and the nearby area, irregular mounds left by the melting of an ice sheet. They are flat-topped hills, a little like giant mole-hills; Beeston Bump, just east of Sheringham, is the most dramatic. The third feature is the Blakeney 'esker', best seen at Wiveton Down. It extends for about two miles from north-west of Glandford across the western watershed of the Glaven valley to Morston. This was once the bed of a river flowing underneath a glacier. As the climate warmed, the edge of the glacier retreated north and the material carried by the river was left behind as a long ridge of sand and gravel.

The ice age once more gave way to a period of warmer climate and higher sea levels. A low cliff at the northern edge of the chalk hills of the North Coast mainland was formed at this time. It was much lowered by the later ice age, but it can still be seen as a feature of the coast along the 25 miles between Holme and Weybourne, especially in the eastern half: Wells Quay is on the cliff and it can also be seen in low features at Warham, Stiffkey and Morston. From Cley to Salthouse the A149 follows the line of the cliff and at Weybourne the chalk can be seen at the base of the more recent cliffs above. The raised beach still to be seen at Morston (just to the north-west of the

4 *The Blakeney 'esker' at Wiveton Downs.*

village) was probably formed by the sea at this time: it lies between earlier glacial deposits and the deposits of Hunstanton till described below.

In the most recent wave of glaciation, the Devensian, a mere 18,000 years ago, the ice did not reach as far south as Norfolk but it still had its effects as the ground was permanently frozen. A tongue of ice did just touch the Norfolk coast in the extreme west, depositing the soil known as Hunstanton till, which occurs between Heacham and Morston, is brown in colour and includes erratics from the Cheviot area of northern England; it forms low ground at the foot of chalk slopes or in the valley bottoms. The drift only occurs inland where the coastal relief is low, as in the small river valleys draining into the North Sea.

Ringstead Downs is a steep, curved valley created by water overflowing from a small glacial lake at the south end of what is now Hunstanton Park, and is now a beautiful nature reserve. As the ice retreated slowly north it left behind another feature that is still visible, the Hunstanton Park esker, a 1.2-mile-long sinuous ridge, laid down within ice and settling as the ice melted; some of the smaller material in the esker originated in Scandinavia.

This glaciation produced another feature that is still visible today – the lower Stiffkey valley. The present valley is long and winding eastwards, reaching the North Sea west of Morston. It is very likely that originally the river flowed due north, between Warham St Mary and Warham All Saints, and reached the sea east of Wells; the course was blocked during the last ice age, forcing the water to flow eastwards to find a route to the sea.

For the last 11,000 years the ice has been in retreat as the temperature has risen. East Anglia slowly became covered in oak forest. About 5,000 years ago there was another rise in sea levels and parts of the coast disappeared under the sea, with their trees: these are the 'drowned forests' off the present coast-line of north Norfolk. The Roman coastline was on average two miles north of the present coastline.

5 *Ringstead Downs in summer.*

6   *General view of the sand dunes at Blakeney Point.*

COASTAL CHANGE: THE LAST MILLENNIUM

For more recent events, it is best to go to the central part of the coast, perhaps to Blakeney. The effects here are caused by currents in the sea. The natural current in the North Sea runs south, hitting the Norfolk coast at the easily eroded glacial cliffs east of Cromer and then being forced westward, depositing material alongside the coast as it travels. These deposits mean the build-up of sandy spits and bars, Blakeney Point and Scolt Head being the two most dramatic. This tends to block the mouths of the rivers of north Norfolk, forcing them to turn westwards before they can find a way through the sands to the sea. E.A.M. Powell describes the scene:

> Between the cliffs at the east and west ends of the coast, lie the marshes; take any large scale map you like, and running out to sea between Blakeney and Cley, passing Wiveton, beneath whose churchyard wall, now some distance from the river, may still be seen the rings to which returning sea-going boats were wont once to tie up, you will observe a river whose meandering course leads it finally to the sea at Blakeney Point. This is the focal point of the wide area, and its construction is important.
>
> Once this river met the sea at what is now Cley beach, but silt brought down by it, meeting the contrary force of winds and tides, or, as some suggest, deposits washed westward by the strong inshore currents from the cliff erosions taking place further eastward, in course of time deflected the river's course, and gradually its outlet moved further and further west. As it shifted, so the tongue of land between it and the sea – really a continuation of Cley beach itself – moved westward, until today we have a long promontory, some six miles long in all, and still yearly growing longer, the only direct access to which is a tongue of land some 50–100 yards wide at the Cley end. Eastward of Cley beach lie the Salthouse marshes – westward at the other end of the promontory is Blakeney point – both today properties of the National Trust and preserved forever from the hand of the spoiler – and inland from the Point vast areas of rough grazing intersected with dykes, strangely like their counterparts in Holland, and indeed wrested from the sea by Dutch Engineers in the eighteenth century.[2]

The sands along the coast are often marked on maps as 'Meals', a word also found on the Lincolnshire coast where it is more commonly spelled 'meols'. In 1853 it was said that 'Brancaster Meals, Blakeney Meals and Wells Meals are among those most dreaded by the mariner'. The *Oxford Dialect Dictionary* refers to 'the fascinating but little known region of the "meal marshes" belonging more to land than sea, but wholly under the dominion of the salt water, which intersects them in creeks broad and narrow, and at spring tides floods the whole', and refers specifically to low sandy land lying between Holkham and Blakeney.

Today, the coast and the land behind it make up four very different regions. Along the coast itself is the alluvial plain, 25 miles long and up to two miles wide. This is the most recent part of the landscape, accumulating over the last 1,000 years as sediments were deposited by the rivers at their mouths, and as material was deposited along the coast by the sea. The process has been speeded up over the last 400 years by human activity: farmers have built ditches and walls to hold back the sea and turn marshes into grazing grounds. As David Dymond wrote:

> the area is a fascinating blend of freshwater marshes, mainly grazed by cattle, of salt marshes and winding muddy creeks which are famed for the richness of their birdlife, and subtly curved islands and spits of shingle and sand. Most of the local villages, which lie well behind the alluvial strip, have little harbours or 'staithes' connected by winding channels to the open sea.[3]

Behind this, from Holme to Weybourne, are the northern fringes of what Arthur Young in the 18th century first called the 'Good Sands' region. The land is a region of rolling upland with chalk at the surface or covered by light glacial soils of a sandy or loamy texture. Three rivers run north to the coast – the Burn, the Stiffkey with its tributary the Binham, and the Glaven. Villages in the region tend to be four or five miles apart, with isolated farmsteads and a geometrical road system, which

7 *Seasonal weather? – Easter Bank Holiday in Hunstanton.*

Dymond saw as 'a curious overlapping of rectangles and "spokes" radiating from the principal villages'.

To the west and east of the alluvial plain are cliffs. To the west is the Western Escarpment reaching the sea at Hunstanton. The scarp is at its highest at the coast and is broken up by several rivers draining into the fens. Villages tend to be on the flanks of the ridge and the 'Icknield Way' runs along the higher ground beyond the heads of the small marshy valleys; the way is probably best visualised as a series of winding tracks connecting villages rather than one continuous long-distance way, but it could have been used for the latter purpose. The origin of the word 'Icknield' is not known: it is first found in documents in the early 10th century. To the east is the Holt-Cromer ridge, made up basically of glacial deposits. The highest parts of Norfolk are Roman Camp behind Sheringham and Beacon Hill near West Runton; the actual highest point is 335 feet above sea level. Much of the area is woodland, but there are areas of high sandy heathland. Dymond noticed 'the far more intricate landscape of the ridge with its snaking roads, tumulus-haunted heaths, irregular patches of woodland, loose-knit villages and modern seaside developments'.

The shingle ridge running from Weybourne to Cley is a natural feature, although man has done some work to maintain it. At Cley, the Glaven is diverted to flow alongside the landward side of the ridge. West of this are 12 curved arms of shingle, increasing in length from east to west, the longest being about 985 feet. This is the area called the Marrams. The main bank of Blakeney Point is also a shingle ridge, 9.6 miles long, 655 feet wide and 30 feet high. It has been likened to a dilapidated comb, with the back of the comb the main ridge and the re-curved laterals the teeth. Sand dunes have accumulated on the shingle ridges near the headland and marshes between the arms of the lateral ridges. The ridge is gradually overwhelming the marshes as it is pushed inland, moving at an average rate of a yard a year – as it has

been doing for at least 350 years. Further west, Scolt Head Island forms a beach barrier between the deep channels of Burnham and Brancaster harbours. The higher parts of the island are large sand dunes, with more sand dunes extending landwards accumulated on gravel ridges between which salt marshes have developed, a low-energy shallow water environment. These marshes are completely inundated at spring tides, when Scolt Head is quite a narrow island, and at low tides it is separated from the mainland only by two narrow stretches of water, Norton Creek and Trowland Creek. As E.M. Bridges says:

8   *Scolt Head Island from the air.*

there is very good morphological evidence that Scolt Head Island has steadily moved landwards and also grown westwards as shingle has been added to the main beach ridge and then carried westwards by longshore drift. This evidence is in the form of marsh sediments which occasionally crop out when the beach is combed down, and the presence of the re-curved ridges which extend landwards from the main beach ridge. These ridges represent the former western ends of the island where the shingle ridge has been swung around the Headland by the waves to form a re-curved shingle ridge, just like the present western end of the island.[4]

At the east end of the coast, there are more cliffs but very different in character. At Weybourne the base of the cliff is white chalk, but this is below ground level further east. Above the chalk at Weybourne, and making up the whole of the cliff further east, are the deposits pushed southwards by glaciers thousands of years ago. This explains how the cliffs erode. Where there is chalk at the base this forms a relatively hard rock (compared to the soils above) for the sea, and pebbles in the sea, to attack. It slowly acts on the lower parts of the cliff, forming a wave-cut notch with an overhang. The overhang eventually collapses onto the beach. For a while this forms a natural defence, but soon it is washed away and the sea's attack on the cliff begins all over again. Many cliff collapses, however, are caused by a different process – slumping. This is caused by heavy rain which leads to the water-logging of the glacial material, which then slips down the slope onto the beach, once again acting as a natural barrier until it is washed away.

In recent centuries, people have tried to halt the onslaught of the sea, and they continue to do so. At one stage a continuous line of baskets full of shingle defended the cliffs at Weybourne, to break the force of the sea before it reached the cliffs. However, heavy scouring underneath the baskets eventually made them dangerous to people on the beach, and they were taken away in 1998. Sheringham has been protected by a sea wall for over a century, the first being erected by the Upcher family in 1895 to defend their home, Sheringham Hall; it was extended eastwards in 1900. Parts of the wall were lost during a storm on 1 February 1983, and other parts eaten away later, forming a wave-cut notch in the wall. The notch was covered in around an inch of concrete in 1988, and much of the wall was replaced by a new one in 1993-4.

A wide beach with shingle slows the sea and thus acts as a defence. The wall of 1895 has lasted better than the extension of 1900 because there is a wider beach in front of it. In 1988, some 12,000 tonnes of flint were put against the sea wall along the East Beach at Sheringham – originally they were so sharp that it was very difficult to walk on them, but attrition soon caused the flints to become smooth and round.

However, some effects often thought to be due to erosion are actually due to the Second World War. Coastguard cottages on the cliff at Weybourne were removed to allow machine-gun emplacements a wider field of fire. The word 'Sheringham' on the plaque erected by the Upchers in 1895 to commemorate their sea-wall has disappeared, not because of erosion but because it was scratched out so that invading Germans would not know where they had landed.[5]

These patterns make up the landscape of the coast, and they also determine the materials that give the shapes and colours to the churches, houses and barns that help to make the region's villages and towns so picturesque – and so unique. There is no limestone locally, so it has to be imported either from beyond the Fens or from Normandy – only the largest churches and greatest houses could afford to do this. There are three forms of local stone, each with its own distinctive character and colour. In the west of the county, above all in Hunstanton, the chief stone used in building is carstone, known to all Norfolk people as gingerbread stone – in fact its colour can vary from café au lait to deep chocolate. It can be used in rough shapes or squared into blocks.

The stone most associated with Norfolk, and especially prominent along the coast between Blakeney and Cromer, is flint. Flints are extremely hard nodules of irregular shape, which, if subject to erosion by the sea, become smooth, forming oval pebbles. Flint can be seen used in several ways. The whole stone, whether rough or rounded, can be built up in layers to form a wall: the rounded stones could simply be picked up from the beach (this is now illegal). As the flints are not square, a great deal of mortar is needed to embed the flints. When looking at a flint tower or wall, it is very often possible to see how it has been built up in layers, each layer supported by shuttering, and the mortar of that layer allowed to dry before the next layer is added on top.

Flints can also be cut in half, or knapped, producing a smooth black outer surface; the flint can then be trimmed

9   *Cliff protection work at Sheringham.*

10   *Landing party, Blakeney Point.*

11   *The work of groins, here large cases of stone, in preventing the drifting of sand.*

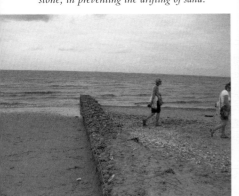

12   *Protection of the beach at Thornham.*

13 *Carstone walls and quoins: Hunstanton town hall.*

to a greater or lesser extent. The most extreme – and most expensive form – of this is to cut the stone into small squares like tiny bricks: as they are regular in shape they can be used with very little mortar. These squares of flint can be combined with another material, most commonly limestone, to create patterns known as flushwork – the gatehouse of the friary at Burnham Norton is a very early example of the technique.

The flints were originally laid down within the chalk beds that formed at the bottom of the sea. Chalk itself is a common building material along the north Norfolk coast, especially in the west: it is often known as clunch. It is a very soft stone and liable to erosion. There is plenty of brick, of course, but it is not as ubiquitous as in many other parts of England. Brick was known to the Romans, but its use then died out until the Middle Ages – some of the earliest local brick used in Norfolk is found in Beeston Regis priory.

All these materials can be used on their own, but they are often combined, so that flint or chalk walls may be edged with brick or carstone. This creates an enormous variety of colour, from white flint pebbles through yellow or red brick, the varied browns of carstone and the black knapped or squared flints. Looking at the infinite variety of building materials making up churches, houses and barns (many of which are now converted into houses) is one of the great pleasures of the north Norfolk coast.

14 *Flint with thatched or pantiled roofs – cottages at Weybourne.*

15 *Chalk as a building material, Old Hunstanton.*

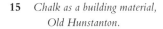

EARLY MAN

Natural developments over millions of years have been interfered with by a more recent phenomenon: mankind. The rest of this book describes his relationship with the landscape of the north Norfolk coast.

The early movements of humankind are very difficult to assess. Man first came to East Anglia well over 700,000 years ago, nomadic peoples advancing during warmer periods and retreating during the ice ages. The evidence is in the flint tools that they used and the places where they made them, but it is very difficult to put dates to these finds. Early man seems to have favoured marine sites, no doubt because of the ease of obtaining shellfish and similar foods, and this, combined with the easily available flint, made the north Norfolk coast an attractive area – but, as we have seen, the actual coastline was not always where it is today. Some sites were worked throughout the Stone Age, like one on Kelling Heath which has produced over a thousand different kinds of tools and microliths; finds have included worked flints and waste from flint workings. Titchwell had an upper palaeolithic settlement site on the present coast – flint implements have been recovered from parts of the beach only visible at exceptionally low tides. When in use, this was an open inland site, perhaps close to a river. Evidence of Stone-Age activity of all dates has been found at Weybourne, in the cliff face or in an exposed layer of peat and clay on the beach. Discoveries at Runton include palaeolithic flint axes and choppers, also mesolithic and neolithic tools and arrowheads. Hunstanton has also produced prehistoric flint artefacts from all periods. Other palaeolithic finds include flints and a flint scraper at Brancaster and a flint axe head at Holkham.

By the fourth millennium B.C., the Mesolithic or Middle Stone Age, farming was beginning to develop. At Hunstanton a group of round houses has been found beside a rectangular timber enclosure. Two mesolithic occupation sites have been discovered on natural mounds at Holkham near to the present coastline, perhaps seasonally occupied. The number and range of mesolithic flints at Morston suggest that flint was being worked there – they were found in deposits overlying a palaeolithic raised beach, which provides evidence for where the coastline would have been during the last ice age. There is evidence of a mesolithic flint-working site at Ringstead.

There are also several neolithic or New Stone Age sites, of which Hunstanton is the best researched: late neolithic pits at Redgate Hill have produced shells of snails that prefer woodland, hazelnuts, bones of red and roe deer – as well as evidence of cattle, sheep and pigs, and cultivated wheat and barley. The settlement continued in use into the Bronze Age, by which time it was functioning as a stock farm. An early neolithic site in the south of the parish of Weybourne can be seen on aerial photographs, probably a mortuary enclosure. Neolithic and later pottery has been found at Blakeney Eye, the site of a possible neolithic enclosure with pits and post holes. There is a neolithic long barrow south of Stone Hill in Runton, and two neolithic skeletons were found at Woman Hithe in the parish. Neolithic flint hand axes, scrapers and pottery have been found at Brancaster, Burnham Market and Ringstead.

The need for caution is shown by an exciting prehistoric find at Runton – a saddle quern from ancient Egypt! However, it is not an indication of ancient trading links between this coast and the land of the Pharaohs: it was probably dumped on the beach thousands of years later by a collector of antiquities who no longer wanted it.[6]

THE BRONZE AGE

After the development of farming, the next revolution in man's technology was the discovery of how to use metals, beginning with bronze. At this time, the sea was several miles further north than it is today. A large area of peat exposed at very low tides along the coast between Hunstanton and Brancaster contains small tree trunks, roots and branches from a Bronze-Age forest. This forest was 'explored' almost two centuries ago by Philip Watson:

> A very striking instance of the mighty agency of tides and currents, or by some other natural causes, may be seen off the coast of Hunstanton, and Holme, at dead neaps. For there commenced at Brancaster Bay, and stretching by Hunstanton and Holme, across the Wash, and extending all along the coast of Lincolnshire, from Skegness to Grimsby, a submarine forest, which in ages far remote abounded in trees and plants indigenous to the district. This now submerged tract was once inhabited by herds of deer and oxen, as is evident from the remains of their horns and bones, which have been occasionally found there. The foot of man has also trodden these now ruined wastes, for works of art have been met with, buried with the forest between the waves.
>
> It is difficult to reach this overwhelmed forest from Hunstanton without assistance of a boat, but in the autumn of 1831, accompanied by a friend, the writer managed to visit on foot.
>
> About two miles north of the cliff, and a mile and a half from highwater mark, we arrived at the prostrate forest, consisting of numberless large timber trees, trunks, and branches, many of them decomposed and so soft that they might easily be penetrated by a spade. These vegetable remains are now occupied by an immense colony of living photades and other mollusks [*sic*], and lie in a black mass of vegetable matter, which seems to be composed of the smaller branches, leaves, and plants of undergrowth, occupying altogether a space of about five to six hundred acres. Many of the trees, however, are quite sound and still fit for domestic purposes, and indeed are sometimes used by the proprietors of the neighbouring lands for posts and rails. But the most extraordinary thing we met with in this submarine forest was a British or Celtic Flint Axe embedded in the trunk of one decomposed tree; this curiosity is now deposited in the Norwich Museum.[7]

The Bronze Age in north Norfolk produced the first works of man in the area still visible – burial mounds, or barrows. These barrows survive most strikingly on the heathland behind Salthouse, where over sixty are still visible, and also on watersheds in the north west, where they may have marked boundaries of territories. There are more on the Holt-Cromer ridge. The largest group of Bronze-Age barrows in Norfolk is on Salthouse Heath, spreading into Kelling and Cley, where there are at least nine bowl barrows, including Three Halfpenny Hill and Three Farthing Hill. Gallows Hill in Kelling is the largest and probably the earliest barrow in the group; a complete Beaker period pot found on Kelling Heath may have come from here. The reason that the group have survived so well is that the area has never been ploughed. There are six round barrows in Cley, and at least three more were ploughed out in the 19th century. There are other Bronze-Age barrows in Weybourne, one in Hundred Acre Wood within Kelling Heath Holiday Park and another on a promontory overlooking the sea in Weybourne Wood. Barrows at Burnham Market include a large bowl barrow into the side of which a Second World War pillbox has been built. A barrow can still be seen at Howe Hill, Holkham, and others at Cattle Hill and Brent's Hill are shown on a map of 1590. A Bronze-Age round barrow can still be seen on heathland in Holt Country Park, and a round barrow at Fiddler's Hill, Warham.

It also gave rise to one of the most spectacular finds in modern British archaeology – Seahenge. This exciting recent discovery was at Holme, consisting of an oval circuit of timber posts surrounding an upside-down tree. It was found in spring 1998 by John Lorimer and Gary Wright while out searching for crabs. Lorimer noted the upturned tree stump as a likely spot, naturally assuming it had been washed up; he then spotted a Bronze-Age axe head close by. Later, the chairman of Holme Parish Council said that he had known of it earlier – it had been revealed during the autumn gales of 1997 and again the following year. The *Eastern Daily Press* recorded its discovery on 11 January 1999, to the superlatives of archaeologists. Dr Francis Pryor, President of the Council for British Archaeology, said when he visited the site: 'I had goose pimples. It really was like stepping back 4,000 years. It's of enormous importance.' Mark Brennand of the County Council's Archaeological Unit added, 'I really do find it eerie and profoundly moving. All the hard-bitten archaeologists who saw it out there felt the same.'

A full survey conducted by archaeologists in November 1998 decided that the circle had been built in a salt marsh environment, probably on an island in the marsh, and would have been between one and three miles from the coast at the time. Thanks to

16   *Seahenge – the wooden circle discovered on Holme beach.*

the wonders of dendrochronology, or dating from tree rings, the monument can be dated with incredible precision: the main tree trunk was felled between April and June in the year 2050 B.C. and the other trees in the spring of the following year – 2049 B.C. The most likely purpose of the uprooted tree seems to be as a place where the bodies of the dead were exposed while flesh rotted or was taken by birds.

The discovery caught people's imagination, with 1,500 visitors in one weekend in January 1999 alone. The problem was that, once having been exposed to the elements, it could not be preserved where it had been found – the elements that had exposed it would now destroy it. Some people thought that this was what should happen, such as Hazel Crow, a spiritualist and environmental campaigner. She commented that, 'my reaction upon first seeing the circle was surprise at how small it was, but then on entering how vast it feels and how powerful'. Protesters, known to most people under the broad name of 'Druids', tried to prevent archaeologists from moving the circle. They were allowed to celebrate midsummer at the site, but in July an injunction was obtained to prevent the protesters from interfering: the timbers were lifted, culminating with the central upturned tree on 17 July. They were taken to Flag Fen, near Peterborough, for cleaning and conservation. In 2009, the timbers of Seahenge found a new, permanent, home at the museum in King's Lynn.

THE IRON AGE AND THE ROMANS

This was a rich countryside in the Iron Age, as shown by forts at Warham, Holkham and South Creake, and the gold torcs at Snettisham. The most impressive fort is Warham, the finest in the east of England: double ramparts and ditches surround an enclosure of 3½ acres that could have contained perhaps a thousand people. That at Holkham is barely above sea level, and was probably on a coastal sand-spit when it was first constructed well over two thousad years ago. There was probably another hillfort in Stiffkey, where an earthwork survived into the late 18th century: it is shown on Faden's map of 1797, where it is called Walbury Hill and described – wrongly – as a 'Roman Camp'. Bloodgate Hill in Creake was excavated in 2003 (the origin of its name is not known). The outer ditch of the monument was dated to about 280 B.C., but the central features to 1600-1800 B.C.: it is probably a fort surrounding a much earlier settlement. There is now an interpretative panel on the site, with a very lively recreation drawn by Sue White that is well worth a look: the Iron-Age forts along the coast would all have looked much like this. Warham Burrows, a rectilinear enclosure excavated in 1959, may be an unfinished Iron-Age hill fort. An Iron-Age or Roman fort at Thornham is prominent on the hill behind the town; it was probably built after A.D. 43, but by natives rather than Romans. Aerial photographs of Thornham show possible round Iron-Age houses, and an Iron-Age brooch has been found. Skeletons found there show that the site was used as a cemetery in the Saxon period.

Torcs are heavy circlets of gold, silver or electrum, presumably worn as neck ornaments. More than a hundred have been found in Snettisham but it is not known if they were made here or if they were placed here for some (unknown) reason. The whole area was part of the kingdom of the Iceni, of whom the warrior queen Boudicca is the most well known. Her revolt against the Romans in A.D. 60 is known

17   *The Iron-Age camp at Warham.*

to everyone, but that had been an earlier revolt by the Iceni in A.D. 47 and the final battlefield of this rebellion could perhaps have been the fort at Holkham.

Other Iron-Age objects include a large number found at Weybourne, especially hoards of coins: two gold coin hoards were discovered on the beach in the 1940s and 1950s, and other gold coins have since been picked up in the same area. A horse-harness hoard has been found at Ringstead very close to Green Bank ridgeway, perhaps a prehistoric route running to Holme; it includes bridle-bits and other pieces very similar to those Boudicca and her warriors would have had on their chariots when they fought the Romans. Two Iceni coins have been found at Holme, and there is evidence of a Bronze-Age farmstead at Brancaster where a relatively rare late Iron-Age silver coin was found. Iron-Age coins found at Runton include two gold coins of the Iceni tribe. There have been large numbers of finds at North Creake, probably an area of some importance in the Iron Age. New finds are always turning up: the first evidence of Iron-Age settlers at Wells was found in 2005 during excavations at Corner House – part of a quern and pieces of a salt-making briquette.

There is evidence of Iron-Age and Roman farming. The area around Burnham appears to have been extensively farmed in the Iron Age, judging from the field systems that show up on aerial photographs. There are traces of large-scale rectangular field systems between Holme and Brancaster and near Wells, where this may be the ultimate cause of the grid pattern that still dominates the centre of the old part of the town. The pattern is one of large blocks of 200 to 240 acres, divided into smaller units of 25 to 35 acres. The landscape historian W.G. Hoskins suggested that this is a Roman landscape, an attractive idea especially as the Roman roads are incorporated into it: if it was a pre-Roman pattern then the roads would cut across it as Roman roads are known to do elsewhere in Norfolk, especially in the Scole area.

There are several Roman roads, of which the most well-known is the Peddars Way, reaching the sea at Holme: the word 'Peddars' is medieval rather than Roman and just means 'footway' – other tracks in the region have very similar names. There is another Roman road running near Holkham and forming the western boundary of the much later Holkham estate. This road crossed yet another Roman road at the place now called Haggard's Lodge. These roads can still be seen on maps and walked on, but they may well, as Tom Williamson suggests, have been primarily military roads, to assert Roman control over the defeated Iceni. These roads, built in a series of straight alignments, make very different walking to the older, winding, 'Icknield Way'. The only known Roman villas in Norfolk in fact developed alongside the latter, on the high ground south of Hunstanton, sophisticated structures of stone with mosaic floors and bath-houses, each no doubt the centre of a farm. There was continued occupation of Warham Camp and Burrows: tiles and possible field systems have been found.

A probable Roman town, including a Roman temple site, has been uncovered at Walsingham. Megan Dennis of the Norfolk Archaeological Unit writes:

> at the temple site over 6000 coins have been recovered, many of which may have been deposited there as gifts to the gods. The discovery of three figurines of Mercury, the Roman messenger god, suggests that the temple may have related to him. Other finds relating to satyrs and cupids also suggest Bacchus, the god of wine and debauchery, may have been worshipped here. Gifts of food and wine may have been left in pottery containers and ritual feasting may have taken place.

As the Romans came under threat from across the North Sea, they constructed the defences known as 'the Saxon Shore forts'. Brancaster – *Branodunum* – is one, erected in the late second century (from the evidence of coins and pottery found on the site) and still just visible immediately north of the main coast road. The fort was almost square, measuring 574 feet by 583 feet. Its walls, which were still standing 12 feet high in the 17th century, were of sandstone around a core of rubble, with rounded corners and backed by a wide rampart. There were defensive ditches outside the walls, and a pattern of regular rectangular Roman settlements to the east and west of the fort have been revealed by aerial photography and excavation: fort and settlement probably lay alongside a then-navigable inlet.

Other finds along the coast include those at Weybourne: a Roman pottery kiln excavated in 1857, with about fifty pottery vessels, and a cult object featuring a peacock, a symbol of the goddess Juno. There was probably a small Roman settlement at Blakeney from the evidence of coins, brooches and pottery, and a first-century brass coin hoard has been turned up at Runton. A hoard of between 1,300 and 2,000 Roman silver coins was found at North Creake in 1799. Other finds in the parish include a razor handle in the form of a horse with a crocodile's tail, a pair of tweezers, a cosmetic mortar, coins, brooches and pieces of pottery.

On the north-west coast, Roman pottery and a brooch have been found at Titchwell. Finds at Thornham include coins, brooches, pottery, a cosmetic pestle and a Roman urn containing a human cremation. There are several possible Roman occupation sites in Ringstead and some good-quality brooches have been found. An iron-socketed spearhead was also found on Ringstead downs. A rectangular enclosure near Old Hunstanton is a probable Roman settlement. Saxon pottery, a bead and a coin show that the site continued to be used in Saxon times.

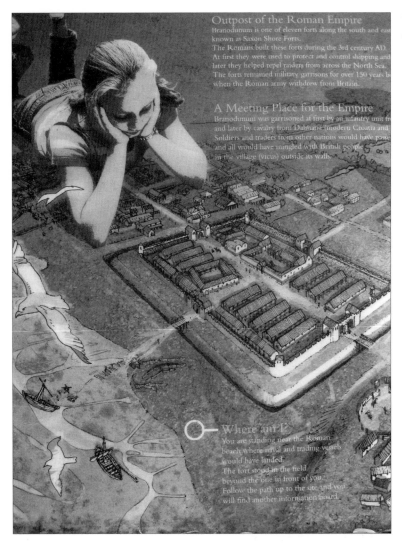

Outpost of the Roman Empire
Branodunum is one of eleven forts along the south and east
known as Saxon Shore Forts.
The Romans built these forts during the 3rd century AD.
At first they were used to protect and control shipping and
later they helped repel raiders from across the North Sea.
The forts remained military garrisons for over 150 years be
when the Roman army withdrew from Britain.

A Meeting Place for the Empire
Branodunum was garrisoned at first by an infantry unit fr
and later by cavalry from Dalmatia (modern Croatia and
Soldiers and traders from other nations would have passe
and all would have mingled with British people
in the village (vicus) outside its walls.

Where am I?
You are standing near the Roman
beach where naval and trading vessels
would have landed.
The fort stood in the field
beyond the one in front of you.
Follow the path up to the site and you
will find another information board.

18   *Information signpost at Brancaster Roman fort.*

Discoveries continue to be made. Three Roman pits, uncovered when building the new esplanade at Hunstanton in 1879, contained oyster shells and pottery. Other pieces of Roman pottery have been found on the beach after cliff erosion. A Roman building in Kelling was discovered in 1957 and excavated by Gresham's school in the late 1970s and early 1980s; they found two ditches and a collapsed wall of wattle and daub sitting on a mortared flint foundation. The skeleton of a young man and Roman pottery were found at Langham during the construction of a new water pipe in 1976.

SAXONS AND VIKINGS

Apart from archaeology, another important form of evidence for early settlement is that of place-names. The very earliest are British, also called Celtic, dating from before the Saxons took over the countryside and drove the former inhabitants into the western fringes of Wales and Cornwall. There are very few of these in north Norfolk. The river name Glaven is a possibility, perhaps deriving from the British word 'glan', meaning pure and referring to the sparkling water of the stream. The 'wey' in Weybourne could be derived from the Celtic word 'war', meaning water. 'Bran' in the name Brancaster may be a Celtic name for the place where the Romans built their fort or *castrum*.

Nearly all names in the area are Saxon, or Old English, many ending in 'ton' or 'ham'. Both these words mean settlement, but 'ham' often seems to imply land hemmed in by water and marsh: not surprisingly it is far more frequent than 'ton' along this coast. 'Ham' can also imply a central settlement from which outliers named 'ton' developed. Burnham is a classic example. The names of the Burnhams suggest a large Saxon estate based on a settlement, 'ham', close to the river Burn, east of the present Burnham Market. From this centre, outlying settlements were founded to the north (Norton), to the south (Sutton), to the west (Westgate) and over the river (Overy). The archaeologists have found evidence of several phases of farming at Burnham: Romano-British enclosures have been covered by a later pattern of open-field strips, and in a third phase more open-field strips have been found, but turned through 90 degrees, into alignment with those of nearby furlongs. There may well have been similar large Saxon estates along the coast, but place-name evidence has only survived for this example.[8]

Some Saxon names capture the landscape of the time. 'Eye' is a Saxon word for an island of dry ground surrounded by marsh: the word is still used for small humps along this coast. It has also produced two place-names: Blakeney (black island) and Stiffkey (tree stump island). The word Holt simply means wood, and captures the wooded nature of the Holt-Cromer ridge. Shipden is the dene or valley where sheep are kept – it was formerly a parish, of which Cromer (which itself means 'crow's pool') was originally a part. Thornham is 'hawthorn settlement'. 'Wells' relates to springs, as in Wells itself and in Titchwell ('the spring of the young goats'). The word Holkham is from the Saxon 'holc', a hollow, probably the large natural depression from which a stream flowed into a tidal creek. The hollow is visible today because it was dammed in the 18th century to create the present lake.

A few of the place-names reflect other early activities by man. Brancaster, of course, incorporates the Roman word for camp, and Salthouse reflects the extraction of salt from the sea, an important early element in the coast's economy. Glandford is a curious one: the ford is the river crossing over the

19 *A timeless scene: searching for cockles on the north Norfolk coast.*

Glaven, but Glan could come from a word meaning 'merriment', reflecting some form of ritual activity that once took place here. For Weybourne, too, there is an alternative suggestion to that already mentioned. Ekwall thinks that the 'wey' element comes from the Old English word for felon, so that the name Weybourne means 'criminal stream', suggesting wrongdoers were drowned here. Morston, the settlement in the marsh, suggests a marginal settlement and perhaps indicates a very early attempt to improve the marshes for farming purposes. Other settlements with farming connotations include Beeston (the farmstead where bent/rough grass grows), Cley (the word is the same as clay, the nature of the soil) and Langham (long homestead or enclosure).[9]

Some popular derivations of place-names are simply false, such as that often given for Hunstanton. According to legend, Edmund set out to claim his kingdom, supposedly heading for Burgh Castle to travel up the Waveney. Diverted by the wind, he instead landed at St Edmund's Point on Christmas Day in A.D. 855; he was 14 years old. There were springs where he landed, whose water tasted as sweet as honey, which, according to tradition, led to the name Hunstanton. In reality, the name simply means 'Hunstan's ton'.

20   *Cliffs and marshes: north-west Norfolk, from Faden's map of 1797.*

Some place-names in Norfolk are later, reflecting the waves of incomers into England from Scandinavia. The place-names ending in '-by' on the east Norfolk coast are sure signs of Scandinavian influence and are discussed in my book on Great Yarmouth. It is significant that there are no such names along the north coast, suggesting that this area was little disturbed by these newcomers. Two possible Norse names are Holme (an Old Norse word meaning island, or firm ground in marsh), and the 'Thorpe' element in Burnham Thorpe. However, both these place-names appear to have been used by Saxons as well as by Scandinavian settlers.

More local names can also be of interest, such as Agar Creek in Morston: according to Forby, the first word means 'eager' and is used to describe a dangerous aggravation of tide in a river. Another name reflecting local speech is Swacking Cuckoo Lane in Cromer, the word 'swacking' meaning huge. There are also later names, such as the field name Spanish Pits, in Salthouse, derived from the guns defending the coast in 1588. Some names, however, are simply wrong, most notably Roman Camp at the highest point of the ridge behind the coast: there is nothing Roman here, the earthworks being defences from the time of Napoleon.[10]

Early Saxon finds show continued use of Warham's Roman settlement and at Blakeney. Rare early Saxon gold bracteates (coins or medals of beaten metal) have been found during excavations at Blakeney Eye. In 2003, a metal detectorist's work led to the discovery of an early Saxon burial in Glandford: the skeleton, which was six feet tall, was accompanied by a skillett, or cooking utensil (the detectorist's original find), a spear, a knife, a bucket, two fifth- or sixth-century buckles and several pottery vessels. A Bronze-Age barrow near East Hall farm in Langham, excavated in 1936, was shown to have been reused for an early Saxon burial – a spear and shield boss were found. Brooches found by another dectorist at Holt led to the discovery of an early Saxon burial site there.

Walsingham continued to be an important settlement in early Saxon times, as Megan Dennis makes clear:

> an Early Saxon cemetery was excavated in Great Walsingham in 1658 by Sir Thomas Browne. This is the earliest recorded excavation of a Saxon cemetery in Britain. The only problem is that we do not know where the excavated cemetery was! There are two possible locations. It is possible that Sir Thomas excavated the cemetery without mentioning the Roman temple beneath it. Metal detecting and fieldwalking on the other possible site found virtually no finds. This might be explained if the site was completely excavated and all traces of the cemetery removed. An Early Saxon cremation urn found in a railway cutting may be a clue to the location of the site. A set of two brooches and some rings were buried with the urn. At another site a rare brooch from Lombardy and other metal detected finds including pottery and more brooches suggest this was an area of Early Saxon settlement and burials.

There may well have been a Saxon religious centre with a mint at Walsingham: two late Saxon coins have been discovered with the inscription ON WALSI.[11]

The Saxons undoubtedly exploited the natural resources of the area. Weybourne Pits, in the south-west of the parish, are ironworking pits making use of the debris dropped by glaciers thousands of years earlier; they are probably Saxon in origin and were still used in the Middle Ages. Two submerged linear features at Stiffkey look like fish traps or structures relating to mussel beds – they could be Saxon, or much later. At Holme, Saxon fish traps have been found on the beach. Saxon coins from France and Kent as well as East Anglia have been found, so Holme was probably already functioning as a port. Middle Saxon pottery and high-quality metalwork at Burnham Overy suggest it was the site of an important market, perhaps preceding that at Burnham Market itself, which developed in the later Saxon period and where high-quality continental metalwork has been found. High-status finds at Binham suggest the probable residence of a Saxon thegn – a disc brooch decorated with enamel and garnet, and an early Saxon gold bracteate depicting a warrior fighting a beaked beast.

There are some indications of a Viking presence in the area, or at least of trading activity between Saxons and Vikings. Late Saxon finds include objects in Viking styles – a buckle frame, a box mount depicting four animal heads, a finger ring, a Borre-style strap end and a Viking-style terminal have all been found at North Creake. Possible Viking presence at Walsingham is suggested by the discovery of a Viking trefoil brooch, and finds at Ringstead have included a key handle of Viking design.

In terms of standing buildings, Saxon towers survive as part of the later church structures at Weybourne, Ringstead Saint Peter and Burnham Deepdale, but these are best described in the next chapter.

TWO

The Middle Ages

THE NORTH NORFOLK coast in the Middle Ages depended on three forms of economic activity: fishing, maritime trade and farming. The importance of fish in the medieval diet cannot be imagined today. It was cheap and many kinds of fish could be preserved, a vital factor in an age before refrigeration. The importance was enhanced by the fasting practices of the medieval church: no meat could be eaten during Lent, nor on other holy days – which altogether made up perhaps one third of the days in a year!

Perhaps surprisingly, over-fishing is by no means a modern phenomenon. The first crisis of over-fishing occurred about a thousand years ago and forced a change from river fishing to sea fishing. This is shown in the archaeological evidence – primarily fish bones in rubbish pits. Before A.D. 1000, freshwater fish were predominant – the carp family (roach and bream), pike and sturgeon. By the 900s, the bones show that the sizes of some freshwater fish eaten, like pike and eel, decreased in size, and others, like sturgeon, shand and grayling, disappeared completely. The beginning of the new millennium saw the appearance of cod, haddock and herring, all sea fish not river fish. Within about a hundred years these sea fish became a major food source, which must have been the result of a commercial revolution in catching and trading fish from the sea rather than from rivers and lakes. This change took place at about the time of Domesday Book, described later: the only fisheries recorded in it along the north Norfolk coast are at Hunstanton, possibly 'round the corner' in the Wash. Alternatively, they could be inland resources: according to Domesday, Hunstanton has 3½ mills and 3½ fisheries, the coincidence leading Hamon le Strange to suggest that the fisheries actually *were* the mill-ponds.[1]

Of course, there were still plenty of freshwater fish, and monasteries and manor houses often had their own ponds. The monastic ones are best recorded, such as those belonging to the estates of Norwich Cathedral priory. The fish-pond at West Hall in Sedgeford was renovated in 1279. It was 'fied' (cleaned out), using 20 buckets bought especially for the purpose, hurdles were bought to trap the fish (eel and pike), a nesting place was made for swans, and a boat bought just five years earlier was repaired. The pond was stocked with 1,200 pike in 1285–6. Fifty years later, it was again fied. There were occasional sales of surplus eels and reeds.

Harold Fox, an authority on fishing villages, distinguishes two types of coastal fishermen – 'trappers', who set up snaring devices on the shore and waited for fish to swim into them, and 'hunters', who set out with their moveable nets in pursuit of their quarry. The most basic forms of 'trapping' involved shellfish. This has left few archaeological remains, but there are possible medieval oyster beds at Brancaster, and at the monastic house of Peterstone, founded before 1200, there were pits for storing shellfish.[2]

Sea fish were trapped too, especially along the western half of the coast. Details of fish trapping can be found in a unique series of Hunstanton estate documents, dating from 1554 but specifically enshrining practices that existed 'before time and times out of mind'. Houses in Old Hunstanton had 'lawers' associated with them, areas off the coast where they would put nets, called pokenets, around stakes and trap fish. Cord Oestmann explains how it worked:

> the lawers were in fact stakes which were set into the ground of the sea. Between the stakes, the pokenets were fixed, and each two, or more, stakes holding one net constituted what was described as a 'birth'. The births were positioned and fixed on the stretch of land which was uncovered by the sea at low tide … The area of the lawers was situated to the north of the village, starting at the north end of the cliffs and stretching along the shore towards Holme-next-the-sea. All births for pokenets … were organised in rows. There were about 30 rows in all along the coast, starting near the shore and stretching into the sea. The depth of these rows varied considerably, some containing only 26 pokenets and others reaching as many as 180. Each owner of lawers had a delimited amount of space within the rows where he was allowed to set up his nets … The most common fish caught in this manner were plaice and sole.

These lawers were at first directly linked to the occupation of houses in Hunstanton, and most houses had them, no doubt supplying fish primarily for their own use, but also selling the surplus, perhaps just a few plaice, to the Hunstanton Hall estate of the le Stranges. Later they were treated as personal property and could be bought, sold and bequeathed in wills.[3]

'Hunters' fished on a larger scale, owned herring nets and had access to boats to go out to sea. Many were still not full-time fishermen and had farms as well. John Gibson was such a man. In October 1522, he sold 800 herrings to Sir Thomas le Strange, to be barreled up for Lent. Fishing was in the family: John's son, William Gibson, bequeathed herring nets in his will of 1558. Others who combined fishing and farming included men like William Osborn, who died in 1541: he owned a boat large enough to transport coals across the Wash, sold fish to the le Stranges and bequeathed herring nets in his will, but he also farmed 24 acres of land and left a half-share of ploughing gear and of a cart. A century later, in 1629, Thomas Geyton of Hunstanton died leaving 19 pokenets and 'old herring nets' worth 10 shillings, but his farming concerns were of much greater value: he had 30 shillings' worth of winter corn, 40 shillings' worth of barley and

20 shillings' worth of pease and vetches in his fields, as well as small numbers of sheep, pigs and cows.

The same mixture of farming and fishing was carried out all along the coast, but lawers were only possible where there was a gently sloping coastline. On the steeply sloping shores at the east end of the coast, lines had to be used. Nicholas Evered of Runton was a typical example. According to his probate inventory, he had four fishing lines worth five shillings, but again it was his farming activities that were more highly valued. However, he was farming on a much smaller scale than Geyton, with no crops in the field (this would depend upon the time of year in which the person died of course), and with just two small swine and one heifer.

'Hunters' caught fish out of all the settlements along the coast. Six ports are listed in a licence to buy fish in 1358 – Sheringham, Cromer, Salthouse, Cley, Wiveton and Blakeney. An exemption to fishermen from paying a subsidy in 1384 adds two more – Wells and Holkham, but other records show there were fishing boats in these two ports half a century earlier. There were nine fishing boats at Holkham in 1336, three of 20 tons and six of 12 tons. John de Bilney owned three, including two of the large ones, and John Speller two, each of the other four vessels having a different owner. At the same date, there were 13 fishing vessels in Wells, and in both places the shipowners also owned land. Thomas Balteys, a large landholder in Holkham, for example, had interests in wool, corn and fish: he owned a 12-ton fishing boat, the *Skardeyn*, moored at Wells.

Below these men in the social scale came the full-time fishermen, such as Simon Fawkener and the appropriately named Clement Fysheman, both of Shipden/Cromer. Fawkener, who died in 1449, left two boats and four nets to Thomas Wilyot, perhaps a business partner, drift nets and lines to other legatees, and ordered a third boat and its gear to be sold. He presumably left no family, unlike Fysheman who died 70 years later and clearly expected his to continue the business. He left a six-oared boat, nets and ropes to his wife, Alice, and a second six-oared boat to his elder son, John (who was to pay his younger son, Robert, 6s. 8d. in compensation). The residue of his nets, after Alice had taken the best, was to be divided between the two sons.

Some 'hunters' among fishermen were prepared to go further and further in pursuit of their quarry, most notably from north Norfolk to Iceland, which according to John Dee was a fortnight's sailing with an ordinary wind. Hakluyt says that Blakeney men fished off Iceland in the time of Edward III and Dee confirms that they were granted exemption by the king in respect of their trade to Iceland. Iceland was isolated in the 14th century but men of Blakeney and Cromer certainly were fishing off Norway and Denmark at that time, as a petition of about 1383 shows. Robert Bacon of Cromer is sometimes said to have 'discovered' Iceland in 1400, but he was no doubt just one of many north Norfolk fishermen making the voyage across the North Sea in his period. By the second decade of the 15th century, men were trading directly between England and Iceland, although they should in theory have traded through Bergen, as a letter from the King of Denmark to the King of England in 1415 made clear. The House of Commons noted that, since the fish had deserted their former haunts off Norway and were now to be found in great plenty off Iceland, the fishing boats naturally followed them. The prohibition demanded by Denmark's king was indeed proclaimed in 16 ports along the east coast of England, but it was generally ignored by both fishermen and merchants and had to be repeated in 1430. It was still ignored, so the English government began to seize the ships engaged in the illegal trade, including some from Cromer. A flourishing licensed trade then grew up, with the Crown receiving payments for the licences; the occasional Cromer boat owner took out such a licence, although no doubt many north Norfolk coast boats continued illegal fishing. The trade was at its height in the middle of the 15th century. The ships were very small – Cromer and Blakeney men told the King that their vessels were of 10 or 12 or, at most, 20 tons – but they may have been exaggerating how small the boats were as they were trying to convince the Crown that they could not be used to carry horses across the English Channel for the King's army.[4]

Jonathan Hooton, the historian of the Glaven Valley ports, says that each ship normally did the voyage just once a year, heading out in spring with five to ten fishermen, with provisions to last all summer, and with salt to preserve the fish on the homeward voyage. They would return between July and September, with 15 lasts of stockfish (dried cod) which might be worth almost £100, an enormous sum in the Middle Ages. There was some trading, too: provisions for the Icelanders and occasional return traffic, such as the 20 whale fins imported in 1601 and sometimes gerfalcons, a bird much prized by falconers.[5]

21   *The marine world in medieval images (left to right): a ship on a bench-end formerly in St Nicholas' Lynn; a 'cog' shown on a Lynn charter; and a mariner on a brass at Beeston Regis church (note the whistle). All are early to mid-15th-century.*

THE SHIPS

There are no documents that tell us what the ships on the coast looked like. The small boat known as the Sheringham crab boat was first illustrated in 1820, but E.W. White points out:

> they were probably quite unchanged as long ago as the Middle Ages; for they illustrate at least two of the characteristics which we are compelled to associate with English boats of medieval days. They were equal-ended, i.e. sharp at both ends, and the oars, instead of being worked from thole pins or rowlocks secured to the gunwale, projected through holes, or oar ports, cut in the sheer strake. These oar ports also served a further purpose in removing the boat from the water to the shore; for the oars were passed through corresponding ports on each side, and provided a means of carrying these lightly-built boats up the pebble beach which, at Sheringham, shelves so steeply.

The boats bequeathed five centuries ago by Fawkener and Fysheman would have been of this type.

There are many names for different types of medieval ships. The earliest were 'cogs', with a single mast, high sides and distinctive stem- and stern-posts: they were ideal as bulk carriers. By the early 15th century, the 'carrack' was being developed, with two or three masts; these both increased the size of the ship and made it easier to manoeuvre – and meant that the mariner was no longer dependent upon a single sheet of canvas. It was these ships that made the long journeys to Iceland practicable. Other types that show up in medieval documents include the 'dogger', of Dutch origin, two-masted, of 30 to 100 tons, and used mainly for fishing, and the 'crayer', a smaller (30 to 50 tons) two- or three-masted square-rigged merchant ship.

MARITIME TRADE

Blakeney was the most important of the north coast ports in the Middle Ages. In 1242, Eustace Morel of Flanders obtained permission to retrieve seven bags of wool from Blakeney, which he had left in store there after buying it from local merchants – this is the earliest known documentary reference to trade with the Continent, but, as it implies, the connection was already well established.

Medieval ships were so small that any coastal village could function as a port, and a ship from overseas might call in anywhere. For example, in 1297, a cog was forced into 'Hunstanton and Holme port' by rough seas; the ship and its cargo were seized by the port keepers. The ship's master was James Coppyn, envoy of the King of Denmark, and he took his case to the King of England. The keepers were ordered by royal authority to return ship and cargo to James and the merchants of Flanders and 'Almain' whose property it was. The port at Holkham could also trade across the North Sea, as shown by a dispute of 1302 recorded in the patent rolls in the National Archives. Olaf Iveri, a merchant of Norway, brought a legal case against Adam Silk of Holkham. The two men had agreed that Olaf would load a ship in Norway with logs of specified length and breadth and export them to Holkham. Olaf claimed that the value of the cargo was £147 8s., but that Adam had only paid him £40 and was refusing to pay him the rest. The case went up to the highest level, involving three years of correspondence between the King of Norway and King Edward I of England, but Olaf does not seem ever to have got his money.[6]

The Crown would commandeer ships for its naval campaigns. Four ports on the north Norfolk coast were ordered in 1301 to send ships to Berwick-on-Tweed: Blakeney and three at the western end – Thornham, Holme and Heacham. In 1345, the ships used for the transport of Henry of Lancaster's troops to Bordeaux included two ships from Blakeney (the *Nicholas* and the *Blythe*), crewed by 37 men and two boys. Blakeney also supplied two ships and 38 mariners for the great fleet that besieged Calais under Edward III in 1347. The total number of ships present on this occasion was 710, with 43 from Yarmouth alone.[7]

By the 14th century, trade between Blakeney and Norway was well established. In 1321, a ship exported wine and corn on this route, and in 1369 wheat and malt were being shipped in exchange for fish. Five years later, John Halle was granted a licence to ship 100 quarters of wheat and 100 quarters of malt, as well as barley and oats, from Blakeney to Norway, returning with a shipload of herrings. In 1361, the bailiffs of Cromer were ordered not to allow the export of falcons and in 1364 of gold, silver or jewellery.

On 30 March 1405, Robert Bacon of Cromer, already mentioned in connection with Iceland, captured James, the 11-year-old son of King Robert of Scotland, driven ashore near Cromer in a storm. He was sent to London where he remained a prisoner for the next 20 years, eventually being released to become King James I of Scotland. Men of Cley also claimed the honour of the capture. In 1417, Adam de Horn of Cley obtained a licence to export grain from Cley to the Low Countries. Hanseatic League merchants are said to have traded with Cley to such an extent that a section of the church was reserved for burials from among their number. The double-headed eagles on coats of arms on the south porch could represent the arms of the Hanseatic League, or they could relate to Anne of Bohemia, the wife of Richard II, whose emblem this was as well; in either case, the rich decoration of the porch suggests Mediterranean influence. A merchant by the name of Lumen Henrikson, who may well have been connected with the Hanse, wrote to the Pastons from Cley in about 1490 concerning their purchase of Rhenish wine and 'half a hundred oranges'. In 1523, provisions were shipped from Cley and district to Calais for the army and navy stationed there.[8]

Trade along the coast would probably have been of even more importance but, as royal licences were not required, is very poorly recorded. However, we know that grain from Thornage was carted to Snitterley and shipped to Newcastle, and that grain from Stiffkey was carted to Holkham and then shipped around the coast to Lynn. Blakeney was the busiest of the ports, carrying wheat and barley to the ever-increasing London market by the late 14th century. The barley was probably shipped as malt, cheaper to transport than unprocessed grain, as it certainly was in later centuries; if so, maltings were already a feature of the economy of the north Norfolk coast. There is a reference in the Paston letters to shipping malt at Blakeney from their manor at Guton, in Cawston, in 1465. No doubt, Brancaster and Wells offered similar trading opportunities.[9]

PIRACY

The risks in maritime trading came not just from the elements but also from rivals from other countries or ports. In 1327, four men, three of them Holkham owners of fishing vessels (Walter Osborn, John le Speller and John de Bylneye) were accused of piracy but produced royal pardons that said they had been of service to the king against the Scots. There were many fights between Norfolk men and men of the Hanseatic League. According to Hakluyt, two 'confederates of the Hanse', Godekin Mighel and Stertebaker, with their accomplices, were involved in several attacks on vessels from north Norfolk ports between 1395 and 1398. In 1395, they captured the *Friday*, captained by Laurence Tuk and owned by John Dulwer, both Cley men. They took the ship into Maustrond in Norway and robbed it of artillery, furniture and salt fish worth 500 nobles. In the same year they captured a ship of Simon Durham called the *Dogger-ship*, and the *Peter* of Wiveton, laden with salt fish. They took the dogger and its contents and the salt fish, worth £170. They murdered the master and 25 mariners, saving just one lad whom they took away with them to Wismer. Three years later, they captured a Cley crayer, also called the *Peter* (captain, Thomas Smith; owner, Thomas Motte) at Langsound in Norway; the ship was worth 280 nobles.

La Eleyne had been out at sea fishing for over five weeks when, on 12 March 1344, she was captured by men from the Low Countries. They killed the captain, John Toly of Wells, stole the cargo of fish and sunk the ship. She was owned by Simon Lambright of Heacham, who claimed compensation of £300, including £60 for tackle and gear and £110 for the fish; the ship itself he presumably valued at £130. In fact, this was only part of a total claim of £3,000 that he made for ships owned by him that he claimed had suffered similar fates; was this a normal level of risk for a north Norfolk merchant in the 14th century, or was he exceptionally unlucky?

A few wealthy captives might be held for ransom, but murders of whole crew were common. A gang of pirates murdered 36 men on a ship called *Saint Edmund* grounded at Le Nes off Hunstanton and stole the cargo of wax, leather, oil and timber, but perhaps the worst atrocity in terms of numbers was in the early years of the 15th century. One hundred men from Cromer, Blakeney and other Norfolk towns were fishing in the North Sea when enemy ships were seen approaching. They landed at Wynforde in Norway seeking shelter but 100 armed Hanse men from Bergen came upon them, bound their hand and legs and threw them all into the sea.

Similar acts were undoubtedly committed by north Norfolk men. In 1285, an action was brought by German merchants against Thomas Burgeys of Blakeney and others for seizing and taking by force a vessel loaded with cloth and other merchandise, and driving it ashore. In 1318, the sheriff of Norfolk was ordered to take into the king's hands a ship from Flanders and Zeeland whose crew and cargo were being held by Henry Burgeys of Hunstanton after being captured on a voyage from Scotland to Zeeland; the common surname of the two men is presumably just a coincidence. It was claimed that the arrested men had robbed two ships, one from Salthouse and one from Cley, and murdered both crews, 39 men in all. They were from Zeeland and were 'adherents of the Scots, the king's enemies, supplying them with victuals' – in wartime, almost any atrocity could be committed.

In 1405, the Admiral of the Fleet was ordered to investigate an incident in which it was alleged that men of Blakeney, Wiveton, Cley, Cromer and elsewhere had seized two Amsterdam ships coming from Prussia, throwing 36 mariners and merchants into the sea to their deaths. They brought the captured ships back to England and sold them, one at Blakeney and one at Scarborough. An agreement of 1409 includes among its list of damages to be repaid: 56 nobles due to Henry Culeman from men of Scarborough, Blakeney and Cromer, whose captain was John Jolly of Blakeney; and 68 nobles due to Nicholas Wolmerstein of Elbing from John Bilis 'neere unto Cromer'.[10]

Even living on the coast was not always the peaceful experience it is today: enemy ships might swoop in and kidnap people for ransom money, as happened at Cromer in 1450. Perhaps a similar raid was unsuccessful at Sheringham 12 years later, as 16 Frenchmen were taken prisoner in the town.[11]

THE SEASHORE

Along most of the coastline, the small ships of the time could navigate their way along channels through the marshes and moor at 'staithes'. These were made of wood and stood parallel to the stream. A few relics of medieval staithes survive, for example at Holkham where there was once a settlement called Holkham staithe, shown on a 16th-century map: the navigable stream ran east into Wells harbour until it was finally closed by a new embankment in 1719. Wilfrid Wren says that there are some remains of the staithe and of mud berths beside the main road, just west of what is now Lady Ann's Drive (Ordnance Survey grid reference 892440); the name is also preserved in the nearby Staithe Wood. More successful staithes survive as present-day settlement names at Brancaster and Burnham Overy.[12]

The towns directly on the sea's edge would benefit from a jetty or pier to moor alongside and to provide protection from storms. The earliest known is at Shipden or Cromer. Shipden is now beneath the sea; as early as 1337, it was said that the greater part of the churchyard had been washed away by the sea over the previous 20 years, and that the church itself was under threat.

The first written record of the pier is in a document of 1390; this is also the first known use of the word 'pier' (albeit spelled 'pere') in the English language. In the document, the King grants the men of Shipden the right, for five years, to levy duties on ships coming into the harbour to build the pier. Fishermen were expected to contribute and a levy was placed on their catches: twopence for a last of herring, 12 pence for every ten-score (120) of 'orgoys' (it is not known exactly what these were), sixpence for lob, ling and cod – and also a penny for every boat called 'Fissher' laden with merchandise. There were also levies on other imports such as timber from Riga, corn, malt, salt and sea coal. Every load worth over five shillings had to pay duty except wool, leather, fells, lead, tin and wine. These lists give an impression of Shipden/Cromer as a port through which a wide range of products was being imported. Such a pier needed continual maintenance, and this was a community effort. Twenty-one Cromer men left money in their wills for the pier between 1453 and 1535, as did one woman, Matilda Coye in 1483. The largest sum bequeathed was eight

22 *Blakeney church, with its second smaller tower.*

shillings, the smallest eight pence. John Sparks in 1483 left money specifically to place 'great stones' to support the pier. By the 16th century, the pier was in decay: Camden, writing in 1536, says that the inhabitants of Cromer endeavoured at great cost to maintain a small harbour, but in vain. Under a royal patent of 1582, the people of Cromer were permitted to export 20,000 quarters of wheat, barley and malt for the upkeep and rebuilding of an 'ould decayed peere'. In 1580, a Worstead widow, Dyones Flegg, left forty shillings for the 'building, maintaining and repairing of the new begun and erected Peere', a bequest suggesting a replacement was being built, and showing its construction was a matter of importance to a fairly wide hinterland, as Worstead is almost twelve miles inland from Cromer.[13]

Ships were guided into their harbours by beacons on the hills above. Some still have the name 'Beacon Hill', that above Thornham being recorded as early as the 13th century. Several were later maintained by the county authorities, showing the importance of maritime trade to the Norfolk economy. A 17th-century document lists the county beacons: those on the north coast are at Thornham, Burnham, Wells and Weybourne. Church towers also acted as guides to ships at sea, hence the great height of Cromer church tower, at 160 feet the tallest in the county apart from Norwich Cathedral, and the two towers at Blakeney. It is not known if a fire was lit in the second (eastern) tower, or whether the presence of two towers was intended to enable easier identification from out at sea. Wren suggested that their alignment marked the (old) entrance to the Glaven estuary.[14]

On any stormy day on the coast, 'you hear the grating roar / Of pebbles which the waves draw back, and fling / At their return, up the high strand'. Often, the waves return with flotsam or jetsam, too. There have always been wrecks along the coast. The local lord of the manor usually had rights of wreck, and there are frequent cases in manor courts of people being fined for helping themselves; no doubt many others got away with it. Robert de Montalt was one man who had difficulty in keeping control of his rights along his coastal manors: in 1317, he complained

23 *Cley church from the south: the quay has now become the village green.*

24   *Wiveton as a port, as portrayed by Godfrey Sayers.*

that people in Hunstanton stole goods out of a ship that he had captured from the Scots, and in the following year that William de Sedgeford and other men had carried away goods cast ashore by the sea at Thornham, Titchwell, Hunstanton and Heacham. A generation earlier, in 1281, there was another legal case, this time about a whale which had been washed ashore between Thornham and Titchwell – local people had cut pieces off it and carried them away.[15]

Wreck was so profitable that along the coastline of Runton and Beeston it was divided up among four local manors – 50 per cent went to Beeston manor, 30 per cent to Beeston priory, 15 per cent to Runton Felbriggs and five per cent to the manor of John de Plumstead. Among many opportunists in the Runton and Beeston manors, Adam Silk's sons, John and Thomas, took goods from a wreck in 1347, while Richard de Hindringham was a repeat offender, being punished for theft of objects of wreck in April 1345, January 1347 and March 1349.[16]

Another important coastal resource was salt, necessary in the preservation of fish. Curiously, there are only two saltings recorded on the coast in Domesday Book, both at Burnham; none is mentioned at Salthouse, despite its name. There are physical remains of saltings at Cley – rectangular earthworks and low banks on the edge of the Glaven and the area is labelled 'Salt Pans' and 'Saltings' on an early 20th-century Ordnance Survey map, but such indeterminate features are impossible to date.[17]

FARMING

The first documentary record of life along the coast is that of Domesday Book, written in 1086 and recording what the King should receive from the manors of his newly conquered realm. The picture is already that of an economy based on corn and sheep. The corn can be seen not so much from counting the numbers of ploughs as the number of mills – in Domesday these are all watermills, and all used for grinding corn. The settlements in the hills had large numbers of mills, five each at Holt and Sedgeford, for example, and the coastal settlements also exploited the rivers: there were watermills at Blakeney and Thornham, to take just two among many. The flocks of sheep are recorded directly, and are especially large in the north-west corner on the chalk downs: 200 at Ringstead, 300 at Sedgeford, and no less than 500 at Thornham.

Apart from pigs the numbers of other animals – goats, horses and cows – are minimal; however, there was a flock of 40 goats at Salthouse. The Domesday description of Salthouse has been written onto a plaque in the churchyard so that visitors and residents can see what was said about the village nine hundred years ago, an example other villages could usefully follow.

A quirk of Norfolk Domesday is that woodland is always recorded not in area but in terms of the number of pigs that it could support. The largest woods were at the east, up on the Holt-Cromer ridge, where Holt had woodland for 60 pigs, Salthouse for 100 pigs, and Beeston and Runton for 30 pigs between them. There was also woodland still at the Hunstanton end of the area, with Hunstanton itself having wood for 64 pigs (on two different manors) and Sedgeford wood for 60 pigs. This, it should be stressed, does not mean that these pigs existed: these are measurements of the size of woodland.

The entries in Domesday record changes between the situation in 1086 and that of 20 years earlier. Some are indications of increasing prosperity: the number of sheep had gone up from just one to 40 on one manor in Hunstanton, and from three to 100 on Bovi's manor in Ringstead. Others indicate social and economic changes: at Hunstanton, a free woman held 30 acres of land before 1066 but she has no parallel in the Norman period. At Sedgford one watermill had been 'taken away' by a man called Anand, no doubt a reference to the opportunities offered in a time of lawlessness.

One fact often noticed is that Cromer is not mentioned at all in Domesday; presumably it comes within the entry for Shipden, where there was woodland for 30 pigs in the main manor, a further six pigs in an outlying portion of Gunton manor, and where St Benet's Abbey had a small estate 'for the supply of the monks', no doubt being exploited for shellfish, sea fish and salt.

The basic unit of land was the manor, with the lord in his manor house, an area

25 *The Domesday record for Salthouse, a sign in the churchyard.*

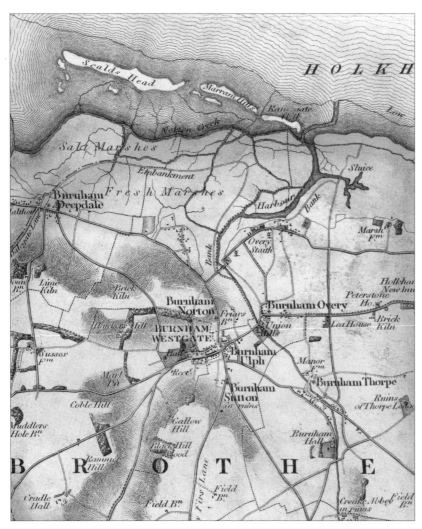

26   *The seven Burnhams,*
in origin a large Saxon estate.

27   *Medieval traditions continued or revived?*
Outside the Old Coach House, *Thornham.*

of demesne land farmed by him, and large fields farmed in common by his tenants, who also had to render services to their lord, such as working in his field and repairing his farm buildings. The basic records are manor court books and related documents, but there is also an extraordinary visual record of farming life: the wonderful Norman font at Burnham Deepdale with carvings depicting one farming activity for each month of the year. They include digging in March, scything hay in June, binding a harvest sheaf in August, slaughtering livestock in November – and feasting in December. Rarely can the harsh life of a medieval peasant farmer be seen so clearly depicted as on the images around the sides of this font.

The records show that the medieval pattern continued to be one of sheep-corn husbandry, a mixture of grazing and growing corn and barley. Holkham is a well recorded example of a large estate. The arable fields were in strips, often described as pieces (which could comprise just one strip or a group of them, so that one piece could be as little as a quarter of an acre or as much as four acres). Pieces were grouped together into larger units called *cultura* or *quarentena*. People would own pieces of land scattered throughout several cultures. The importance of manure was recognised: transports of loads of dung are mentioned in a 1273 custumal, suggesting the systematic practice of enriching the soil.

Holkham women mainly appear as market traders, paying fines for breaking the assizes of bread and ale. Others were land-holders, either single women or widows. Often they rented out the estates they had inherited from fathers or husbands, or had bought from their market trading activities. They occasionally appear in legal disputes, most commonly against other women: they were involved in five cases of *hamsoken* (property disputes) in the 1330s and 1340s, in one case Margaret Crane being successful against her own son. Women were also fined for sexual activity outside marriage, and if giving birth to a child outside marriage they had to pay by themselves the fine that was otherwise paid by a parenting couple. Alice Carpe, for example, paid a fine of 32d. in January 1336 when she gave birth out of wedlock, and another fine of the same amount 13 months later when a second child was born; there was no support for a single mother in 14th-century Holkham.[18]

Many estates were owned by religious institutions and farmed for profit. Norwich Cathedral manors at Hunstanton and Titchwell and the Bishop of Norwich's manor at Langham practised the most intensive of cropping regimes, substituting the sowing of legumes for periods of fallow. The Cathedral's estate at Hindringham and the le Strange's estate at Hunstanton had grain yields of more than eight bushels an acre, although the same cropping system at Langham produced

28 *Norman carvings of the labours of the months on Burnham Deepdale font.*

yields of 5.2 bushels per acre. This was probably because the Bishop still relied on customary services from his tenants whereas the other two manors were more advanced economically, employing hired labour.

Norwich Cathedral also owned estates at Sedgeford (West Hall and East Hall) and another at Thornham. Accounts show the details of farm life. At West Hall, hemp, garlic, leeks, shallots and beans were grown, and surpluses of apples, pears and plums were sold. The garden at Thornham was also planted with vegetables. Marl was spread on 50 acres of land at Thornham in 1265-6. West Hall had at least three barns. In 1255-6, the granary was roofed with oak boards and 50 years later boards of fir were bought for a solar at the head of a new barn. In East Hall, over 250 spars of fir were purchased at Lynn for repairs to farm buildings. A rope 90 feet long was bought for the well at Thornham in 1294-5 and the well repaired with boards in 1349-50. By the second quarter of the 14th century, each estate at Sedgeford, with its light soils, was using four teams of just three horses to prepare an annual sown area of about 400 acres.[19]

In 1432, relations between Binham priory and its tenants (who comprised almost everyone in the village) were formalised. An agreement was drawn up settling a large range of issues and lists 30 leading tenants, all men, one of the first lists of names of village inhabitants. It halved the fee that tenants had to pay on admission to copyhold land, which must have been very welcome to the peasants. It also settled issues of rights of pasture in the common, and thereby gives us information on the uses of the north Norfolk coast commons, some of which – Beeston for example – are still important features of the landscape. At Binham, the tenants were permitted to pasture their cows on a common called Middlegate, and to fence them in with stakes, from 29 August through to the following 25 March. They could also put their sheep there from 29 September to 24 June. The number of sheep was limited, however: each tenant could pasture four sheep for each acre that he held. The priory agreed not to put their pigs and 'piglings' on any common in Binham between 25 March and 1 August.[20]

A vineyard was established at West Hall in 1263-4, using vine stock brought from Ely. This was a major venture: no fewer than 139 men were employed to plant the young vines in a single day. A decade later, two further journeys were made to Ely for more vines, but the vineyard is not recorded after 1327-8: it had lasted 65 years before becoming a victim of the increasingly cold winters leading into the period sometimes known as the Little Ice Age.

Watermills and windmills both occur in the medieval record. The pond for the watermill at Thornham was repaired

29   *A deserted medieval village: the ruined church at Little Ringstead.*

in 1273-4 but it is not mentioned again, so it had perhaps given way to the latest technology, the windmill. A mound had been made for one in Thornham as early as 1263-4, the first documentary reference to one on the north Norfolk coast. The mound cost 14s. 6d. to construct and the mill itself cost £4 11s. 10½d. There is a reference to a windmill in Langham in 1278: it was bought by the Bishop of Norwich two years later. These windmills were all post mills, being built around an enormous wooden post with the whole of the mill turned into the wind.[21]

Wells is a planned town. A charter of 1202 allowed Ramsey Abbey to develop the town for use as a port to export grain from its estates. The plan consists of long, straight, parallel streets, connected by a series of very narrow passages: the pattern is a gridiron, very like that of the more famous Rows of Great Yarmouth – or like New York. Wells was a success, but not all settlements stood the test of time. Along the hills are four deserted villages, where sometimes only the churches now can be seen, almost alone among fields. The best example is Little Ringstead, a village which may well have been deserted as a direct result of the Black Death. In 1332, there were 17 people paying lay subsidy here, but after the Black Death it was exempted from tax because there were fewer than ten households. The other villages seem to have declined more slowly in the 15th century. Waterden was granted no relief in the 1350s, but by the lay subsidy of 1424-5 it had ceased to be a separate community. Egmere also received no relief in the 1350s, but had fewer than ten households in 1428. Egmere and neighbouring Quarles together were allowed a reduction of 40 per cent on their payment to the lay subsidy of 1449. The most dramatic of these churches are the ruins of Saint Andrew, Little Ringstead, in a field of corn not far from Hunstanton, and Egmere where the tower stands close to a single farm. Earthworks are still visible on aerial photographs of the sites of Egmere and Quarles. The desertion of Egmere was exploited as early as the 1550s, when a former parson of the parish and the lay occupier of the rectory stripped the lead from the roof and took the largest bell out of the tower, intending to transport them to the coast and sell them overseas; then, as now, a deserted Norfolk church was a temptation to an unscrupulous thief.

The only deserted settlements actually on the coast are where erosion has physically destroyed the site, as at Shipden: rumours abound that the church tower still stands and that the sound of the bells can still be heard from beneath the water if you stand on Cromer Pier. Snitterley could be a lost village north of Blakeney but it may well just be an alternative name for a part of Blakeney that gradually dropped out of use.

Three substantial medieval houses survive, at least in part. Blakeney 'Guildhall' is really a 14th-century merchant's house; the plaster on the walls shows signs of having been modelled with rose ornament and birds and beasts. Hunstanton Hall was built in the 1480s as a manor house inside a moat; the brick gatehouse can still be seen, although the rest of the present building is later. Baconsthorpe 'Castle' is another moated house, begun in about 1450 by John Heydon and completed in 1486 by his son Sir Henry Heydon. It originally consisted of two courts within a moat, but was then altered to one large court. The gatehouse and part of the curtain wall make an impressive ruin.

Other survivals include Hanover House, or Shipden House, the only medieval house in Cromer but concealed behind a later façade – a 16th-century ceiling was uncovered in the house in the 1980s. Old Hall, Holt, was a medieval and later manor house with a 12th-century chapel and two ponds. In the mid-19th century the hall was demolished, the ponds enlarged into the present lake and the chapel moved to Holt Hall. A 17th-century flint and brick cottage in Church Street, Stiffkey, is on the site of a medieval guildhall, marked on a map of about 1600. The Longhouse in Cley is a late medieval house with a wall painting of that date inside, while Cley Old Hall is on the site of a medieval manor house.

30   *The parish church at Heacham.*

Moats from medieval houses can still be traced on the ground, or seen in aerial photographs. They include Kelling Hall, a medieval structure, now in ruins. Parts of the moated structure were excavated in 1986 and 1987, when a turret stair, garderobe (lavatory) and possible fore-building were recorded, along with earthworks of banks, terraces and a possible hollow way. Aerial photographs show a medieval moated site with surrounding enclosures and a fishpond south of Rosedale Farm in Weybourne – there were two moats, the larger being still visible as an earthwork. Hale's Manor Stiffkey has standing and buried remains of a moated site with associated earthworks, including fishponds, alongside a tributary of the Stiffkey. Berry Hall, Great Walsingham, is another example of a medieval moated site, and there are more in Burnham Thorpe, one with a 17th-century manor house within it.

Medieval archaeological finds are sometimes the possessions of people of relatively high status. Finds at North Creake include a gold half-ryal coin of Edward IV, flasks for holy oil and a 13th-century buckle plate depicting a lion. Those at Wiveton include a silver finger ring, a French coin converted into a brooch, and a seal matrix with a bird motif. An inscribed silver ring and a bell were found in a ditch at Runton. Discoveries at Ringstead have included a lead 'Boy Bishop' token, a harness pendant, and a bronze seal matrix with a French inscription that reads 'I am a nuisance'.[22]

MEDIEVAL RELIGION

The lives of most country people were based upon the manor, and the lives of all people were centred around their parish church, which they would attend at least once a week throughout their lives, and where they would be baptised, married and buried. Most of the settlements in north Norfolk probably had churches by the time of Domesday Book, although very few (such as Blakeney and Beeston) are specifically mentioned; many survive with their characteristic walls of flint, and often with the round tower so much a feature of East Anglia. They provided spiritual comfort to their parishioners, all of whom would have believed strongly in the Christian faith – and from whom the church received tithes. Many churches were owned by a monastic house which would put in a vicar to run the church – and take the profits from the greater tithes (corn, hay and wood). A typical example is Shipden. There appear to have originally been two churches, one called Shipden-next-Felbrigg, presumably where the present Cromer church now stands, the other Shipden-next-the-Sea, now lost beneath the waves. The income of Shipden church in 1385 was £78 10s., almost all from tithes: the tithe on the corn brought in £15 a year, and the tithes on wood and on herrings each raised almost as much. Everything grown or produced in the village was tithed – lambs, wool, suckling pigs, heather and hay, the mills, eggs, dairies and dovecotes, hemp and brushwood. There were also general seasonal tithes to cover other items too small to calculate individually, such as fruit from garden trees. The church belonged to the monastic house of Hickling, who paid a chaplain £6 14s. 4d. to run the parish. With £2 for his clerk, and just under £5 for other expenses such as candles, bread and wine, repairs to the church, and bulrushes and straws to cover the floor, Hickling made a profit of just under £65 a year.

The evidence of wills, and of occasional inscriptions in the churches themselves, enable us to build up a clear picture of later medieval parish life along the coast, with local people taking great pride in improving their parish church. At Cromer, for example, we can trace the building of the chancel at the end of the 14th century and beyond. In 1388 John Gosselyn left £10 for putting stained glass into the large three-light window, and three years later Simon Chyld left six marks to repair the south window at the east end of the chancel. In 1402, James Harmer left a further 20s. for the chancel and by 1420 the work was almost complete as Richard Bishop bequeathed money to add battlements to the wall, a decorative rather than defensive feature; he also left £5 for work on the tower.

31 *Burnham Deepdale church, with a characteristic Norfolk round tower.*

At Salthouse, the windows in the south aisle and the large east window of the church were re-glazed in 1503, but the main concern of the parishioners at this time was providing new bells for their church. Three parishioners left money for the bells between 1481 and 1504, and William Grene's humble four pence towards the tower, left in 1483, was probably used for the same purpose.

Within the church, local people commonly left money to the repair or improvement of rood screens and rood lofts: being made of wood, these needed frequent repairs. The most beautiful surviving screen is probably that of Beeston Regis, paid for at least in part by the £4 bequeathed by Thomas Rooke in 1519. In other cases the evidence is not from wills but from inscriptions. That on the screen at Thornham tells us that it was paid for by John and Clarice Miller; no date is given, but it is known that John Miller died in 1488. Their gift, 16 saints and prophets of a very high quality of painting, can still be appreciated in the church today. The pulpit at Burnham Norton, with its beautiful paintings of the four doctors of the church, was the gift of John and Katherine Goldalle in 1450.

Sir Henry le Strange, who died in 1485, had seen and admired the Morley family monument in Hingham. He left £20 for a monument to himself in his church at Hunstanton, which was to be modelled on it. Other members of the family are commemorated in brasses. The Felbrigg family also favoured brass. There is a very fine brass in Felbrigg church in honour of Simon de Felbrigg, his son Roger and their respective wives, Alice and Elizabeth. Simon, who died in about 1351, is in civilian dress, although he wears a short sword. In his day, everyone would carry a knife or sword for self-defence: knife-crime was far more common in the Middle Ages than today, despite the impression given by the modern press. His son Roger is in military garb, as befits a man who was a prisoner of war in France in 1355, and who died in Prussia in about 1380. Their wives wear kirtles and head-dresses, but the lower half of Alice's brass does not survive. There is another magnificent brass to Simon, Roger's son, one of the very few depicting a Knight of the Garter. It was presumably erected after the death of Simon's wife, Margaret, in 1416; the date of his own death is left blank. However, when Simon died he was not buried here but in a friary in Norwich with a second wife by his side.

Both Wiveton and Cley churches now stand above fields and marshes, but when they were built they were churches in busy ports, and were the local churches of merchant traders. In 1437, John Hakon left 200 marks (£133 – a very substantial sum) for a new 'church' at Wiveton. This is the present nave of the church. The chancel is over a century earlier, and the flushwork panelling on the outside walls is an early example of this form of decoration. Cley is clearly intended to be seen from the south, where the quay was, with its splendid decorated clerestory of alternating circles and two-light windows, and the south transept with its beautiful south window. This is the more dramatic now as it is roofless – as it has been since about 1600, a dramatic indication that the port was already in decline.

Monastic houses were another form of devotion. The Norman Conquest brought to England men who were used to the idea of establishing large Benedictine monasteries. They saw the foundation of a religious house as a concrete act towards the salvation of their own soul and those of their relatives. It took a generation for the Normans to feel sufficiently secure in their estates to begin founding monasteries. That at Binham was the first in the county, founded in about 1091 by Peter de Valoines. In its day, it was probably the most advanced building in England. The window of the west front has bar tracery, the pattern formed by intersecting ribs of stones; all earlier windows used plate tracery, where the shapes are cut through the solid stone. It was built by the prior Richard de Parco, between 1226 and 1244, and thus predates the bar tracery at Westminster Abbey, constructed from the 1240s onwards: monastic Norfolk was leading the way in 13th-century design. Most unfortunately, this window was allowed to fall into disrepair and was bricked up, probably early in the 19th century.[23]

32 *Binham Priory, showing the west window.*

These monastic houses were not always the peaceful places that we imagine, as two incidents of Binham history illustrate. In about 1212, in the reign of King John, the priory was besieged by Robert Fitzwalter. The monks were reduced to great hardship and compelled to eat bread made from bran and to drink rainwater from the roof. Eventually the king sent troops to break up the siege, and Fitzwalter fled for his life. Also in the early 13th century, one prior of Wymondham, Alexander de Langley, was driven mad by studying too hard. His outbursts eventually became intolerable to the other monks there. He was flogged until the blood flowed copiously, and then taken to Binham priory where he was kept in chains in solitary confinement until he died. He was buried in his chains.

Other smaller monastic houses were those of Augustinian canons. Weybourne priory was founded in about 1200 by the local lord of the manor, Sir Ralph Mainwaring. The abbey at Creake began as a family chapel for the Nerfords, founded in about 1206, and was elevated into a hospital by Alice de Nerford in 1217. In 1226, the Archbishop of York granted an indulgence for those who gave to it, and commented that many needy folk went there and that very great misery was alleviated. Some of the houses of Austin canons on the coast were not part of the mainstream of their order: Beeston and Peterstone were part of an independent grouping known as the Order of Peterstone. Their prime purpose seems to have been to house travellers, chiefly pilgrims visiting Walsingham. They were small and very remote; the friar John Capgrave described them in a sermon as 'not in the world, as they say, but in Norfolk'.

Binham and Weybourne were unusual monastic houses in that the priory church was also the local parish church; in effect the parishioners had the nave and the monks had the chancel. Because of this, the naves of both have survived intact, and the monks' part of the two churches can still be seen as ruins beside the present parish churches. The arrangement could cause problems, some of which were sorted out in Binham by the 1432 agreement between the priory and the villagers already mentioned. The villagers were permitted to put up a bell to announce their services in the nave, provided it did not weigh more than 800 pounds. It was not to be rung before six in the morning or

33   *The two towers of Weybourne church and priory.*

after six or seven in the evening except in an emergency (a church bell would be rung in a crisis such as a fire, a pirate raid or an invasion). The monks walked in procession through the church every Sunday and on some other days, and it was agreed that the vicar would suspend his service while they did so.

Walsingham was the most famous and most visited priory in the country and probably in Europe. Even the Milky Way in the sky came to be called the Walsingham Way because it was supposed to point across the heavens the route to England's Nazareth in the Holy Land of Walsingham. The priory as such dates from about 1155, but the site may already been a revered one for almost a century: a 15th-century poem dated its origins to 1061. More probably it began in the first third of the 12th century. A lady called Richeldis had a vision here of the Holy House in Nazareth, where the Annunciation had taken place and where Jesus had been brought up. The Virgin Mary herself appeared to Richeldis in Walsingham and told her to build an exact replica of the house. It was decided to build it between two holy wells there; however, when craftsmen tried to build the house they ran into problems. On arriving for work on the following day they found that the foundations which they had begun had been moved 200 yards during the night, and that the house had been miraculously completed to a perfection that they could never have achieved. This shrine became known as the Chapel of Our Lady of Walsingham. The holy wells also had power to work miracles: the sub-prior was once saved by grace after he had fallen into one of them. There was another miracle on the site in 1314. Sir Ralph Boutetourt, fully armed and on horseback, being pursued by a deadly enemy, rode at full speed towards the small doorway on the north side of the precinct, which was closed. Praying to the Virgin for deliverance he found himself miraculously inside the precinct and in sanctuary. The entrance was known afterwards as 'the Knight's Gate'.

King Henry II's brother William gave the priory some land but the first monarch to visit was Henry III. He first came in 1226 after visiting Bromholme in north-east Norfolk, another place of pilgrimage. He made 20 visits over the next 30 years and his many gifts included oak trees for use in constructing new buildings and vast quantities of wax and tapers: on the feast of the assumption in 1241 he gave 3,000 tapers for the chapel. Five years later, he gave 20 marks for a golden crown to be placed on the head of the statue of the Virgin Mary in the shrine. He last visited Walsingham in September 1272, not long before his death.

His successor, Edward I, visited Walsingham on a least a dozen occasions, often with his queen, Eleanor of Castile. He was especially keen because of an incident that had happened in one of the royal palaces when he was a young man. He was playing chess with a knight when he left the table for a short while (to relieve himself?). At that moment, a huge stone fell from the ceiling on the very spot where he had been sitting; had he not got up he would undoubtedly have been killed. Edward attributed this miracle to Our Lady of Walsingham. In 1296, he signed a treaty with the Count of Flanders in the chapel of Our Lady in the priory on the Feast of the Purification. Every monarch, with the possible exception of Richard III, whose reign only lasted two years, visited Walsingham. Henry VII was a frequent visitor, last coming in 1506. When he died three years later, he left instructions for silver statues of himself at prayer to be placed facing the three most important shrines in England: Edward the Confessor in Westminster Abbey, Saint Thomas Becket in Canterbury Cathedral – and, of course, Our Lady of Walsingham. His son Henry VIII and his first wife, Katherine of Aragon, were also pilgrims. Supposedly, Henry walked barefoot from Barsham Manor, two miles away (where he was staying), and hung a circlet of gold around the statue's neck. He visited Walsingham after the birth of his son Henry in 1511 and again after the infant died. Katherine owned property in the town and, on her death, she provided in her will for a pilgrim to travel to Walsingham, distributing the sum of 20 nobles to charitable cases on the way.

There were many other important visitors, including David Bruce, King of Scotland, who was given safe conduct by Edward III to come with 20 knights, and Queen Isabella of France. When Sir John Paston was ill, his wife came to Walsingham to pray for him and her mother dedicated an image of wax – of the same weight as John Paston – to the shrine. Even Cardinal Wolsey was a visitor and pilgrim, drinking the water from the holy well in an attempt to cure his weak stomach.

The village was developed to provide facilities for pilgrims – a medieval planned town. Excavations in the 1950s revealed an inn or almonry under the present Anglican shrine. Medieval buildings include Shire Hall, now a museum, a leper hospital which

34 *Walsingham priory: the east end of the church, with the medieval gatehouse behind.*

became the police station in the 17th century, and a now-gone cross in Common Place. Medieval pilgrim finds at Walsingham have included lead flasks for holding holy water (ampullae), a reliquary for holding parts of the true cross, an ornate piece of horse harness, and a medieval boot found in a trench dug for sewers in the High Street. An old boot may not sound the cause of much excitement but in fact it is extremely rare for a leather object not to have decayed over the centuries.

The Dutch writer Erasmus visited Walsingham in 1511. He tells us that the chapel was:

> built of wood, and pilgrims are admitted through a narrow door at each side. There is but little or no light in it but what proceeds from wax tapers yielding a most pleasant and odoriferous smell, but if you look in you will say it is the seat of the gods, so bright and shining as it is all over with jewels, gold and silver … To the east of this is a chapel full of wonders. A joint of a man's finger is exhibited to us. I kiss it, and then ask, 'Whose relics are these?'. He says, 'Saint Peter'. Then observing the size of the joint, which might have been that of a giant, I remarked, 'Peter must have been a man of very large size'. At this, one of my companions burst into a laugh, which I certainly took ill, and pacified the attendant by offering him a few pence.

Other people were becoming even more cynical by the 15th and 16th centuries, one Norfolk man in a heresy trial going so far as to refer to 'Our Lady of *Falsingham*'. This attitude was far from universal in Norfolk, however, as we shall see in the next chapter.

There was a new religious movement in the 13th century: the friars. These were men who deliberately adopted a life of poverty and dedicated their life to the service of God, preaching, hearing confessions and providing a decent burial to the dead, even the poorest. There were many orders of friars, but only two reached the north Norfolk coast. First was the Carmelite Order, who had friaries at Burnham Norton and Blakeney. The order originated in a group of hermits who lived on Mount Carmel in the Holy Land; as regime change in the region made it impossible for Christians to remain, they retreated to Western Europe. Burnham Norton was founded in 1241, the gatehouse, which can still be seen, being one of the earliest buildings to make use of flushwork. The house at Blakeney was founded in 1296, and the precinct wall can still be seen just south of the low 'cliff' that was the coastline in medieval times.[24]

The other order of friars to reach north Norfolk was that of the Franciscans, followers of Saint Francis of Assisi. They had a friary at Walsingham, founded in 1346 to minister to the many thousands of pilgrims – many desperately poor – who visited the town. The priory in the town saw the Franciscans as a rival and objected, but they failed to have it closed down or moved out of the town as they wanted.

Some of the monks and friars from north Norfolk were men of great learning. John of Baconsthorpe was a friar at Blakeney, who went on to spend most of his life at Padua University and became one of the most important theologians of the first half of the 14th century. Thomas of Walsingham was a Benedictine monk of St Albans; his *Chronicles* and related works, written in the last quarter of the 14th century, are an essential source for the history of the period. John Bale was a Carmelite friar and writer at Burnham Norton in the years before the Dissolution.

TRAVEL AND TRADE

Travel was more common in the Middle Ages than might be thought, much of it for reasons either of trade or of pilgrimage, and it has left a few mementoes. A well-defined medieval hollow way or sunken road survives in the south of Sheringham parish. Wiveton bridge was built in 1292, although the present bridge is 15th-century; Robert Paston left money for a bridge chapel here in 1482. There are several wayside crosses in the area, the best-preserved being those at Titchwell and Binham. Evidence of pilgrimages includes the finding of the base of a medieval pilgrim's badge from Walsingham at Kelling, and a pilgrim bottle at Weybourne. Other people would move to improve their prospects, then as now usually to the big cities of Norwich or London. Two lord mayors of London came originally from Cromer, and both made important bequests to their home town. William Cromer, lord mayor in 1423, left the substantial sum of £40 to the parish church, while Bartholomew Rede, a goldsmith, founded the free school at Cromer, maintained thereafter by the Goldsmiths' Company.

Many travellers would come by sea, and manor courts regulated travellers along the coast. In 1389, for example, two men were fined at Beeston for carrying off wreckage and for being 'common travellers on the sea'. Another man was fined two shillings just for being 'a common traveller on the sea by night', a journey in the dark presumably suggesting criminal intent. Travel across the seas was also common. Coins from Gelderland (now part of the Netherlands) and Flanders have been found in Sheringham, showing medieval continental contacts. Coins found at Holme include

35 *The slipper chapel at Houghton, on the pilgrims' way to Walsingham.*

one from Scotland, jettons from France, and a brooch found there features a coin of Philip IV of France.

Another notable traveller was William of Cley, son of Ralph of Cley, who in 1240 took up the cross, that is became a crusader; no doubt he was one of the two parties of men who went set off with Richard, Earl of Cornwall, and Simon de Montfort in June of that year. Before leaving, William leased his property in Gateley for a term of three years; in return Thomas of Gateley gave him six marks of silver towards the journey. People who went on crusade sometimes found it difficult to reclaim their land on their return, and William prepared for this: he had more than a dozen named witnesses on his charter, including many clerics. We do not know if William did successfully complete his crusade, or whether he died during the venture.[25]

One possible Holt resident also 'made good'. Tradition associates Alice Perrers with Holt, mainly because one of the manors within the town is called Perrers. In fact, Alice was probably the daughter of Sir Richard Perrers of Hertfordshire, although her opponents variously alleged that actually she was the daughter of a thatcher or of a Devon weaver. She was a lady-in-waiting to King Edward III's wife, Philippa, and became Edward's mistress in around 1364. After Philippa's death in 1369, Edward showered Alice with jewels and land; in 1375, he exhibited her as the Lady of the Sun at a tournament in London. In the following year she was banished from the court by Parliament, but she soon returned and remained with the king until his death in June 1377; she is alleged to have stolen the rings from his fingers as he lay dying. After her death, much of her property and jewellery were confiscated and she spent the rest of her life trying to recover as much as she could. She died in 1400 and was buried in Upminster church. She had married Sir William Windsor, probably in about 1374, but her three children – John, Jane and Joan – were almost certainly not his but Edward's. There does not seem anything to suggest that she ever visited Holt, but local people like to think of her as a daughter of the town.

The wealth of the coastal area is reflected in the number of medieval markets; there were goods to sell and money for purchases. Markets were set up by manorial lords as commercial ventures. The lawyer Henry Bracton thought that markets should be at least 6.6 miles apart, otherwise they would not be profitable, but markets in Norfolk in general, and along the coast in particular, were often much closer than that. The earliest known is Holt. Mentioned in Domesday Book, it was in existence for almost a thousand years before its closure in 1960. By the beginning of the 13th century there were also markets at Wells, Wighton and Binham. Burnham Market was established in 1209 and by 1250 there were others in Hunstanton, Little Walsingham, Thornham, Docking, Langham, Snitterley and Sheringham. The flood continued in the second half of the 13th century with new markets at Heacham, North and South

36 *Market day in medieval Burnham, as shown on the town sign.*

Creake, Fakenham, Stiffkey, Cley and Shipden, along with a second market at Little Walsingham and two markets at Burnham Overy. By then the great age of the market was over. Two were set up in the first half of the 14th century, at Weybourne and Kelling, but few markets were established anywhere after the Black Death; the only one in north Norfolk was Felbrigg, established in 1353. The first known record of a market in Cromer is in 1402, but this was probably the one established at Shipden in 1285, forced inland by erosion of the coast.[26]

THE BLACK DEATH

Two national events in the 14th century had a great impact in north Norfolk: the Black Death and the Peasants' Revolt. The Black Death or great plague spread across England from the summer of 1348, reaching Norfolk the following year. Deaths and burials were not recorded in the 14th century, but it is a reasonable guess that half the population of the region died of plague during the summer and autumn of 1349.

Two forms of document survive that give an idea of the devastation – the appointments of clergymen and the records of manor courts. In June 1349, new incumbents were required at Morston, Blakeney, Langham, Wighton, Holt and Letheringsett. In July 1349 the Burnhams were clearly struck with a sudden disaster: new incumbents were appointed to Burnham Westgate, Burnham Norton, Burnham Deepdale, and to both churches in Burnham Overy (St Andrew and St Clement). The appointment at Deepdale was in the gift of the abbot of Ramsey, but there was no abbot; had he, too, died of the plague? The king stepped in but the man he appointed was a mere acolyte, because of the shortage of qualified priests available. Other places needing new priests in July included Binham, Titchwell, Brancaster, Stiffkey, Cockthorpe, North Creake and Great Ringstead. A new prior was also needed at Walsingham. August was almost as bad, new incumbents having to be appointed twice in the month at Great Ringstead, at Binham again, and also at Burnham Sutton and at Shipden. There were fewer changes in September but Warham St Mary and South Creake needed new appointments, as did Beeston Regis, West Beckham and Burnham Westgate, once more, in the following month.

Thus, most of the churches along the north coast had to appoint new clergy in the summer of 1349, Binham and Burnham Westgate twice and Great Ringstead three times; the last was Richard Alword, who was also not fully qualified, being described as a clerk with first tonsure. Although the Black Death is never mentioned in the record, it is clear that it was sweeping through the north Norfolk coast towns and villages. Indeed Little Ringstead was abandoned at this time, one of the very few villages in England which we can be sure was deserted as a result of the Black Death.[27]

Manor records also show the effects of the plague, for example in Hunstanton and Holkham. The former was a large manor and the court was held every month. In April 1349, the plague had not appeared: the death of just one tenant is recorded. At the April court, 16 men were ordered to attend the next court in May to resolve disputes; when the day came, 11 of them were dead. In May, when three cases of debt were due to be held, four of the six people involved had died in the previous month. In October, the court found that in the previous two months, 63 men and five women had died. These are people who held land of the manor; the deaths of other family members and the landless would not be recorded in the court records. That whole families were dying is shown by the fact that in nine cases there were no heirs at all, and in a further 31 cases there were only women or children to succeed. Augustus Jessopp, who looked at the manor court rolls for Hunstanton, lets his pen flow:

> Incredible though it may sound the fact is demonstrable, that in this one parish of Hunstanton, which a man may walk round in two or three hours, and the whole population of which might have assembled in the church then recently built, 172 persons, tenants of the manor, died off in eight months; 74 of them left no heirs male, and 19 others had no blood relation in the world to claim the inheritance of the dead.

Inevitably, some people took advantage of the crisis: Catherine Busgey of Hunstanton was caught with a leather jerkin that she had stripped from a dead man; his friends recognised it and took it back.[28]

Holkham is one of the very few manors where the cause of the disruption is actually mentioned. A hayward's account for one Holkham manor records rents for the year starting September 1349 as just 3s. 6¾d., *causa pestis* – because of plague. The figure is just one penny more in the following year, and the explanation then is *causa pestilentia*. The court of October 1349 shows an exceptional number of holdings becoming suddenly vacant, undoubtedly because of the Black Death. Again whole families had died, so that in many cases there was no direct heir. Bartholomew de Holgate died without any surviving family: his six acres passed to his sister, Cecily. Matilda Abraham left no heir nearer than a cousin. No heir came forward to claim the estate

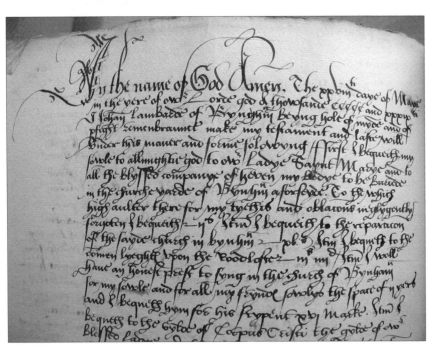

37   *The will of John Lambarde of Binham, 1539, leaving money to the local church.*

38 *St Edmund's chapel on Hunstanton cliffs, with the lighthouse behind.*

of William de Barney; Richard Bakhouse had also died without an heir. Some people benefited – survivors, like the Balteys family, mentioned earlier as shipowners, were able to increase the size of their holdings by taking over unclaimed estates.

Building work at Cley church is traditionally said to have been interrupted by the Black Death. There is certainly a long gap in time and style between the pre-plague clerestory and south transept and the post-plague south porch. Once in the country, the plague recurred over the next three centuries, sometimes with devastating results to an individual community: Creake Abbey came to a sudden end in 1506 when all the canons died of plague within a single week.

THE PEASANTS' REVOLT

The Peasants' Revolt broke out in the summer of 1381, the immediate cause being a protest against the imposition of a Poll Tax (echoes of the 1980s). Rebels entered Norwich on 17 June, but were finally defeated in a battle at North Walsham on 26 June; this was a massacre as peasants armed with pikes were mown down by professional soldiers – led by none other than the Bishop of Norwich.

The leader in the Norfolk revolt was Geoffrey Lister of Felmingham but other key players included two men from north Norfolk, John Lister of Binham (presumably a relative of Geoffrey's) and Sir Roger Bacon of Baconsthorpe. The latter, described by one authority as a 'notorious and murderous captain', shows that some smaller landowners joined in the revolt. He was one of the leaders of the peasants camped outside Norwich on 17 June; two men, Simon Cook and Henry Sherman, turned up and urged the peasants to come to Walsingham. They may have wanted to organise an attack on the priory or perhaps the area was seen as fertile ground for the uprising: there was an outbreak of violence at Wighton that day. Two landowners, John Holkham and Edmund Gurney, were attacked at Holme by a group of rebels led by Thomas Kenman on the following day; they and a servant were able to escape by boat. They were pursued as they headed for Burnham but managed to get away. The monks at

Binham Abbey were attacked and forced to give up their manor court rolls; these were publicly burnt on 21 June. These rolls recorded the customary fees and work duties owed by the peasants to their lords, and the peasants hoped that by destroying the records they could rid themselves of these hated impositions.

Even after the defeat at North Walsham, there were still outbreaks of violence. On 8 July, Robert Fletcher of Hunstanton rode to Heacham with a gang of men armed with bows and arrows, and tried to stir up rebellion. It was too late – just a week later, Fletcher was executed for his part in the revolt. Bacon was imprisoned, but was eventually pardoned by the king.[29]

We know in great detail how the revolt played out along the eastern part of the north Norfolk coast thanks to research by G.F. Leake. Most of the manors in question were owned by the Felbrigg family; Roger de Felbrigg had recently died and the estates were being administered by his attorneys, one of whom, John de Wulterton, was robbed during the revolt. The peasants seized manor court rolls of three manors – Runton Felbrigg, Aylmerton and Felbrigg – and set fire to them. The rolls of a neighbouring manor – Metton Parnow Hall, held by the Carbonel family – were also burnt.[30]

Three men led the way in their opposition to their lords in the Beeston/Runton area – Robert Bully, John Abbe and Vincent Grom – but there were many other malcontents: at Felbrigg in October 1381, there were nine presentments for damage to the lord's corn and four for leading beasts into the lord's pasture. At the same time, eight men were presented at Aylmerton for damage to the lord's corn there. Bully was charged with a variety of offences. He had trespassed on the lord's land by leading his horses, cows and sheep over his demesne, 'trampling, destroying and reducing to nothing' the corn growing there. He was fined a total of seven shillings but continued to offend. One year later, he was charged with breaking a gate onto a common, and in 1387 he was before the court of a neighbouring manor in Runton accused of having failed to do autumn work when summoned by the lord. In 1390, he was before the court at Beeston for failing to put his sheep on the lord's field as he was supposed to do – the sheep would act as living muck-spreaders providing fertility to the field.

Another local troublemaker was Vincent Grom. He was a tenant of several manors, and he and his wife also brewed ale and sold bread. The accusation made against him at Felbrigg was that 'he was in the company of those who caused damage in the manor at the time of the Rising'. He paid 6s. 8d. to be readmitted as a tenant. Five years later he was before the court over debts on woollen yarn and skins – clearly a man with fingers in many pies. His son was also in trouble in 1381. He had dug up flaggs in the soil in Metton Parnow and carried them away without licence. However, this may not be directly related to the troubles of 1381 as the court heard that Vincent junior had been just one of a group of men who had been doing this for the previous five years. Another 'rebel' was John Abbe. He was accused of damaging barley grown in the lord's fields. He was also charged with possessing a white dog called 'Fetch'. No crime in that, but it was claimed that he used the dog to take rabbits from the lord's warren. In 1385, he and two other tenants were presented for not using the lord's mill to grind their corn.

The revolt failed. New rolls were started in each of the manors where they had been burnt. They have headings such as 'First court held after the burning of the court rolls'; many of these are now in the Norfolk Record Office.

CRIME

Much can be learned about a society from the way in which it deals with its criminals: the medieval coast is no exception. Minor infringements were dealt with at manor courts, but for major crimes the judges came up from London and held trials at Norwich castle for the whole of Norfolk. The accused might be in the castle for several months awaiting trial, but, if found guilty, the sentence followed immediately: death by hanging.

In 1286, according to the Assize roll, two Hunstanton people, Christina Gamot and Nicholas, the son of Mariota Bagge, were arrested for theft. They escaped from custody. Christina sought sanctuary in Hunstanton church, acknowledged herself as a thief and abjured the realm. Later, Nicholas did the same. This meant that both went abroad and were liable to immediate execution should they return. Nicholas did return and was caught burgling the house of another Hunstanton man, John Norman. Execution was inevitable, but unusually he was beheaded rather than hanged, the only known person to suffer this kind of execution for theft.[31]

The court rolls for the period 1308-16 have been transcribed by Barbara Hanawalt, and show us the kinds of criminal cases that were typical of the Middle Ages. In 1315, five people from the hundreds of North Greenhoe and North Erpingham appeared before the court on a range of offences. Agnes Vincent was accused of burglary: she stole 24 red herrings and a bushel of grain, worth in total three shillings. Margaret, her mother, was charged with receiving the barley, which we are told was worth 18d., so that the herring must have been valued at 18d. too, or three farthings a fish. John Lenyne of Hindringham was charged with stealing three sheep, valued at 2s. 6d. John Pratt was charged with breaking into three different houses. Margaret Gryffyn stole five bushels of malt and other goods from the house of Eustace Gryffyn (who must surely have been a relative). All five were found guilty and sentenced to be hanged. Four were immediately executed. However, there was a complication in the case of one of the Margarets: she told the court that she was pregnant. The standard medieval procedure was followed: she was examined by matrons, found indeed to be pregnant, and returned to the castle to await the birth of her child. This was only a temporary stay of execution: if she survived giving birth, Margaret would be hanged very soon after.

In the following year, John of Framingham and Christina la Sutere were charged with breaking into the barn of the Bishop of Norwich at Langham and stealing four bushels of wheat and four pence worth of fish. They were acquitted. On the same day, John Loly was accused of two offences – breaking into the church at Holt and also breaking into a house at Edgefield, from which he stole some barley. Asked to plead guilty or not guilty, he refused to do so, so he could not be tried. He was returned to Norwich castle *ad dietam*, that is, to be fed only bread and water until he gave in and agreed to plead; the case does not come up again, so he no doubt died under this harsh treatment. Beatrice of Warham was found guilty of stealing barley worth three shillings from a house in the village, and was hanged. Some of these people may have been literally starving as this was a time of famine in Norfolk after a succession of failed harvests.

Criminal records survive even for the settlements which have disappeared. In 1316, Joan of Brundal was accused of breaking into the house of Roger Dene of Shipden and stealing bread, herrings and other goods worth nine shillings. In the same year, it was a Shipden man, Simon Cateline, who was accused of theft, charged with stealing six sheep worth nine shillings from James le Clerk at Overstrand, and also for burglary from James' house. However, Joan and Simon were both found not guilty. Geoffrey Lonegod, a resident of Snitterley, had linen cloth, worth the considerable sum of 40s., stolen from him in 1310; a man called Clement Loby was found guilty of the theft and hanged. Another Snitterley resident, Martin Skot, was accused of the murder of John le Sire of Morston, who was killed at sea. Another man was taken at Snitterley for stealing property from Northrepps church: was he hoping to escape by ship? Both the last two were acquitted: the high acquittal rates show how difficult it was to prove guilt in an age before forensic evidence. If you were not actually caught in the act, or in possession of stolen property, you had a very good chance of getting away with your crime.

Crime amongst clergymen is exceptionally well recorded. Not all clergy were honest, naturally, and indeed clergymen might get away with their crimes because of the medieval practice known as benefit of clergy: a cleric could not be tried before a civil court. When six men were charged in 1316 with breaking into Hindringham church at night and stealing wax and towels, one of them – Roger of Weybourne – claimed to be a cleric. Of course, his claim had to be checked: letters from the Bishop of Norwich were produced before the court, proving that he was indeed in holy orders. Roger was thus released into the hands of the Bishop: he would be held in the Bishop's prison in Norwich and eventually sentenced to some form of penance. Better than being hanged, but in this case he was the only one of the gang to suffer at all as the other five were acquitted at their trial before the civil court.[32]

In 1286, the local blacksmith at Hunstanton was assaulted. Five men were accused of the crime: William Dunny, the vicar of Hunstanton, along with his brother, his chaplain and his clerk, and a man called Alexander le Eskermiscur. William's case went to the church courts, Alexander was found guilty, and the others were fined for being present. In the same year, a chaplain from Hunstanton was accused of the murder of another chaplain at Barsham.

Lesser crimes came before manor courts as we have already seen. However, it was not just peasants who broke manorial laws. The parsons of Runton and Beeston and the chaplain at Aylmerton were all charged in 1386 with hunting hares on the lord's manor at Beeston. Two years earlier the same offence had been committed by no less a figure than Sir Thomas Erpingham, the future hero of Agincourt, friend of kings – and the owner of many manors himself.

THREE

The Tudors and Stuarts

AS WE HAVE seen, King Henry VIII was originally a supporter of the Walsingham shrine. In fact, he made a yearly payment of 200 shillings for a priest to sing before the statue of Our Lady of Walsingham, and a further 46s. 8d. for a candle to burn continuously on the shrine. The payments are recorded in the royal accounts down to 1538, when a final entry reflects the new situation: 'For the King's Candle before Our Lady of Walsingham, and to the Prior there for his salary, NIL.' The Reformation had arrived.

In 1536, Cromwell's delegate had visited Walsingham. The locals protested at the prospect of the shrine being destroyed, and this peaceful protest became known as the Walsingham Rebellion. Eleven men were sentenced to death, two, including the sub-prior of the monastery, being burned alive in Walsingham itself; the place of execution is still known as Martyrs' Field. In June 1538, the statue was dragged away to London and burnt. The little Holy House was torn down, the priory church stripped of its lead and furniture, the stone, slate and tiles sold off in lots for £55 15s. 11d. Some local people still had faith, however. In January 1539, a woman from Wells was arrested for coming on pilgrimage; on Market Day, she was paraded around the town in the cart, with a paper on her head describing her as a 'a reporter of false tales', and she was then put in the stocks for the rest of the day.

Kett's Rebellion of 1549 was another peaceful protest in Norfolk, not primarily religious but about the rights of villagers and manorial tenants. The rebels included four tenants of the manor of Burnham Thorpe – Edward Combes, John Water, Robert Palmer and Walter Buckham. They forfeited their lands for 'collecting together at Rysing Chase and Mussold Heath with William Kett'. No doubt a thorough search of the manor records would reveal the names of other 'rebels'.[1]

The Reformation led to the dissolution of all the monastic houses in north Norfolk, their sites, and the thousands of acres of land they owned, being sold to lay owners. It affected every parish church as well. The church authorities sold off the equipment that was no longer needed under the new regime, and used the proceeds to repair the church, to whitewash its interior walls, and often for secular purposes as well.

39   *The pump at Walsingham.*

Inventories drawn up in 1552 show the process at work. At Blakeney, for example, money was raised by selling chalices, censers, a cross and a cope. It was spent on lead for the church roof – and also on mending the sea road and repairing a drainage channel. At Holt, £14 was raised by the sale of silver and gilt items. Half was spent on glass for the church windows, surplices and whitewash – and on road-mending. The rest was to be split between church repairs and money for the town's paupers. Sometimes the money was used for military purposes, a reverse of turning swords into ploughshares. The clearest case was at Weybourne, where the Marquess of Northampton ordered proceeds from the sales to be used to make 'a great dike and a sluice to drown withal a certain marsh belonging to the said town joining to the most dangerous place for the enemies to land at in these parts which if it be done shall be greatly annoying to our said enemies if they should chance at any time hereafter to land therein'. Langham contributed £4 to the making of the bulwark at Weybourne and to the beacon there, and also equipment for two soldiers. Glandford raised £5 by selling a chalice and a cross: 30s. were spent in repairing the nearby bridge, and 23s. 4d. on kit for soldiers.[2]

Money was being spent because of the fear of war with Catholic Spain; as always, the north Norfolk coast was seen as a likely place for an invasion. The Holt church register records that:

> in this year [1588] was the town of Wabourne fortified both with a continual garrison of men both of horse and foot with skonces [earthworks], ordinance and all manner of warlike appointment to defend the Spannyardes landing there. Sir William Heydon, being lieutenant, appointed Sir Christopher Heydon his prime captain, with many other gentlemen which in order came in with their companies.

The Heydons had a direct interest as their Baconsthorpe home was only three miles inland. A plan 'drawn up in haste' on 1 May 1588 shows an entrenchment along the firm ground behind the salt marshes, with a fort at each end: Weybourne Fort due north of the village church and Black Joy fort at the mouth of Cley Haven.[3]

Monastic houses had provided an opportunity for education for local boys. This disappeared when they were dissolved, leading to the emergence of grammar schools shortly after the Reformation. John Gresham may well provide a direct link as it is likely that he was educated at Beeston priory. Gresham bought the manor house in Holt for £170 and converted it to a school to teach grammar to boys. He endowed the school with land, including two manors in Holt, land in nearby villages, and also the *White Hind* and the *Peacock* in Cripplegate in London, and appointed the wardens of the gild of fishmongers in London as governors. The school finally opened in 1562, six years after Gresham had died. A later headmaster, Thomas Tallis, left his private library to the school on his death in 1640.

Some people eagerly embraced the new form of faith, such as John Bale, who left the friary at Burnham Norton when it was dissolved and became a Protestant writer. Not everyone did, however: the le Stranges at Hunstanton Hall remained loyal to Roman Catholicism, for example, and at least one north Norfolk man was prepared to die for his religious beliefs – Henry Walpole. Walpole was born at Docking and was present at the execution in London of the priest Edmund Campion, which inspired him to become a priest in 1583. After spending time in France, Italy and Spain, he was sent – as he wished – to England, landing in disguise in Yorkshire on 4 December 1593. He was captured within 24 hours, and was sent to the Tower of London where he suffered torture no less than 14 times, more than any other of the Roman Catholic martyrs. He was eventually returned to York and was executed there on 7 April 1595. The present Catholic church at Burnham Market is dedicated to him.[4]

The Civil War divided the people of north Norfolk as it did everywhere. There were no battles in the area, but the L'Estrange family were heavily involved in the one conflict in Norfolk, the siege of King's Lynn. On 13 August 1643, the town declared its support for the King, and Sir Hamon L'Estrange was appointed as its Governor (he was also the man who changed the spelling of the family name from le Strange to L'Estrange). The town was blockaded by Parliamentarian forces led by the Earl of Manchester, and he sent word to the defenders that he would storm the town on 16 September unless the garrison surrendered. It capitulated on the day before the attack. Sir Hamon was held responsible for damage in the town he had briefly governed. His Hunstanton Hall estate was already under sequestration and had been plundered of sheep, corn and horses. Claims against him continued until 1650.

Sir Hamon's son, Roger L'Estrange, had fought at Lynn with his father and at the end of 1644 embarked on a reckless scheme to recapture the town for the Royalists. He was captured and sent to London for trial. He was tried on 26 December and sentenced to death, his execution being fixed for 2 January 1645. However, he was reprieved and committed to prison in Newgate. In 1648 he either escaped or was set free, and then went to Kent where he was involved in another uprising. One monument to these events survives, a powder magazine at Sedgeford, built for Sir Hamon in about 1643.

In 1649 a party of Royalist prisoners were being taken by boat from Lynn to Boston when they overpowered their guards and ordered the man

40 *Sir Roger L'Estrange of Hunstanton Hall.*

steering the boat to take them to Scarborough. He said that that was impossible, and landed at Heacham, telling them that a local Royalist would help them. This was Sir Hamon at nearby Hunstanton Hall, but he refused to see them and sent for the chief constable of the hundred; the escaped prisoners were soon rounded up. On their way back to Lynn, they passed by Hunstanton Hall, and, as it was an extremely hot day, asked for a drink, which Sir Hamon's butler gave them without his master's knowledge. He was reported to the London authorities by the constable for this act of common charity, but does not seem to have been further punished.[5]

In 1650, there was an attempted Royalist rising in Norfolk. Encouraged by a man named Smith alias Kitchingham, the Royalists met at Easton Heath, but were easily dispersed and it soon emerged that Smith had been a traitor; on his evidence many Royalist supporters found themselves in prison. The events showed the splits in the views of north Norfolk men, too. One of the leaders of the suppression was Colonel Robert Jermy, the Puritan squire of Bayfield near Holt, but three Royalist leaders were also closely connected with Holt: Thomas Cooper and William and Edmund Hobart. Cooper was born at Edgefield and was rector of Little Barningham in 1631. He was probably ejected from there on political grounds and in 1643 he appears as usher at Holt School. The Hobarts were younger men, the sons of James Hobart, lord of the manor of Holt. The Royalists were tried in Norwich, at Saint Andrew's Hall, in December 1650. Cooper's trial actually took place on Christmas Day, a deliberate policy on the part of the judges to show their own dislike of that day and to upset the Royalists. He was found guilty and a few days later he was executed in Holt, probably outside the door of the grammar school. William Hobart is said to have given evidence at Cooper's trial. If so, it did him no good: he was executed in Dereham Market Place, and was buried in Holt in January 1651. His brother Edmund was more fortunate, managing to escape his Royalist pursuers by hiding for three days in the roof of a wood shed in Holt belonging to a local currier, Anthony Riches. He then made his way to London, where he lived in disguise as the servant of a shoemaker. When the disturbance had died down he surrendered and was very heavily fined. He returned to Holt after the Restoration, and is said to have brought the shoemaker with him and to have provided for him. Edmund died in 1666 and his tomb can still be seen in the chancel of Holt church. Sir Roger L'Estrange also survived the war, and went on to publish one of London's first newspapers and translate *Aesop's Fables* into English before his death at the age of 88 in 1704.[6]

MARITIME TRADE

Maritime trade and fishing continued to be the main planks of the economy of the coastal region. According to Jonathan Hooton, trade with the Mediterranean began in 1589 when two ships left Blakeney and Cley bound for Marseilles. In the following year, Ben Bishop sent two of his ships, the *Ambrose* and the *Laundrel*, both of 100 tons, to Crete. The *Laundrel* took provisions for 30 men for a 10-month round trip, while the *Ambrose* carried 40 men and was to be away for a year, no doubt calling in at additional ports. Between them, the two ships took 900 stones

41 *Ships of the Elizabethan period, a plaque designed for the* Ship *at Brancaster.*

of beef and pork, 2,500 fish, 5,000 biscuits, 35 quarters of wheat, 20 quarters of peas, plus a quantity of butter, cheese and meal – and 15 tuns of beer.[7]

The port book for Blakeney survives for the period 1587 to 1590, and from it we can see what this port was like in the days of the first Queen Elizabeth. It distinguishes very clearly between foreign trade and home coastal trade.

For foreign trade, the record runs from Christmas 1588 to March 1590. In this period, 28 ships engaged in foreign trade in and out of Blakeney, ranging in size from 100 tons down to the *Swallow*, a mere five tons. Seventeen were from the Glaven ports (13 from Cley, three from Wiveton, one from Blakeney). Two were from London, four from Scotland and five from Dutch ports. Trade with Holland dominated the port – of 30 foreign voyages from the Haven, 20 were to Rotterdam and two to Amsterdam. Much of the trade was organised by a Rotterdam merchant, Gaillen Blaifote, usually through his factor, another Dutchman, Adam Kindt. The other voyages were to France, Scotland and two further afield – one to Danzig and one to Iceland. There were many more outgoing cargoes than incoming ones: in one full year, 27 ships loaded up at Blakeney but there were only 13 incoming cargoes.

Three ships arrived from Scotland in June 1589 alone, with loads of white salt. Exports included seven tons of beer sent to Culross. An unnamed Scottish ship was wrecked off Runton in 1589, and the goods sold out of it included prunes, honey, alum, liquorice, aniseed, two gross of playing cards, pins (described as 'wet and rusty'), wool combs and cards, and pepper. The *Gift of God* went to Iceland once, carrying cloth and cotton, while the *Mary James* brought 1,000 'stockfish called cropling' from that far-off country. More exotic imports include two goshawks and ten pairs of tables with their tablemen (ivory chess pieces?).

We can take the *Jonas* of Cley, 30 tons, as one example of a ship trading across the North Sea. On 4 February 1589, she sailed for Rotterdam with 19 lasts of barley and a pack of dornix with thread, containing 240 yards. She was back in Blakeney on 27 March with 600 hoops and 400 crusses of stone. On 9 April she set sail for Rotterdam once more with the same kind of cargo as before – barley and dornix. Presumably she returned empty as she is not mentioned again until 12 March 1590, when she sets off again for Rotterdam with a load of barley. Other exports apart from grain and cloth were not common. The *Speedwell* of Cromer took a hundredweight of nails as well as a load of barley on one journey, and on 14 April 1589 the *Rose* of Cley set sail for Danzig with a freight of skins: 300 'black and seasoned' rabbit skins, 8,000 grey rabbit skins and 200 lamb skins. Trade to France in 1589 was more varied. The *Gift of God* of Wiveton and the *Levoret* of Cley set out together for Rochelle on 14 October 1589, between them carrying 30 chalders (an old measurement of weight) of coals, five dozen pairs of hose and 1½ hundredweight of yellow wax. The *Gift of God* also carried three lasts of herring of 'her owne takeinge': fishing and trade could still be carried on by the same ship. Imports from Rotterdam included hops, Flanders bricks and onions.

A detailed record for coastal trade covers a six-month period between April and September 1587. A total of 43 ships are mentioned in this period, varying from 70 tons down to a mere five tons. Of these ships, 36 were from north Norfolk coast ports – 19 from Blakeney, nine from Cley, two from Wiveton, one from Salthouse, four from Cromer and one from Burnham. The other seven were from elsewhere in Britain, including several from Sussex ports bringing in sawn timber. A total of 51 coastal ships came into the port during the year (some coming more than once), peaking in June when a dozen ships arrived during the month. In contrast, only 22 departures are recorded, so that many ships made outward journeys empty, especially those engaged in the Newcastle coal trade, which made up the great bulk of business. Some items in the coastal trade originally came from further afield: salt from Spain coming on a ship from London, and Madeira wine from Yarmouth. In July 1589 two 'fowlers' and 10 pieces of cast ordinance arrived from Yarmouth, perhaps connected with the fears of invasion by Spain. The main export to Newcastle was malt, while large quantities of fish were exported in season. On 27 September 1587 four ships left for London, between them carrying 51,000 fish (cod and ling), 3½ lasts of stockfish and also 30 barrels of butter. On the same day another 16,000 cod and ling went to Lynn. A typical coastal trader was the *Mathew* of Blakeney. She arrived from Newcastle on 27 April 1587 with 25 chalders of coals and was one of the ships carrying fish to London in September. Another typical ship was the *William* of Cromer, arriving in Blakeney with coal from Newcastle four times between May and August. Most of her return runs must have been empty, but on 16 August she left Blakeney for Newcastle with a load of rye originally from Danzig.[8]

Wells and Burnham were not ports in their own right but creeks of Lynn; however, the record does not always separate the creeks from the main port. We can take as

Port	Haven	Householders	Ships for Ireland	Crayers and boats of burden	Mariners	Fishermen
MUNDESLEY	[unnamed]	16	0	3	0	10
CROMER	Cromer Pier	117	0	0	0	48
SHERINGHAM	The Hythe	136	0	0	0	69
WEYBOURNE	The Hope	35	0	0	0	14
SALTHOUSE	[unnamed]	58	0	0	0	21
CLEY	Blakeney Haven	100	9	14	35	25
WIVETON	[unnamed]	80	1	5	0	53
BLAKENEY	Blakeney Haven	80	4	8	30	18
WELLS	[unnamed]	90	7	7	0	60
BURNHAM DEEPDALE and OVERY (at Burnham Norton)	Two creeks together named Burnham Roadstead	56	0	2	7	5
HEACHAM	Creek called Heacham Haven	76	0	1	3	2
For comparison:						
LYNN		542	5	12	90	30
YARMOUTH		553	7	104	150	250

Figure I *Ships and ports of the north Norfolk coast in 1565. Source: A survey of the ports, creeks and landing places of Norfolk, 1565, held at the National Archives.*

an example one year that does make this distinction, 1614. The most frequent visitor to the creek, whether to Wells or to Burnham Overy Staithe we cannot know, was the *Estrich* of Camphire (Veere in the Netherlands), of just 15 tons. She arrived in January from Veere with a cargo of oats, leaving in the following month with pewter. She was back in March laden with Dutch cheese, tar, three copper kettles, and wine, leaving at the end of the month with 20lb of saffron. She was back in May to unload rye and wine and to load with more saffron, and then in July, again with rye and wine, leaving the same month with lead. She was back yet again with rye and wine in August, leaving in September with 'trayne' oil (the blubber of whales or seals), and returning in October with rye, hops, herrings and wine. Her last trip for the year was in November when she left with a load of saffron and sea coal.

Other ships were much less frequent visitors. Two came in February, one from Amsterdam and one from Rotterdam. They brought Spanish salt, some earmarked for the year's expedition from Wells to Iceland, 30 barrels of white herrings, three hundredweight of prawns, a barrel of raisins, Dutch cheese, and deals from Norway. In March, the *Fortune* of Sneak (Sneek, also in the Netherlands) arrived from Rotterdam with wine and Spanish salt, including more salt for the Icelandic expedition. This departed later in the same month and consisted of the *Mewne*, *John* and *Newyere*, all of Wells and of between 36 and 80 tons. All three carried salt that had come over from the Netherlands. The salt was, of course, for preserving fish caught on the expedition, and it is significant that the shipowners preferred to import it from Spain rather than use local salt.

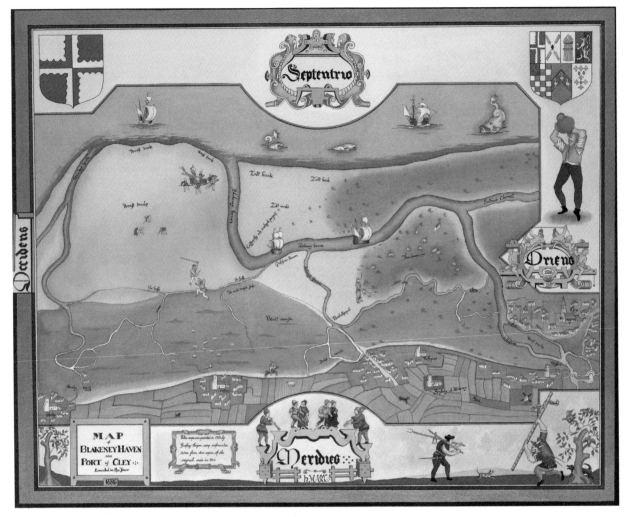

42 *Map of 1586 showing part of the north Norfolk coast, including Blakeney and Cley.*

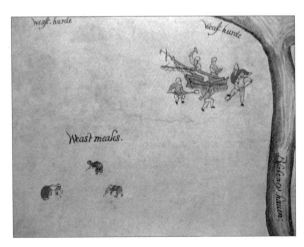

43 *Detail of 1586 map: the men work on a stranded ship while the women gather cockles.*

Two ships arrived in April from Flushing and Rotterdam. They brought in more salt, tar, pitch, spars, Norway deals – and one and a half chests of white Normandy glass. In June the *John* of Kinghorn arrived from Kinghorn with 25 tons of Scottish coal. In August, the three ships on the year's expedition to Iceland came back with cargoes including Icelandic cloth, called wadmal, and also hawks – gerfalcons, tercels and merlons, usually between six and nine of each breed on each ship. The ships were presumably also loaded with fish stored in salt, but this is only very erratically recorded, being regarded as fishing business rather than imported produce. The *Robert* of Wells, 20 tons, arrived at the end of August from Leith in Scotland, carrying white salt and Scottish linen. After that there were no more ships from foreign ports for the rest of the year apart from the *Estrich*.[9]

So the port was only a small one, with one ship a month or so coming in from abroad, peaking at four in August. Of course this is just the foreign trade; smaller local ships would be arriving with coal and leaving with grain.

The government also made surveys of local shipping at this period, in case the vessels were needed in time of war. One was made in 1565, and another, carried out in 1580, survives among the Bacon papers and names the ships, 70 in all, in the coastal ports, and also gives the names of their owners. The ports have the following numbers of ships: Cromer, three; Sheringham, two; Weybourne, two; Cley, 11; Wiveton, 13; Blakeney, 11; Wells, 19; Stiffkey, one; Burnham Norton, one; Burnham Deepdale, one; Brancaster, one; Holme, one; Hunstanton, one; Ringstead, two; Heacham, one. The largest of the ships are the *Clementes* of Wells, of 160 tons, and the *Marie Grace* of Wiveton, 120 tons. There are a total of nine ships of 100 tons or more, all based at either Wells or the Glaven ports. Ships to the west and east of this were smaller: those at Hunstanton and Ringstead were each of 30 tons, none of those at Cromer or Sheringham was more than 20 tons. Several people owned or part-owned more than one vessel, and the greatest of the shipowners in the survey was William Sabbe of Wells, who owned four ships, including the *Clementes*, and part-owned a fifth. At Cley, Richard Ralye owned two ships and part-owned a third, as did James Graye at Wiveton. At Blakeney, the Page family owned three ships between them: family members owning the ships included Katherine Page, widow. The only other female shipowner in the survey was Rose Rooke, who owned both ships plying out of Weybourne, the *Peter* of 70 tons and the *Rose* of 60 tons. These were quite large vessels, especially considering the lack of a haven. It was common for one person to own all the ships plying from the smaller ports: Eustace Rolfe owned two of the three ships at Heacham, and Thomas and John Read jointly owned both the Ringstead ships.[10]

Maritime trade was flourishing, but pirates from France – Dunkirkers – were a great problem. In 1602, the inhabitants of Wells petitioned the Commissioners for Musters to provide a ship to protect their vessels. Dunkirkers had taken a Wells ship on its way home from Iceland; the ship and its cargo were worth £700 and the master and part-owner, John Housigoe, was ruined by the loss. The Dunkirkers had also captured a barque belonging to John Green on its way to Newcastle, and were holding the master in pledge for some of their own men imprisoned at Lynn. The situation was worsening:

> whereas the Dunkirkers were wont to come upon our coasts with small boats, now since their prizes have been taken from them they come in very great ships of 200 tons apiece, very well furnished with men and munitions so as the coast is no way able to resist them.

The importance of the sea in local transport arrangements can be seen from Felbrigg documents. In the early years of the 17th century, John Wyndham decided to put

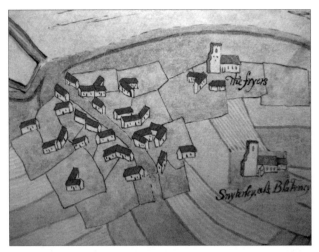

The fryers

Snykerley alt Blakeney

44   *Blakeney in 1586: note the two churches, one belonging to the former friary.*

up monuments in Felbrigg church to his predecessors Thomas Wyndham and his sister Jane. He commissioned effigies in brass embedded in Portland stone. These were of the best possible quality, made in London in 1612, and were brought by ship to Yarmouth, by barge to Coltishall Bridge, and from there carried in two carts to Felbrigg.[11]

Graffiti in both Salthouse and Wiveton churches include drawings, perhaps by bored choir boys, of ships in harbour or in full sail; those at Wiveton have only recently been uncovered. These reflect the romance and adventure of sea voyages, as the boys dreamed of the day when they, too, 'went down to the ship, set keel to breakers, forth on the godly sea'.[12]

The Wells parish registers show that the Icelandic trade continued into the Tudor period. They also show the dangers involved in maritime pursuits – and the popular superstitions of the time. The register for 1583-4 records many deaths at sea. In July, nine men perished in Iceland in a dogger belonging to the *Symons*, a ship owned by Ambrose Fiske of Wells. On Boxing Day 1583, 14 men from Wells perished on the west coast of England coming from Spain. It might be thought that their deaths were caused by attempting such a voyage in the middle of winter. However, the vicar of Wells recorded in his register that their

> deaths were brought to pass by the detestable working of an execrable witch of King's Lynn whose name was Mother Gabley, by the boiling or labouring of certain eggs in a pail of cold water. Afterwards approved sufficiently at the arraignment of the said witch.

Clearly she was tried and convicted – and no doubt paid the penalty of execution. January 1584 also saw the burial in Wells of Admeson, a boy from Iceland, and another Icelandic boy, Gwilloner or William Johnson, was buried there in 1599. It is interesting to speculate whether these boys had taken to the maritime life by choice or whether they had been kidnapped by the crew to assist them; it was a common complaint of Icelandic people in the Middle Ages that their young men were captured and enslaved by British boats.

Deaths at sea were plentiful over the years. To take just three examples of many, seven men from Wells were lost in April 1586 in a crayer called the *Matthew*. At the end of 1588-9, it was recorded that Ambrose Burwood 'this year being left with a ship in Norway was never heard of since'. In August 1602, Andrew Fornas was coming from Iceland in the *Susan*: 'as she was under sail [and] entered within the haven, was slain with the shot of a gun by a ship of war [be]longing to Dunkirk, and buried the same day'.

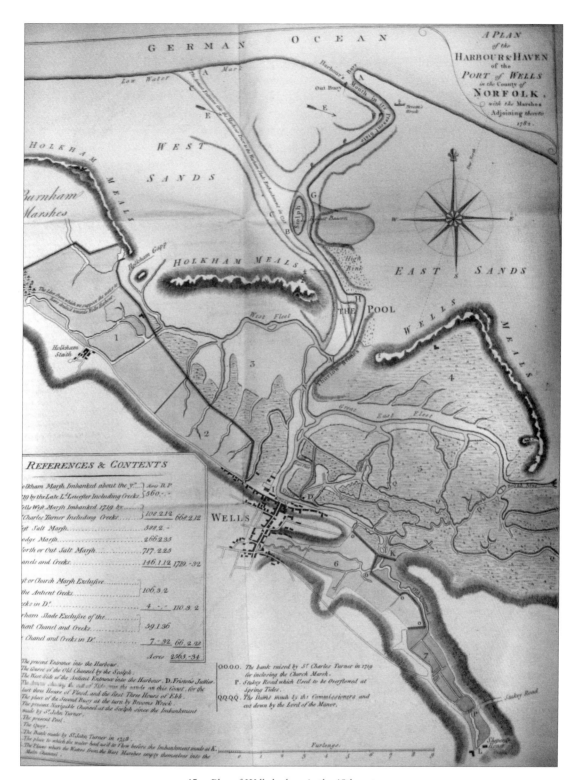

45 *Plan of Wells harbour in the 18th century.*

In 1624 the vicar made a separate list of men of Wells lost at sea. Two boats had been lost on that year's return voyage from Iceland in August. The *Cyst* of Wells sank on 24 or 25 August: the master was Christopher Anderson. Three other men from Wells were also drowned in the disaster, along with five 'strangers' (which might mean foreigners, but probably simply means men not from Wells). A week later, at 'about the end of August', the *Jeane* was lost in Iceland. This was a family disaster: the master John Pells was drowned with his two sons James and John, along with two other men from Wells – Thomas Mowes and John Hodds. Five strangers were also lost on the *Jeane*. Later in the same year, on 12 or 13 November, four Wells men were lost on a voyage to Holland on board a Flemish ship.

Not all the burials at Wells were of seamen of course. One man who took a risk as great as that of any mariner was buried in October 1589. The burial register records:

> George Matthew, a shoemaker being an adulterer was stabbed into with a knife by the husband of the adulteress even as the filthy deed was in doing, and so killed, out of hand and without speaking any word, the 8th October between the hours of five and six o'clock in the morning.

Men in port were liable to be press-ganged into the navy. On 31 July and 1 August 1599, some 106 men were pressed in Wells, Wiveton and Sheringham. They included 19 from Wells and 11 each from Cley, Cromer and Sheringham. In 1602, 30 men were press-ganged at Burnham and 26 at Sheringham. Each man was given four shillings press money and a shilling for conduct money. Not all of them went. It was possible to get out of it by greasing the right palm, as three cases before Nathaniel Bacon in March 1598 demonstrate. William Starkin of Wells was dealing with his father's affairs when he was press-ganged; he paid 10s. to a Mr Sharpe for his discharge. Clement Mangle of Cley spoke on behalf of Richard Kendall, 'being boat master for his voyage this year to Iceland'. Because Kendall was 'a necessary mariner for his ship's voyage', Mangle paid Dr Burman 20s. to discharge him, and a further half a crown to Burman's servant who acted as go-between in the negotiations. John Beane of Sheringham was also press-ganged by Dr Burman; he had himself discharged by giving 10s. to John Emerson, marshal of the Admiralty.

Wells was given separate status as a customs port in 1676. It also administered the creeks of Thornham, Brancaster and Burnham Overy Staithe. Its neighbour Cley took responsibility for Blakeney and the beach landing ports at Cromer and Sheringham. There was already a stone quay at Wells, which was in disrepair by 1662 when local merchants and mariners petitioned Parliament to authorise the raising of money to repair it and maintain the harbour. This led to the Wells Harbour Act of 1663, which allowed the levying of charges on cargoes loaded or unloaded in the port by two people chosen by the merchants and mariners of the port.

In the late 17th and the 18th centuries there was a decline of international trade, balanced by growth in coastal trade – in 1700, 14 ships went from the Glaven ports to London; by 1780, the number had increased to 86, mainly loaded with barley.

THREE NAVAL HEROES

Christopher Myngs

Christopher Myngs was baptised at Salthouse on 22 November 1625: his father was John Myngs, a shoemaker originally from Cockthorpe, and his mother Katherine, daughter of Christopher Parr. In later life, Myngs liked to stress his humble background, calling his mother a hoyman's daughter, but in fact he inherited land in Salthouse from his property-owning parents. Myngs probably served in the navy during the Civil War and was second in command on the *Elizabeth*, which fought in the first Dutch War; her captain was killed in May 1653 and Myngs was promoted to replace him. In October he met a Dutch convoy and captured about twenty merchant ships. In October 1655 he was chosen to captain the *Marston Moor* and take her to the Caribbean. The ship had only just returned from Jamaica, and the crew mutinied at the prospect of such a swift return. Myngs took drastic action, sacking them and putting together an alternative crew out of men from other ships. He took part in an unsuccessful attempt to capture Spanish treasure ships and helped boost the new English colony in Jamaica by bringing in 400 settlers from the island of Nevis. He was badly wounded on his flagship the *Victory* at the Battle of North Foreland against the Dutch in 1666; he was brought to Whitechapel where he died, and where he is buried. His daughter, Mary, is buried in Salthouse; her memorial describes her father as 'valiant and renowned'.

John Narborough

John Narborough was baptised at Cockthorpe on 11 October 1640, the son of Gregory Narborough. He was probably related to Myngs, and, according to legend, began his naval career as Myngs' cabin boy. His first commission was as lieutenant of Myngs' *Portland* in October 1664. In April 1666 he became lieutenant of the *Victory*, and when Myngs was mortally wounded, Narborough took command. His success led to his first appointment as captain of the *Assurance*, in which he fought in the engagement at Martinique in June 1667. He was wounded in the thigh at Surinam on 7 October 1667. In 1669, he was captain of the *Sweepstakes*, in which he served in South America and the Pacific Ocean. He was noted for his concern for his crew, and also his sympathy for Peruvian natives, of whom he wrote, 'the poor miserable Indians groan under their heavy burden'. He fought in the third Anglo-Dutch War of 1672, became an admiral and received a knighthood in 1673. In 1674, he was in the Mediterranean defending English shipping against African pirates, and led an attack on Tripoli in January 1676 which resulted in the signing of a treaty with Tripoli in March. However, hostilities soon broke out once more, and in 1678 he was back in command in the Mediterranean with 35 ships, but was unable to control the activities of the pirates. He returned to England in 1679 and bought an estate at Knowlton in Kent. From 1682, he interested himself in salvaging a lost Spanish treasure ship, which had sunk in the West Indies in 1641. He financed a successful salvage trip led by William Phips, from which he gained over £20,000. In September 1687, he himself sailed to the site. Fever broke out aboard the ship while they were in the West Indies, and Myngs died on the ship on 27 May 1688; he was buried at sea. He left a wife, Elizabeth, two sons and a daughter.

Cloudesley Shovell

Cloudesley Shovell was baptised at Cockthorpe on 25 November 1650, Cloudesley being his grandmother's family name. He was closely connected with both Myngs and Narborough, becoming Myngs' cabin-boy in 1663, and Narborough's cabin-boy after Myngs was killed. He may have been with Narborough on his voyage to the Pacific, and was certainly present with him at the battle of Sole Bay. He was also with him at Tripoli, where he earned praise for his actions: James Greeve, who was with him, is buried in Cley church.

Shovell was appointed to his first command, the *Sapphire*, in September 1677. Over the next five years he was in command of several ships in the Mediterranean, and assisted in drawing up the treaty that led to the end of the war with Algiers in April 1682. He was knighted after the battle of Bantry Bay against the French in May 1689, and was promoted to rear admiral of the blue in 1690. In 1691, he married Narborough's widow, Elizabeth.

Shovell commanded the rear division of the central squadron at the Battle of Barfleur on 19 May 1692. He was able to break through the French line, and followed the French fleet to La Hogue, where he was unable to attack because of sudden illness, probably blood poisoning from a splinter wound he had received in the thigh. However, he recovered and his later achievements included the bombardment of Calais in 1696 and command of the Channel Fleet in 1697. In 1707 he took part in an unsuccessful attack on Toulon, after which he took the fleet into Gibraltar. It was on his return voyage that disaster struck. The fleet reached the Scilly Isles on 21 October, but three ships, including Shovel's flagship *Association*, struck the rocks and sank. Of the 1,315 men on the ships, just one survived. Shovell's exact fate is not known. His body was found at Port Hellick Cove on the south side of St Mary's Island. His two stepsons, a pet dog and the flagship's captain were found nearby, so they had presumably reached the cove together on one of the ship's boats. Tradition says that Shovell was still alive when he was found by a local woman, who murdered him for the sake of an emerald ring on his finger; she is supposed to have confessed to this on her own deathbed in the 1730s. Shovell was laid to rest with great ceremony at Westminster Abbey on 22 December 1707, the last and greatest of the three admirals of Salthouse and Cockthorpe. Elizabeth, his wife, lived to a great age, dying in April 1732.

POCAHONTAS

The ability of Norfolk people to cross and re-cross the Atlantic can be illustrated by a romance, the story of Pocahontas. She is probably the only person with a Norfolk connection to feature in a Walt Disney movie, even if the films (*Pocahontas* and *Pocahontas II: Journey to a New World*) do take considerable liberties with her story. Her formal name was Matoaka, but she was early given the nickname

46   *Pocahontas on the Heacham village sign.*

47   *Plaque in Heacham church to Princess Pocahontas.*

of Pocahontas, or 'wild one'. She was the daughter of Wahunsunacawh, an Indian chief of the Powhatans who ruled an area in Virginia. Their contact with Englishmen began in May 1607, when colonists arrived in Virginia and began building settlements. One of the colonists, John Smith, told how he was captured by a group of Powhatan hunters. He was laid across a stone and about to be beaten with clubs, when Pocahontas, then aged about thirteen, intervened: 'Pocahontas, the King's dearest daughter, when no intreaty could prevaile, got his head in her armes, and laid her owne upon his to save him from death'. There must be some doubt about Smith's story, as he did not put it into writing until 10 years later, and he had earlier told a very similar story when he had been captured by the Turks in Hungary and a beautiful girl had intervened to save him.

However, it is certain that Pocahontas did often come to the English settlement and play. On one occasion, when the English were suffering from hunger, she bought supplies to Smith that saved the life of many of the colonists. She may have saved him on a second occasion, too. When Smith and some others had a meeting with the Indian chief, they missed the tide that would have taken them back and had to stay the night. During the night Pocahontas came to Smith's hut to tell him that the chief planned to murder the Englishmen when they were unarmed. They kept their arms and no attack came.

In 1609, Smith was injured in a gunpowder explosion and returned to England. The English told the natives that he had died, inventing a story that he had been captured by a French pirate ship that had been wrecked on the Brittany coast, with the loss of all hands.

Four years later, Pocahontas was taken prisoner by one of the colonists, Samuel Argall, who held her to ransom, offering to return her to her father if he gave back some prisoners he had captured, together with weapons and tools that had been stolen by the natives. Powhatan returned the prisoners but not enough weapons to satisfy the English; Pocahontas remained a prisoner. She was baptised into the Christian faith and took the name Rebecca. It was at this time that she met John Rolfe.

Rolfe was a Norfolk man baptised at Heacham on 6 May 1585. In 1608 he married a woman whose name is not recorded. They set sail for Virginia on the *Sea Venture* in the following year. Their ship ran aground on Bermuda where the colonists were stranded for 10 months. While there, Rolfe's wife gave birth to a daughter whom the couple named Bermuda; she died while they were still on the island. The couple finally reached Jamestown in 1610 where Rolfe suffered another tragedy, his wife dying shortly after their arrival. Rolfe brought to Virginia a much improved variety of tobacco, and this new crop was the beginning of the great tobacco trade between Virginia and England.

Rolfe wrote a letter to the governor, asking permission to marry Pocahontas, saying that he was not motivated by:

the unbridled desire of carnal affection, but for the good of this plantation, for the honour of our countrie, for the glory of God, for my owne salvation, and for converting to the true knowledge of God and Jesus Christ, an unbelieving creature namely Pocahontas, to whom my hearty and best thoughts are, and have been a long time so entangled, and enthralled in so intricate a labyrinth that I was even a-wearied to unwind myself thereout.

He described his Princess as 'one whose education hath bin rude, her manners barbarous, her generation accursed'. The couple married on 5 April 1614, and lived together on Rolfe's plantation, Varina Farms. They had a child, Thomas Rolfe, who was born on 30 January 1615.

In 1616, the couple returned to England on the *Treasurer*, bringing about a dozen other natives with them. They landed at Plymouth on 12 June 1616, and went by coach to London. They stayed in England for 11 months, living at first on Ludgate Hill. By the autumn the Rolfes had moved out of London to Brentford, and also spent time, according to a strong tradition, at Heacham Hall. Pocahontas met King James I at the Banqueting Hall in Whitehall Palace in January 1617; apparently, she was not very impressed with him. She also met John Smith once more, at a social gathering at Brentford.

In March 1617, Rolfe and Pocahontas boarded a ship for Virginia, but Pocahontas was already sick, suffering from tuberculosis or pneumonia; she was taken ashore at Gravesend and died. Her funeral took place at St George's Gravesend on 21 March and a statue is now there in her honour. Rolfe then continued to Virginia, where he became a member of the governor's council, and was later on the council of state. He died in 1622, either during a native uprising or of sickness. Their child Thomas had been left behind in London in the care of his uncle, but he migrated to Virginia in the 1630s. He married Jane Poythress there and many Americans claim Pocahontas as an ancestor through the couple's children.

Another person to cross the Atlantic more than once was Thomas Cornwallis, whose family owned land at Burnham Thorpe. Cornwallis played a leading part in the foundation of the province of Maryland in America. He made his money exporting tobacco to England and became the richest man in the colony. He returned to England in about 1660 and lived in Burnham Thorpe until his death in 1676.

FISHING AND FARMING

Besides these great voyages, local fishing continued – and remained a dangerous occupation. The Wells burial register tells us that in January 1584 three men perished in an 'oysterfare', and later in the same winter Robert Herrison and his servant Thomas Hindson were lost with their gear in a coble. Cobles are a type of boat, apparently peculiar to eastern England, designed to be launched straight from the beach into the water, always a dangerous venture in rough seas. An entry for 1622 in the same register gives an insight into the contributions made by women and children to the fishing industry. On 19 September, 17 people were drowned together in a boat rowing down to the Meals to dry fish. There was just one man among them, and five adult women: the other eleven are described in the register as 'son of …' or 'daughter of …',

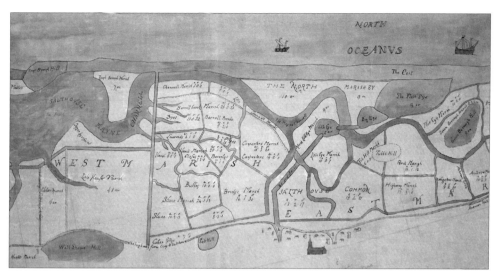

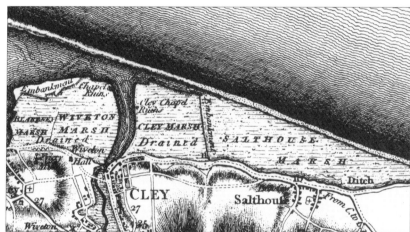

48 a–c *Channels and marshes east of Cley, shown on a map of 1649 (Salthouse church is shown), with the same area shown on maps of 1797 and 1826. The marshes are now a Norfolk Wildlife Trust reserve.*

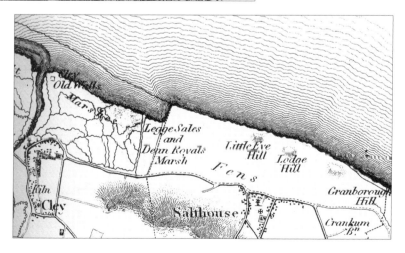

so they were presumably children. The body of one woman was never recovered but the rest were buried in the churchyard.[13]

Freshwater fishing was still important. On the Felbrigg estates, William Windham treated his fishponds as part of his income. He:

> recorded details of his carp, noting when ponds were restocked, the numbers involved and the size and growth of the fish, which he measured from 'eye to tayle'. He moved carp from one pond to another to prevent overstocking, and tried to keep the same size fish in each location to ensure an even growth pattern. He enlarged existing ponds by removing gravel, and built extra ponds to accommodate the surplus.[14]

Farming naturally continued in importance, relying on an ever-increasing production of barley, much of which was exported to London on local ships. The 17th century saw the first attempts to extend the area of farmed land by enclosing and draining the marshes along the coast, described by C.L.S. Linnell:

> Inspired by the example of Vermuijden, reclamation was begun along the Norfolk coast under the supervision of another Dutchman, Van Hasedunck. The area in question is the strip of coast between Cromer and Wells where several small streams find their way into the sea by means of creeks which during the medieval times afforded the transit of shipping to the prosperity of such places as Blakeney, Cley-next-the-Sea, Wiveton and Salthouse; places which are now, thanks to the reclamation, small villages from which, although they bear many and considerable traces of a sometime prosperity, anything in the nature of export trade has vanished.

Van Hasedunck made use of the three high pieces of land known as Little Eye, Great Eye and Flat Eye, which were islands at high tide before the embankment. The bank meant that Kelling and Weybourne were cut off from the sea. The towns brought a legal case in 1638, claiming that they were excluded from their chief means of livelihood and from fishing in their channel and in the creeks, so that they were forced to beg or to move elsewhere.

Further west, Sir Henry Calthorpe enlarged the marshland at Blakeney in 1637, throwing a bank across the marsh between Wiveton and Cley. This threatened to obstruct shipping to Wiveton entirely, and to that part of Cley near the church. The inhabitants of the two towns protested to the Privy Council, cleverly appealing to royal self-interest:

> That the same haven hath had many good ships of burden belonging to it which have been set forth from thence to Westmonie and Iceland and to trade with Holland Flanders and France and Spain and other small vessels carrying corn and other commodities to Newcastle etc, and bringing in coals, salt and other merchandise for the country hereabout and likewise to the advantage of His Majesty's customs … That the Susan of Wiveton was pressed in Queen Elizabeth's service in 1589 for service into Portugal of which Thomas Coe of Cley went as Quarter-master (as he does testify). Thomas Coe affirms that they have 19 other good ships, some of 140 and one of 160 tons belonging to the same town (six being built at Wiveton near unto the main channel beside many others belonging to Cley) by means of which his late Majesty King James of blessed memory did receive for customs in one year £420, and now his majesty [Charles] only £100.

The petition pointed out the importance of the haven as a refuge, citing the example of the *Jonas* of Housan, which was carrying, among other things, 44 horses 'fit for His Majestie's service'. Had they not be able to find shelter in the haven, men and horses would have perished. The petition was successful and the embanking was removed after two years, but it was too late: Wiveton had ceased to be a port. Two centuries later, priorities had changed. An embankment was put up again on almost exactly the same site in 1823, this time without protest.[15]

The first Coke to live at Holkham was also keen on drainage: this was John Coke, who was living there by 1638. He inherited the manor in 1659 through his marriage to Merial Wheatley, whose grandfather had bought it from Lady Anne Gresham. He went on to buy other pieces of land until he owned almost the whole parish. In 1660, he reclaimed 360 acres of salt marsh from the sea.[16]

We have seen that barley was exported, and also seen some mention of saffron, grown widely in Norfolk from the 14th century onward, both for use as a dye and for culinary and medicinal purposes. The word saffron is still found as a place-name in various villages. A saffron yard is mentioned in a 1623 Sheringham deed and there is a Saffron Yard on a map of Cromer of 1760. There was a saffron garden at Holkham, and the crop was grown in nearby Walsingham; it is mentioned in two Walsingham wills of about 1517. It was also grown at Wighton; in 1556, Richard Elflyght left his saffron close there to his wife Alice for the term of her life, it then passing to their son David. Alice was to keep the close in good repair, and was instructed not to take out the saffron heads unless she replaced them. A lease of 1570 among the papers of the Bacon family of Stiffkey, relating to the manor of Stiffkey Netherhall and Stowes, also includes a covenant about retaining saffron heads; these are presumably the bulbs, rather than the seed heads.

There are many other mentions of saffron among the Bacon papers in the later 16th century. When Nathaniel was walking round the Stiffkey manor estate recently purchased by his father, he found that there were three acres of saffron ground, but could not find out how much rent was received from them. There were a further three rods (three-quarters of an acre) of saffron ground still in the hands of the steward. In 1598, Nathaniel spent 30s. on creating a new saffron ground by putting in ditches, and the expenses of gathering the crop are also recorded. A 1599 legal case indicates that the crop was prepared at home. A girl named Elizabeth Ransome was in service with Mr Fiske of Binham and his wife. One night, 'when saffron time then lasted', Fiske was tending his saffron kiln in his hall; it obviously did not occupy all his time as, according to Elizabeth, Fiske seduced her – even though his wife was asleep upstairs in the house – as a result of which she was now with child.[17]

The papers of the Bacon family of Stiffkey have a great deal more information about life in north Norfolk at the time of Elizabeth I. Nathaniel Bacon was born in about 1546, the son of Sir Nicholas Bacon, the Lord Keeper. He was educated at Cambridge University and at Gray's Inn. In 1569, he married Anne, the illegitimate daughter of Sir Thomas Gresham. He was appointed a Norfolk Justice of the Peace in 1574, holding office for almost fifty years, and was twice sheriff of Norfolk and a Member of Parliament; he was knighted in 1604.[18]

49 *Stiffkey Hall showing characteristic round towers and the proximity of the parish church.*

When Bacon married Anne, the property settled on them by her father included the manor of Langham with Morston. His own father, Sir Nicholas, began acquiring land in Stiffkey, the greater part being purchased from John and Edmund Banyard for £2,000. Nathaniel lived in Cockthorpe until 1578 when he moved into the newly built Stiffkey Hall.

Cockthorpe House itself had to be made ready. Nathaniel agreed to buy eight cows from Edward Stannow, the previous occupier of the house, and to allow Stannow to keep his own animals on the property until Easter, provided he supplied straw to Bacon's cows. He wanted to buy other things from Stannow including brewing and kitchen equipment, dairy vessels and bedding. He also asked his agent to look at one of the chambers to see what length of board could be put there 'to dine and sup at'.

The Bacon records illustrate the continuing importance of marine trade. Edward Goodwin agreed with Sir Nicholas to ship to Stiffkey a salt-house 40 feet long and 18 feet wide. He would charge £25 and erect it as a 'garner', supplying tiles for the roof, and board for the planking and for the doors and windows. Sir Nicholas had to provide nails, including pins for the tiles, lime and sand – and also carriage from where it was landed to where it was to be erected. The agreement was signed on 3 March 1573, Goodwin promising the work would be completed by 25 July. An unnamed merchant agreed with the Bacons in the winter of 1571/2 that he would deliver 'at the waterside at Stiffkey Goat, Wells or Wighton nine score quarters of good, sweet and merchantable barley' at or before the feast of the Purification of Our Lady, each year for the next six years.

In the winter of 1571, Nathaniel reported to his father that a ship had run aground on the sands by the salt marsh at Stiffkey and had broken up. The men were saved and most of the contents washed up in Stiffkey, but some items came ashore in the liberty of Morston. The ship was loaded with iron, Danish board and ordnance. In another letter, he told his father that eight score bars of iron, two pieces of ordnance, three sacks of wet hops, two hundred pieces of clapboard, 'besides other pieces of broken timber', were in the hands of John Mounford, the Bacon's bailiff.

The records describe the cutting of a creek in Stiffkey marsh:

> I have thought since Mounford's going from me that, if the turf which may be cut of the upper sward of the ground where the trench shall go, be laid in form of a little wall on the sides of the trench, I think thereby the earth that is cast out of the trench beyond that wall shall be kept from falling in again when Spring tides come.

It is a mistake to think of fishermen, farmers and mariners as separate groups. I have looked at probate inventories of men from the coastal towns who are described as fishermen, and without exception they are also farmers, with the crops and animals on their farms worth much more than their fishing gear. Another good example is the probate inventory and will of Arthur Browne of Blakeney, who died in 1726. Described as a gentleman, he was a farmer, brewer and shipowner. At the time of his death, he had 140 acres of barley, 40 acres of wheat, five acres of rye, 30 acres of peas and 820 sheep. He was also the owner of a 25-ton sloop, the *Mayflower*, of which his second son William was master. He bequeathed the *Mayflower* to William, and his farm and brewery to his eldest son, Samuel. William Dawson, a tenant of the Windham family, was also both a farmer and a fisherman. He paid Windham eight shillings a year for rent on a piece of land in Runton, normally in cash, but in 1686 he paid in kind for the previous three years' rent, giving Windham salt fish worth £1 4s. in December.[19]

It was natural for people to look to larger towns for opportunity, and many from the north coast went to Norwich. This was fine as long as they could find work, but if they lost their jobs they were soon rounded up by the authorities and sent back to their home parishes. There are many such cases in the Norwich archives, as shown by these examples from the early 1630s. Two men were sent back to Holt, a journeyman shoemaker called John Playne, and William Atkins, a vagrant. Henry Burgess, a tinker from Cromer, was also found a vagrant in Norwich and told to go.

Some cases were less clear cut. Two men from Blakeney, William Jackson and James Pickett, had been in Norwich for five years working for a weaver. When the work came to an end, they were ordered to leave the city within 14 days. Jackson clearly did not do so as he was later set to work in the Norwich Bridewell. Grassington Hodgkyn went from Holt to Norwich with his wife and children. He must have died there, as the family became dependent on the city's charity; they were promptly sent back to Holt and ordered never to return.

The case of Elizabeth Carter of Cley is more complicated. Found begging in Norwich, she was whipped and sent back to Cley where she had been born. However, the inhabitants of Cley were not happy to receive her back and took the matter to the Assize courts. They said that 11 years earlier, Elizabeth had been put into St Augustine's lazar house, probably with mental health problems. The Cley authorities paid the keeper, a man named Hoath, £4 13s. 4d. to keep her there for the rest of her life. The city authorities said that the lazar house had no funds to maintain its inhabitants but sent them 'a-begging into the city'. The judges decided that Norwich had been right to send her back to Cley, and that Cley would have to look after her. If they thought they had been cheated by Hoath, who had left the lazar house, they would have to sue him themselves and try to get their money back from him.[20]

In Tudor times, money that might well have been previously spent on churches or monastic houses was spent on large houses instead. Good examples are Stiffkey and Felbrigg. According to Piet Aldridge,

Stiffkey Old Hall, standing in eight acres of gardens, is a remarkable flint, brick and stone house, dating from 1576 onwards, with additions and alterations in the 16th century (the gatehouse is dated 1640) and 18th century, and restorations in the 20th and early 21st centuries. The hall was built on the site of earlier halls for Sir Nathaniel Bacon, with financial (and possibly design) help from his father Sir Nicholas. It was originally intended to be a four-sided building symmetrically placed around a courtyard, but some parts were never built and others were later demolished. Of the U-shaped structure that stood originally, the west or kitchen range and part of the hall range survive, having distinctive round towers at the northeast, northwest and southwest angles.[21]

The Windhams had lived at Felbrigg for generations. Thomas Windham built his new house in 1621 on the site of the previous residence, and there is medieval masonry in the cellars of the present house. The house was finished by 1624, when a carver named Smith was paid for two four-foot high lions for the parapet, which can still be seen on the gables. The façade is largely unchanged, with the inscription GLORIA DEO IN EXCELSIS ('Glory to God on High') in large stone letters on the parapet. The architect is said to have been Robert Lyminge. Half a century later the house was doubled in size when the west wing was added, designed by William Samwell and built between 1675 and 1678.

The Windhams invested in their estate as well as their house. William Windham was a great planter of trees, some of his planting activity being recorded in his 'Green Book' (a very appropriate colour). His favourite tree was the sweet chestnut. He established his own tree nursery in 1676, sowing acorns, ash keys, haws, holly berries, chestnuts, maple and sycamore keys and a small quantity of beech mast. In the same year he planted over six thousand small trees: 4,000 oaks, 800 ashes, 600 birches, 70 beeches and 50 crab-apples. Ten years later, he was able to use the trees in his nursery to extend his woodland. Some of his sweet chestnut trees still flourish after more than three centuries.

50   *Felbrigg Hall: note how close the flock of sheep is to the house.*

51 *Baconsthorpe Castle: the medieval buildings are in the background.*

Other older houses were redeveloped, albeit in a less drastic manner. The Outer Gatehouse at Baconsthorpe was added by Christopher Heydon after 1551 and became the only inhabited part of the complex after the 1650s when the rest of the building was demolished by the Heydons and sold as building material. At Hunstanton Hall, the earlier gatehouse was retained but the inner courtyard was constructed between 1625 and the early 1640s, probably designed by William Edge. The le Strange household accounts show how well the rich lived: for example, in June 1537, 16 stone of beef was purchased, together with calf tongues, veal, pig, chicken, fish, cockles and eggs. All the same foods were on the menu at Christmas and also cod, geese, and wading birds such as redshank, spoe (whimbrel), curlews, stynts, teal and mallards. A feast at Felbrigg in 1654 included pigs, turkeys, ducklings and partridges, a great amount of seafood – lobsters, crabs, whiting, codlings – as well as river fish, including trout and salmon. The food would have been kept fresh with ice, stored in the deep brick pit of the estate ice-house; there is one in perfect condition on the Holkham estate. The ice would have been scraped each winter from the nearby lake, one of the advantages of the Little Ice Age – how often do these lakes freeze over today?[22]

PLAGUE AND FIRE

The Black Death had not gone away: it reappeared at different times in different places. Plague came to Cley, for example, in September 1579. The average number of burials in the parish in the 10 years between 1579 and 1588 was seventeen. In 1579, there 35 burials and no less than 88 in 1580. As is often the way after an outbreak of plague, the numbers buried in the years immediately following it were much lower than the average, just six in 1581 and eight in 1582; presumably the plague had wiped out the 'weaklings' in the population. In Wiveton, the number of burials was only four or five a year. It rose to 13 in 1578, but fell back to the average in the following year, so the outbreak in Cley in 1579 and 1580 was extremely localised, not even affecting this nearby village.

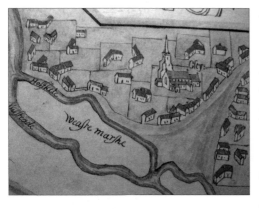

52   *Cley in 1586: the houses near the church were destroyed in the fire of 1612.*

There was plague in Holt in 1592, as recorded in the parish register. In this small market town, there were only six or eight burials a year at this period. Suddenly, everything was different. There were 10 burials in August, 22 in September and 15 in October. In all there were 64 burials between August 1592 and February 1593, 10 times the average. Then, just as suddenly as it had arrived, plague disappeared from Holt: there were only three more burials of any kind in the town in the remaining 10 months of 1593.

We can look at some of the families involved. Four children of James and Agnes Leaman died within 10 tragic August days and James himself was buried on 27 August. Edmund and Cecilia Cooke suffered a similar tragedy in the following month: five of their children died, three being buried together on 16 September. Just two days later, Cecilia followed her children into the grave. Of course, life must go on after a tragedy. The widow Agnes Leaman remarried in July 1593 and in the following month Edmund Cooke also took a second marital partner.[23]

Fire was a real danger in all towns, with thatched roofs, wooden structures and open fires. On 1 September 1612, fire destroyed 117 dwellings in the Newgate area of Cley, the area around the church. Those who lost houses included widow Newgate, who lost 18 dwellings valued at £600; Robert Beales lost 12 houses and John Rayley eight. Widow Fysh lost five houses, 'wherein dwelt fower poor persons'. Thomas Cloudesley, grandfather of the admiral, also lost houses in the fire. The inhabitants appealed to the Quarter Sessions for help, and they awarded the 'poorer sort' of the town £200, authorising Nathaniel Bacon to organise its distribution. In such a disaster, it was customary to issue a royal brief, an appeal for money which was read out in all the churches on a particular Sunday, and the collection put to that purpose. This was an extremely long-winded procedure, and a great deal of the money raised was spent on administration. A brief was issued after the Cley disaster, but the sum collected was only just over £40 – and more than £10 of it had to be laid out on expenses.

53   *Part of a long list of damage claims in Holt after the 1708 fire.*

54 *Plan of Gresham's school, Holt: the wall at the back shows the fire damage of 1708.*

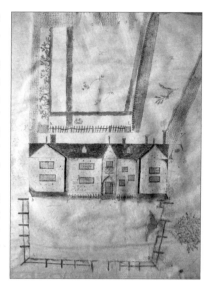

The fire may have benefited Cley in the long term, as Jonathan Hooton points out. In effect the town moved to the north, new buildings going up not beside the church but further downstream, which is why the church is now such a distance from the town centre. This was fortunate as it meant that it was on the seaward side of the bank built by Lord Calthorpe in 1638, unlike Wiveton, which was on the landward side and so ceased to be a port.[24]

Almost a century later, on 1 May 1708, fire broke out at Holt, destroying a large part of the town. It was said that it spread so rapidly that the butchers could barely save the meat on their market stalls. The church was also largely destroyed. Tom Martin, the 18th-century antiquarian, tells us that the fire

> took hold of the chancel first, being thatched, and burnt down the whole roof, melted all the lead, which falling upon the stones crack'd them all in pieces, so that none are remaining. There were two bells which fell down, the frames being burnt in the Steeple.

Naturally, towns nearby helped: the people of North Walsham collected over £32 at once, and also gave a sovereign to one individual sufferer, Thomas Brown, a shoemaker. Because of this spontaneous generosity, when a brief was finally issued and read in the church there, in April 1710, only just over four shillings was collected.

A document at the Norfolk Record Office lists all the claims for losses made by the inhabitants. Public houses mentioned include the *Maid's Head,* for which John Howard claimed £300, and the *Mariners,* for which the claim was £110. Other claims were for houses on Fish Hill and 'near the church', and for the butchers' stalls on the market – 17 butchers claimed for 50 stalls, usually valued at £3 apiece. Money was also claimed for a mill-house and damage to the *Cock* and to the *Lyon.* The Fishmongers' Company claimed for damage to a barn (£65) and to a house (£75). The property claimed for by the Fishmongers was at the back of Gresham's school, which was then, of course, in the Market Place; the damaged buildings are shown on a map of the school drawn in about 1717 by the then headmaster, the Revd David Duncombe. Ten pounds worth of damage had been done to the Quaker Meeting House. The total claims came to very nearly £9,000, an enormous amount of damage to a small market town three centuries ago.

The first brief had been for damage to buildings in the town. A second brief was issued in 1722 for rebuilding the parish church itself; it said that the people of Holt had been trying to make use of the chancel, but it was too small to take more than a quarter of the parishioners. The people of Holt were unable to pay themselves because they had been so impoverished by the fire. The returns from this brief did not come in until 1731, nine years after it was issued and well over twenty years after the

55   *Holt church as rebuilt after the fire of 1708.*

fire – 10,346 briefs had been issued and a total of £1,178 6s. 9¼d. raised (one wonders who gave the farthing). This was not far short of the estimated costs of £1,229. However, the real picture was not so rosy: out of the money raised, the organisers took their commission of £419 and the fees for the patent came to £95: so the actual money that came in was not much over £600. The authorities did not wait for the money. They borrowed £100 from a wealthy local widow in 1723 to buy timber to repair the church. Local tradesmen naturally benefited. In 1725, William Parsons, a Holt joiner, agreed to supply new doors, seats, pulpit, reading desk and communion rails for the church. In the following year, he was commissioned to make a new ceiling and new seats for the chancel. By the early 1730s, it was time for the finishing touches: a weathercock for the steeple cost two guineas and the new clock was made by Isaac Nickalls of Wells. He had estimated this would cost £35, and the eventual cost was £36 15s. Money was spent on replacement plate, an iron chest, upholstery and cloth. The great and the good contributed plate and ornaments, including Sir Robert Walpole, the then Prime Minister, his brother-in-law Viscount Townshend, and George, Prince of Wales, later to become George II. In 1727, the new seats were allocated to the parishioners; the list shows that the men sat on the north side of the church, the women on the south. Seats in the gallery were mainly occupied by the boys of Gresham's and by 'charity children' – pupils at the local charity school. When you look at Holt town and church today, you are looking mainly at what was rebuilt in the 18th century as a result of the Great Fire of Holt of 1708.[25]

THE FIRST 'TOURISTS'

There were already nine alehouses in Cromer in 1602 – magistrates queried if that was not too many. No doubt they were already serving visitors as well as the local residents. The beauty of the north Norfolk coast has been portrayed in poetry and paintings for many centuries, probably from nearby towns like Holt. This tradition could be said to have begun in 1623, when John Taylor, known as the 'Water Poet', was forced to land at Cromer because of bad weather: he was travelling from London to York. The locals were not yet used to tourists, and mistook the poet and his crew for pirates. Taylor put the experience into a long poem, a verse of which already shows an awareness of the problems of coastal erosion:

> It is an ancient town that stands
> Upon a lofty cliff of mouldering sands;
> The seas against the cliffs doth daily beat,
> And every tide into the land doth eat.[26]

FOUR

The Eighteenth Century

THAT MOST OBSERVANT of travellers, Daniel Defoe, came to north Norfolk in the 1720s:

> From Cromer, we ride on the Strand or open shore to Weyburn Hope, the shore so flat that in some places the tide ebbs out near two miles. From Weyburn west lies Clye, where there are large salt works and a very good salt made, which is sold all over the county and sometimes sent to Holland and to the Baltick. From Clye to go to Masham [*sic*, he must mean Morston] and to Wells, all towns on the coast, in each whereof there is a very considerable trade carried on with Holland for corn, which that part of the country is very full of. I say nothing of the great trade driven here from Holland, back again to England, because I take it to be a trade carried on with less honesty than advantage, especially when the clandestine trade, or art, of smuggling was so much in practice; what it is now is not to my present purpose. Near this town [Wells] lie the Seven Burnhams, as they are called, that is to say seven small towns all called by the same name and each employed in the same trade of carrying corn to Holland and bringing back -------------- etc'.[1]

The blank is significant. Defoe did not know what, if anything, was being imported – it was the export trade which mattered in these small ports in the 18th century.

The largest port was Wells, described in the *Norfolk Guide*:

> Wells is a large and populous but indifferent town, situate on a rising ground at the upper end of a spacious harbour, which runs through the salt marshes into the British Ocean, one mile below the town. The import of coals, from Newcastle and Sunderland here and at Blakeney, supply most of the northern hundreds in Norfolk, and are conveyed by land carriage as far up the country as East Dereham. About four or five thousand tubs of oysters are sent annually from this place to Norwich, Lynn etc. Of wine, probably not more is imported than seven or eight pipes annually. The harbour is extremely difficult of access, and a north or north-east wind often proves fatal to the shipping off its mouth.

56   *Cley parish church in the 18th century.*

An anonymous diarist, visiting in 1829, was not impressed:

> the streets in Wells are narrow and badly pitched, no good houses, nor any large looking shops and very little pavement. The river side seems a poor neighbourhood occupied by depots of coals, marine stores and trading warehouses not worth seeing.[2]

Blakeney had declined since its glory days in the 16th century, the *Guide* describing it as 'a small seaport town: [it] was, but is so no longer, a noted town for fishing'. However, in 1817, the Blakeney Harbour Company was formed and a private Act of Parliament passed to collect dues, cut a new channel and improve the quays. The Act's preamble states that Blakeney is 'a very ancient Harbour and much frequented by Ships and Vessells of large burthern'. However, 'the present Channel of the said Harbour is very crooked in its Course, whereby the Navigation thereof is greatly impeded, and the same might be considerably shortened, and improved, if a new Cut was made' through the lands of George Calthorpe. Ships belonging to foreign subjects were to pay three pence a ton, those belonging to British subjects 1½d. – however, fishing boats loading or unloading at Sheringham, Cromer, Mundesley and Bacton did not have to pay dues. Ships laden with grain belonging to Cley or Blakeney had to pay – but not if, instead of using the new channel, they unloaded in Blakeney Pit and conveyed their cargoes to Cley, Morston or Stiffkey. A 500-yard channel was indeed dug through the marshes, and Blakeney, like Wells, continued to be an active working port, as shown by the number of granaries still to be seen near the quay, most now converted into houses.[3]

In a typical week at Blakeney in February 1837, for example, the packet between Hull and Blakeney arrived and left again, taking north a cargo of corn, flour and general goods. Another packet, the *Land*, arrived from Hull and Goole, the *Prudent May* from London and 11 laden colliers also arrived. Two ships, the *Briggs* and the

57 *Wiveton Bridge, Blakeney church and Wiveton Hall.*

Albatross (a steamship), put in for shelter on their way from Yarmouth to Hull. At Wells, five ships arrived from Newcastle and two from Goole in the same February week, while three ships left the port for Hull, two for Newcastle, one for London and one from Montrose, an average of one ship arriving and one leaving each day, even in the depth of winter. In fact, one more ship, the *Gleaner*, left for Wisbech but was forced back by the bad weather, while the *Orion* of Wells, laden with coal, ran ashore when trying to enter the harbour. In the following week, the schooner *Fleming* from Finland also came ashore at Wells; the crew and the cargo were saved, but the ship and its stores had to be sold off.

Cley was less active. In 1822, Thomas Telford was called in to advise on the silting of the channel, but nothing was done. Within a few years there was a setback to the revival of the port: the Cley Inclosure Act was passed, intended to reclaim the marshland on both sides of the Glaven by putting a bank and sluice across the river in a similar position to the bank put up in 1637. C.L.S. Linnell tells us what happened:

> Under the enclosure award of 1823, an embankment was made on the site of the old bank that in times past caused such an offence to the merchants of Cley and Wiveton. This has prevented the tide from flowing up any further than the old Cley quay with the result that

58 *The tools of a miller's trade on the tombstone of Thomas Smith at Wiveton.*

the once wide estuary between Cley and Wiveton churches is completely silted up. The Blakeney Point, made by the dual action of sea and wind, grows in size every year and the channel once a deep waterway is no longer capable of accommodating a boat of any size. So shallow has it become in some parts that it is quite easy to wade across the Cley channel from the fresh marshes to the beach opposite at low tide. To use a local phrase, it is *landed up*.[4]

Cromer was a working port, too, despite its obvious physical disadvantages. Chambers' *Norfolk Tour*, published in 1829, says of it:

> Cromer is principally inhabited by fishermen: it has no harbour, yet a considerable trade is carried on, and much coal, tiles, oil-cake, porter etc are imported in vessels carrying from sixty to one hundred tons: corn is also exported. These vessels lie upon the beach, and at ebb tides carts are drawn alongside to unship their cargoes; when empty, they anchor at a little distance from the shore, and reload by means of boats, a measure attended with much inconvenience and expense, as the carts, though drawn by four horses, owing to the steepness of the road up the cliffs, can only carry about half a ton at a time. In this manner they continue passing and repassing till the water flows up to the horses' bellies, when they are obliged to desist until the return of the tide.

War with France broke out in the 1790s and the coast was again feared to be a likely place of invasion. In 1803, Sir James Craig, who was in command of the Eastern Military District, ordered a Major Bryce to look at possible invasion sites. Bryce thought Weybourne would be too exposed to bad weather for the French to risk a landing, and recommended flooding the marshes as the best defensive measure further west. He recommended two small batteries at Cromer, mainly to train 'sea fencibles' – that is, auxiliary troops recruited from local fishermen. He suggested three batteries at Holkham Bay and others at Blakeney, to prevent deep-water vessels coming into the Pit, and at Wells and Burnham. However, Craig had already sent cannon to Cromer, and thought the rest of the coast could be covered by mobile field artillery based at Cley and Wells.[5]

The gun barrel still to be seen on Wiveton Green, supposed to be one of a convoy being taken from Lynn to Felixstowe during the Napoleonic wars and abandoned when its carriage broke, is a lasting souvenir of these events. At Burnham Overy, the name Gun Hill preserves the memory of an artillery emplacement, and a defensible granary can still be seen on the staithe.

STORMS

One of the greatest pleasures of the north Norfolk coast is its ever-changing weather. At times the sea is so calm that 'the happy ocean lies/ Like an

59   *The fortified granary at Burnham Overy Staithe: note the gun emplacements.*

unfingered harp, below the land'; on other days, the most violent gales stir up the waves. The coast has always been subject to storms, but we know more about them from the 18th century onwards because the records are better. As well as newspapers, we also have local journals and diaries, and some clergymen recorded major events in their parish registers. At Blakeney, for example, a 'great snow' fell on 3 May 1698, starting at 11 a.m. and continuing for five hours. Defoe knew all about the dangers:

> Ships which come from the north leave the shore at Flamboro' Head and stretch away SSE for Yarmouth Roads, and the first line they make is Winterton Ness. Now the danger of the place is this: if the ships coming from the north are taken with a hard gale of wind from the SE, or any other point between NE and SE, so that they cannot, as the seamen call it, weather Winterton Ness, they are thereby kept within that deep bay, and if the wind blows hard, are often in danger of running on shore on the rocks about Cromer on the north coast of Norfolk, or stranding upon the flat shore between Cromer and Wells; all the relief they have is good ground tackle to ride it out, which is very hard to do there, the sea coming very high upon them, or if they cannot ride it out then, to run into the bottom of the great bay I mentioned, to Lynn or Boston, which is a very difficult and desperate push; so that sometimes in this distress whole fleets have been lost here all together.[6]

Defoe tells how in 1692 (he thinks), a fleet of 200 light colliers from Newcastle to London were caught in a storm off Winterton, adding that coastal vessels laden with corn from Lynn and Wells and bound for Holland were also caught in the storm; a thousand men drowned on that dreadful night.

The Blakeney parish register records another storm half a century after Defoe's visit: 'at three o'clock on the afternoon of 25 October 1772, it thundered very much the claps louder than usual, the wind south-west by west'. Half an hour later,

> there fell a storm of hail, the hailstones exceedingly large, some measured (by report) four inches in girth. They broke a part of all the glass windows fronting the west, some of the windows they damaged exceedingly. At Langham they did great mischief to the glass windows, in passing over the fields they cut the turnip-tops. The storm continued no longer than five minutes (I think): it went off to sea, did no damage at Wiveton or at Cley.[7]

Mary Hardy recorded some severe storms in her diary:

> in the violent storm of wind at NE on Thursday last [1 December 1774] … At Wells a ship was lost at the mouth of the harbour, the crew saved … the wreck of a foreign ship was driven ashore at Warham, supposed to be a Hamburger. The same day a light brigg belonging to Sunderland was lost at Burnham, the master died as they were bringing him on shore, the rest of the crew saved.

On 31 December 1778 she recorded:

> a very stormy day … the wind rose higher this night than had been known for many years, accompanyd with storms of hail and snow. Much damage was done to roofs of houses, many trees and barns blown down in the neighbourhood. What damage was done at a distance and at sea have not yet learned but fear it must be terrible.

The storm continued on New Year's Day 1779:

> at Clay [*sic*] the *Cornought* of London and the *Hunter* of Sunderland, light briggs, are drove on shore, the crews saved and the vessels like to be got off. At this place a great many sheep and other cattle were drowned, the marshes are all under water. At Hunstanton the violence of the storm broke down the banks upon the salt marshes, which had been raised at the great expense and fortified with the utmost care and strength by Nicholas Styleman Esq at Snettisham and the sea made its way with irresistible fury along the shore to Wolverton Point, where likewise the banks of Mrs Henley were destroyed and one of her tenants lost his whole flock consisting of 700 sheep … At Brancaster the key is said to be much damaged. Great mischief has been done to the shipping in harbour and stores of the merchants on shore and the oyster boats are almost totally destroyed.[8]

This storm is also described in the Blakeney parish register:

> on New Year's Day in 1779, a gale caused great damage. The wind blew from the north west, swelling the bank that surrounds the marshes of the Great Farm damaging the bank and causing the marshes to flood to a depth of eight or nine feet.

A ship lying in the channel broke her mooring and 'beat down a house and a considerable length of wall upon the Quay'. The roof of the church was also damaged.

One victim of a shipwreck off the coast was Mary Anne Arnold, born in 1825, a cross-dresser. She had signed up as a cabin boy on the *Williams*, a Sunderland collier, in October 1838, when she was only around fourteen years old. She then transferred to the *Annie*, bound for London and Quebec. The *Annie* was wrecked off the north Norfolk coast and the crew brought ashore at Blakeney. Mary Anne then boarded the *Choice* bound for London. She was found out while crossing the Atlantic in 1840 – and disappears from history.

The lighthouses at the two ends of the coast saved lives over several centuries. A hermit called John Puddock is supposed to have erected a wooden beacon over one hundred feet high near Hunstanton in about 1550, to guide ships into the Wash. In 1663, the mayor, shipowners and mariners of Lynn presented a petition to Charles II for the erection of lights at Hunstanton, saying that the coast was 'much infested with many sands, not only troublesome but exceedingly dangerous to all ships passing', especially at night, and that they were willing to pay dues to fund the light. The king granted the patent to John Knight, and two stone towers were erected, aligned to show the channel through the sandbanks. The first lighthouse was erected by Alderman Everard of Lynn: this was a wooden structure, with a coal-burning fire at the top. In 1778, the lighthouse was the first in the world to use a system of parabolic reflectors, and was lit by oil: 'it shone out with a brilliance that made all others dim in comparison'. In 1837, the patent passed to Trinity House. The lighthouse we now see was built in 1840; it ceased to operate in 1922. The nearby coastguard look-out tower was built in 1907. It was used as a Marconi listening post in both world wars, playing a part in the plotting of the movements of German ships prior to the Battle of Jutland.

60 *Hunstanton cliffs and lighthouse.*

61 *The (old) lighthouse at Cromer as drawn by Mr Marten in 1826.*

62 *Cromer: the (new) lighthouse, still in use today.*

The first lighthouse at Foulness on the cliffs east of Cromer was built in 1674 as a private venture by Sir John Clayton, who erected several lighthouses in England but does not appear to have actually lit them. The first functioning lighthouse on the site was built in 1719 by Edward Bowel of Ipswich. In 1825, the Revd Marten, a visitor from London, spoke to Mrs Newstead, the lighthouse keeper, who told him that there were four in the family, and that they took it in turns to sit up during the hours when the lights should be kept burning. There were five lights, which looked like one from a distance and could be seen by a ship thirty miles from land.[9]

A resident told Marten that the cliffs were crumbling: a house, which he pointed out, and which had only a narrow footpath between it and the cliff edge, had only 50 years earlier a carriage way and a bowling green in its front. This applied to the lighthouse as well: it was now too close to the edge of the cliff and was replaced in 1832 by the tower that still functions today, 280 yards further inland. The old lighthouse, now disused, finally collapsed into the sea in 1866.[10]

FISHING

Sheringham was still primarily a fishing settlement, as the following description makes clear:

> The town is divided into Upper and Lower Sheringham, the latter also called Sheringham Hithe, as lying by the sea-shore; the houses in the former being nearly a mile from it, whilst those of the latter are so near the beach, as frequently to suffer by the impetuosity of the tides.
>
> Lower Sheringham is situate on a part of the cliff which is but a few yards from the beach, and the cliff gradually rises on each side to upwards of one hundred feet. The sea gains on the land here considerably; and it is not uncommon to see large pieces of arable land carried away with corn growing, between seed-time and harvest, so near do the people plough to the edge of a cliff, which strikes a stranger with horror to look down it. There is a very considerable fishery from this place, of cod, skate and whitings, but especially crabs and lobsters, with which this place and Cromer chiefly supply the London market, by vessels which take the fish from the boats while at sea. There was a very good inn at lower Sheringham, much resorted to in summer for the sake of eating lobsters. The dining room stood so near the edge of the cliff, that at high water no land could be seen; and from whence a stranger could not but be delighted with the awful but pleasing prospect of the unbounded ocean, peopled with fishermen, or variegated with fleets of colliers. This inn fell a sacrifice to an extraordinary high tide, brought in by a gale of wind from the north-west, on the morning of the 22nd of October 1800; the inhabitants were in some measure prepared for it, and stripped off their furniture with all possible expedition. A new house has since been erected in a different situation.

This was the *Crown*, owned by William Hardy, husband of the diarist Mary; he rode down to it on the day after the sea had washed through it, and saved what he could. The fishermen at Sheringham had a jetty from which to load and unload, though this was badly damaged by storms and the tide in 1797.

63 *Sea fencibles at Cromer in the 1790s.*

The supply of fresh local produce from the sea was one of Cromer's attractions to Marten:

> We dined today on Hot Lobster used by us for the first time as fish for a first course. A good thing is a good thing at all times and hot lobsters, or cold lobsters, are good things, and if a real relish and making good use of hot lobsters – fresh, of course, – and in fine condition, can entitle them to praise ours of today fearlessly claim the title of excellent food.

That same evening he took a walk on the beach and noticed that:

> near to the pier there is, far within high water mark, a strong tank in which lobsters are preserved alive till wanted for use. The boats which go off this town catch cod, soals, turbots and lobsters. The latter are sold by the pound weight, and usually about 8d per pound.

On walking there again the following morning, he:

> saw the boats launching to visit the lobster potts which had been left during the night at sea. A fisherman returned from the visit with a tolerably sized hand basket full of lively lobsters. These potts are baited (as I learned from a fisherman's boy) with butts. On enquiring what butts were, he told me they were like sandlings. As this brought me no nearer to the knowledge I desired I was obliged to renew my enquiry. The good natured boy seemed to wonder at my ignorance and told me they were small fish – flat like a flounder or small turbot – and that they were very good for catching lobsters. He was about to immerse in the sea a basket containing live lobsters – the basket being first made fast to the Jetty. He said that the live lobsters would bite very hard unless they took the precaution which they generally used on first catching them of tying down their claws. He had had his fingers lately bitten – and the lobsters would unless prevented bite one another when they were confined.

64   *Three-master off Cromer. The pattern of the Cromer streets near the church is the same today as on this map of 1714.*

Marten and his family visited a fish curing house, examined the Liverpool salt which was in store, saw men preparing cod for salting, and had a peek into the 'smoaky place whereby the smoak-blue herrings' were converted into red herrings: 'the place was such a dense cloud that the herrings then under operation were wholly invisible'. They took a trip on a crab boat, the boat's master carrying Mrs and Miss Marten to his boat through the waves. They were on board for an hour but made very little headway against wind and tide. When they turned, the wind quickly carried the boat back to shore. Marten bought from the master two large crabs which he had caught in the night, paying nine pence, and also paid 3s. 6d. for the use of the boat and wages to the master and his son. On 25 September, he noted the presence of three French boats, 'the first of some hundreds of fishing vessels which will be here in a few days to intercept the expected annual migration of herrings'.

WRECKS

There were many wrecks along the coast, and locals were often accused of profiting from them. The most controversial incident occurred in 1833. On 31 August, a severe gale caused great damage to shipping, with the loss of many lives along the coast. The *Earl of Wemyss*, a Leith smack under the command of Captain Nesbit, was sailing from London to Leith with 22 passengers aboard when it was caught in the storm. Both anchors were lowered but they would not grip; they had to be cut away and the ship allowed to drift. At about 10.30 p.m., she ran aground at Brancaster, a short distance to the west of the present-day Club House. The ship's crew and some of the passengers, led by Nesbit, waded ashore and sought shelter at the *Ship*. Meanwhile, a large crowd gathered, but unfortunately helping the victims seems to have been the last thing on their minds. Local coastguards watched as the waves drove the ship further up the beach. Newman Reeve, the son of the lord of the manor, went down to look at the wreck as did the local curate, James Holloway. Holloway went to the *Ship*, talked to the crew and then to the passengers, learning for the first time that lives had been lost. He asked Nesbit, who admitted he had lost 'a few' passengers, some ladies having drowned. He said that at about eight o'clock a heavy sea had swept over the ship, carrying away the skylight and filling the cabin with water. He had left the bodies in the cabin, claiming that it would have been pointless to try to retrieve them as they would have been dead for several hours. Holloway went down to the ship just as a waggon was drawing away; it contained 11 bodies. He talked to the coastguard, who said that, if only the skylight had been battened down, all of them would still have been alive. The bodies, six ladies, four children and one man, were laid out on Brancaster church floor: two local women were attending the laying out, and one of them pointed out blood where earrings had been torn from the ears of the stoutest of the women − as dead bodies do not bleed, this must have been done while she was still alive. Holloway felt the bodies: they were still warm, so they must have very recently been alive.

The victims were buried in Brancaster churchyard. They included Susanna or Susan Roche, sister of the composer Alexander Roche and herself 'a young lady of great musical ability'. Her gravestone can be seen still, but can now only be deciphered with difficulty − it reads:

> Sacred to the memory of Susanna Roche aged 32 years and also to her nephew Alexander David Roche aged 4 years, who were unfortunately drowned with many others in the cabin of the *Earl of Wemyss*, Leith Packet, which was stranded on this coast during the dreadful gale of September 1st 1833 on its passage from London. Which melancholy affair has been doubly afflicting for the relatives of the deceased from the fact that no attempt was ever made to rescue them from their situation, and in continuation of such inhuman conduct their persons were stripped of every valuable and their property plundered.

Relatives of the dead, including Alexander Roche, wrote a formal letter of complaint to the Home Secretary, Lord Melbourne. They claimed that Reeve had gone on board and stripped the bodies of their valuables, and the crowd on the beach took the luggage of the passengers and opened it up there and then. In October, Docking magistrates opened an inquiry under the authority of the Secretary of State 'to ascertain for his own and the public satisfaction whether there had been any loss of life by culpable negligence or loss of property by dishonesty'. Nesbit was a witness and claimed that he had gone to the ladies' cabin at about eight o'clock and told them they would be able to go ashore in two hours. Then, he claimed, the keel of the ship had suddenly given way, filling the ship with water. However, one of the surviving passengers, Henry Gooch, contradicted him. He had been in the cabin when the skylight, which had not been fastened down, suddenly blew away. One of the ladies, Mrs Hamilton, seized him and begged him not to leave her. He was just reassuring her when 'the sea a-buried us in darkness'. He himself was saved when the water washed him through the skylight: he tied himself to the mast until it was safe to walk to shore. He blamed the deaths directly on the negligence of those who had been told to secure the skylight but had not done so. Two witnesses said that they had seen Reeve stealing a bag from one of the women and taking rings from dead fingers. Even in the church, the bodies were not safe: Hannah Pike had tried to steal a gold watch from one of the bodies she was laying out.

As a result of the inquiry, Reeve was charged with removing property from the wreck, which he claimed he was protecting for his father-in-law, who as lord of the manor had right of wreck. The case was heard at the Assizes in Norwich in March 1834; the original charge was with theft from the bodies of Susan Roche and

Mrs Pyne, the stout lady, but only the second charge was proceeded with. After a skilful defence, the judge directed an acquittal, saying that there was not the slightest stain on the character of the accused.

In July, three men, Robert Allen, Charles Oakes and James Ward, were charged with stealing from the wreck. Allen was the ship's steward and Ward the cook, while Oakes was a local farmer. John Cutting, the son of the *Ship*'s landlady, gave evidence that he had seen Allen, together with Captain Nesbit's son and a local girl named Fanny Parker, smashing open a jewel box in the brewhouse of the inn. They then appear to have moved to the *Lifeboat* inn, where another witness, Thomas Fiddament, had seen them with more jewellery. The jury was told that Oakes and Ward had no case to answer and, after further evidence was heard, Allen was also acquitted. Nobody was ever convicted of any offence in connection with the deaths on board the *Earl of Wemyss*, or the callous thefts of the possessions of the dead.

Wreckage was generally regarded as their right by coast-dwellers, as Defoe had already noted on his journey from Winterton to Cromer:

> the farmers and country people had scarce a barn or a shed, or a stable, nay, not the pales of their yards and gardens, not a hogstye, not a necessary-house, but what was built of old planks, beams, wales and timbers etc, the wrecks of ships and ruins of mariners' and merchants' fortunes.

The *Norfolk Chronicle* condemned their greed in two further incidents in the 1830s. On 9 November 1835, the schooner *Harriet* on her passage from St Petersburg to Liverpool was lost with her crew of eight off Hunstanton:

> the wreckage washed ashore was immediately broken up, and part of it converted to private purposes. It is shocking to contemplate the lawless scrambling of the wreckers of this coast to obtain possession of their prey, in which they appear to be encouraged by the conduct of persons whose especial duty is to prevent rather than encourage the abominable plunder here carried on.

On 24 February 1837, during a severe gale, the *Raby Castle* came ashore at Salthouse at two in the morning. By 8 a.m. there were 600 people waiting eagerly:

> when she broke up the beach was strewed with spirits, wine, oranges, nuts, packets of tea, toys, hampers, boxes etc. The scene beggared description. The most outrageous and beastly conduct was exhibited. Here might be observed a group broaching a spirit cask, and letting it run into their oil-skin hats, shoes etc. There another stood filling their pockets and handkerchiefs. Plunder, wholesale plunder, appeared to be the order of the day, in spite of contingents of coastguard men. Many who were charged to watch the property became themselves intoxicated. Many were conveyed from the beach literally dead drunk, and it is with disgust we add that many women were in the same state.[11]

SMUGGLING

As Defoe pointed out, smuggling was a large-scale operation all along the coast. Piracy and privateering were also common, and these activities could not always be distinguished, especially in time of war. In January 1780, the *Mary Anne* and the *Richard* left Blakeney for London with cargoes of barley – both were seized by French ships.

In February 1781, a band of 11 men armed with loaded muskets and cutlasses landed at Runton from a boat that carried Dutch colours. Assistance was called from Cromer and the men were overpowered and captured, two of them being wounded in the fight; they all turned out to be English. They claimed to be smugglers, saying that they belonged to a sloop with 30 men that came out of Flushing a month before. However, it was suspected that they were pirates. They were taken to Norwich and committed to the Castle. It was thought that they were part of a gang led by the pirate Fall and that they had come either to plunder houses or to surprise some unarmed vessel, but, despite a lengthy interrogation by magistrates, nothing could be proved against them. They were conveyed under a strong guard to Yarmouth and put on board a tender in order to be sent to the Nore and impressed into the British navy. The *Norfolk Chronicle* commented, 'these are the same desperate fellows that went ashore at Whitby, and were fired upon by the volunteers of that town, who wounded one of them. When they were taken, they said they were only smugglers'.

Smuggling is generally regarded as a crime without victims, but it could lead to loss of life both among the smugglers and those trying to guard the coast. In February 1781, the Trinity House victualler, bringing supplies to customs officers, was grounded on the sands two miles off Cromer, and the crew was stranded on the wreck all night. At eight the following morning, some fishermen determined to rescue them. However, as they were preparing their boat, a very heavy squall caused the ship to shift: she was dashed to pieces and every man on board was drowned.

Two gravestones, now very much eroded, in Old Hunstanton churchyard tell the story of a fatal smuggling affray in 1784. One reads: 'Here lie the poor mangled remains of poor William Green an honest Officer of Government who in the faithful discharge of his duty was inhumanly murdered by a gang of smugglers in this Parish, September 27th 1784, aged 37 years.' The other reads: 'In memory of William Webb late of the 15th Light Dragoons who was shot from his horse by a party of smugglers on the 26th of September 1784 aged 26 years.'

On 21 September 1784, 12 smugglers and a cabin boy sailed from Dunkirk on the cutter *Lively* with a full cargo of tea, brandy, gin and a few packages of silk. The leaders were William Kemball of Thornham and Andrew Gunton. Their plan was to unload the smuggled goods at Hunstanton and conceal them in a public house called the *Cutter*. The *Lively* anchored at Thornham on 24 September. The next day, Saturday, they waited for darkness to fall and then set sail for Old Hunstanton, where they filled a rowing boat with goods and waited for a prearranged signal from ashore that the coast was clear – literally. The signal would come from two of Kemball's men on horseback on the shore.

The signal finally came at about one o'clock on Sunday morning and the rowing boat was brought to the shore by three of the smugglers. As they were unloading the contraband, three men on horses approached, and so the smugglers pushed their boat into the sea and fled back to the *Lively*, leaving the smuggled goods behind.

On board, Kemball resolved to get the goods back, and he, Gunton and six others armed themselves with muskets and cutlasses and set off in their rowing boat.

The smugglers had been betrayed and men from the 15th Light Dragoons were in Hunstanton waiting. The contraband seized by the dragoons was now under guard in a farmhouse occupied by a Mr Cleer. The smugglers themselves hid in wait. As some of the excise men rode past the farmhouse they came under fire: Webb was shot dead and Green received four wounds, in his neck, stomach, arm and head. The dragoons retaliated and the smugglers fled across a field.

Soon after, another smuggler was seen in the hedge near the farm. He raised his musket to fire but it failed to go off and he was captured; he was soon identified as Thomas Williams of Hunstanton. The dragoons then searched the *Cutter* public house, suspecting that more contraband was hidden there, and later rounded up Kemball and Gunton. Green, dying from his terrible wounds, identified Kemball as the man who had shot him; he had seen his face by the flash-pan of his musket.

Kemball, Gunton and Williams were taken to Norwich Castle for trial. Williams turned king's evidence against the other two men, whose trial finally came up at Thetford Assizes in March 1785. Green had died and none of the other dragoons could definitely identify Kemball as the man who had fired the fatal shot. The landlord of the *Cutter*, Thomas Cooper, and a local farm worker, John Smyth, who had been drinking there, supplied him with an alibi: Kemball, they claimed, had been drinking with them at the time of the killings. Smyth added that he recalled hearing the shots as he left the pub: Kemball was still inside. Kemball and Gunton were both found not guilty of murder; had they been convicted, they would undoubtedly have been hanged. A few weeks later they were tried again, this time with the much lesser offence of smuggling: they were found guilty and each fined £350.[12]

THREE NORTH COAST SAILORS

Nelson

Horatio Nelson was born in Burnham Thorpe rectory. A local *Guide* stresses the remoteness of the area:

> We stand and look right across the North Sea to the North Pole. There is nothing to break the tumbling waters, save the fields and cliffs of ice which ring it round. And well do we know all this when the Nor'Easters whistle in off our steel-grey sea every day from January to June; stiffening our backs and shutting tight our mouths. It may be a welcome thing for the wind to reach some land at last; but it can hardly expect a welcome from the inhabitants.

Nelson was born in 1758, the son of Edmund, the rector of Burnham Thorpe. His mother, Catherine, died when Horatio was only nine years old. His father engaged a nurse to look after his family, the youngest child being still an infant. Later she married a Mr High and they ran the *Ship Inn* in Brancaster, where Nelson visited them on occasion.

It is said that, when a mere boy, Nelson strayed from his grandmother's house to go bird-nesting in company with a farm-boy. When dinner time arrived, he

65 *The* Ship Inn, *Brancaster: Nelson was a visitor.*

could not be found, and the alarm of the family became very great. At length, after search had been made for him in various directions, he was discovered alone, sitting composedly by the side of a brook, which he could not get over. 'I wonder, child', said the old lady, when she saw him, 'that hunger and fear did not drive you home.' 'Fear, grandmamma!' replied the future hero, 'I never saw fear; what is it?'

On Horatio's request, his father wrote to his brother-in-law Maurice Suckling, who was a post-captain in the Royal Navy, asking for Horatio to join. Suckling replied, 'What has poor Horatio done, who is so weak, that he, above all the rest, should be sent to rough it out at sea?', adding, 'but let him come, and the first time we go into action a cannon ball may knock off his head, and provide for him at once.'

In 1781, Nelson came back to Burnham for the first time since his boyhood. One of his sisters, Susannah, was now married to a Mr Bolton and lived at Wells. His youngest and favourite sister, Kate, now aged 15, was still at home, and Nelson hoped that she would marry a man of standing: 'Although I am very fond of Mrs Bolton, yet I own I should not like to see my little Kate fixed in a Wells society.' A few months later he was appointed to the *Albemarle*.

Nelson married Fanny Nesbit at Nevis on 11 March 1787. The couple came to Norfolk in the summer of 1788, and they settled in the Parsonage House at Burnham Thorpe. In the spring of 1789, he indulged his favourite hobbies of gardening and collecting birds' eggs in Burnham. Meanwhile Edmund had moved into a cottage in Burnham Ulph to allow the couple full run of the Parsonage House. In 1793 Horatio was finally given a new post, aboard the *Agamemnon*, to his great joy. His naval victories at Cape St Vincent in 1797, the Nile in 1798, Copenhagen in 1801 and Trafalgar in 1805 belong to the story of England, as does his love affair with Emma, Lady Hamilton, whom he first met in Naples when staying with her husband.

Nelson was concerned with the poverty of labourers in Norfolk. He wrote to the Duke of Clarence saying that an average family received yearly earnings of £23 1s. 0d. 'Not quite two pence a day for each person; and to drink nothing but water, for beer our poor labourers never taste, unless they are tempted, which is too often the case, to go to the Alehouse.' Nelson blamed the landlords for 'not making their farmers raise their wages, in some small proportion, as the price of necessaries increased'. In 1797 he wrote to Fanny from Cadiz,

> I intend my next winter's gift at Burnham should be fifty good large blankets of the very best quality, with the letter 'N' in the centre that they may not be sold; I believe they may be made for about 15 shillings of the very best quality, and they will last some person or other for seven years at least … I wish enquiry to be made, and the blankets ordered of some worthy man: they are to be at my father's disposal in November.

It was Nelson's wish to be buried beside his father at Burnham Thorpe. In 1804 he wrote from the *Victory* to his friend the Dean of Raphoe:

> most probably I may never see dear, dear Burnham again, but I have satisfaction in thinking that my bones will probably be laid with my father's in the village which gave me birth. The thought of my former days brings all my mother to my heart, which shows itself in my eyes.

66   *Bust of Lord Nelson in Burnham Thorpe church.*

Even on the morning of his death at Trafalgar on 21 October 1805, Nelson's thoughts were of home: he recalled that it was the day of the annual fair at Burnham Thorpe. Among Nelson's last words were that the nation should look after Horatia, his illegitimate daughter by Emma. After his death, she was cared for by Kate, now Mrs Matcham. Horatia married the Revd Philip Ward in Burnham in 1822. Nelson's importance was recognised immediately in his home area: the public house in Burnham Thorpe, then called the *Plough*, was the first to be renamed after him, and many other public houses and other facilities have followed suit over two centuries.

Frederick Marryat

The great seafarer and writer, Frederick Marryat, was born in London in 1792 and went to sea at the age of fourteen. He bought Manor Cottage in Langham in about 1830, but did not live there permanently until 1843. It was a curious house – the previous tenant had put beds in the drawing room which he would let out to passing tramps at twopence a night. He had let the farm go too, so Marryat built new pigsties and also model cottages for his tenants. As William Dutt comments:

A more fitting place than Langham for a sailor to settle down in after an adventurous life abroad and afloat could hardly have been chosen; for amid its quiet country scenes he could find complete rest and change, yet within a mile or so of the bounds of the village are the tidal flats which border the North Sea, and on stormy nights, if he lay awake and thought of storms and dangers past, he could always hear the roaring of the waves as they broke upon the shingle ridges beyond the meal marshes at Wells.[13]

Marryat had written two of his trilogy of great sea stories – *Jacob Faithful* and *Peter Simple* – before he settled at Langham. The third, *Masterman Ready*, was completed at Langham and it was here that he wrote the only one of his books that is read much today, *The Children of the New Forest*, 'whose sympathetic account of royalist children at the time of the Civil War has influenced generations of children in their views of seventeenth-century England far more than any history book', as Dutt comments. If you think of Royalists as heroic and Roundheads as oppressors, it is probably because of Marryat's book.

Like Nelson, Marryat sympathised with the poor conditions endured by Norfolk labourers, writing in 1847 of a feast he had provided for his labourers at Langham: 'these poor men work hard all the year round, and never get anything to eat but bread for themselves and their wives and children: and they are thankful if, by hard labour, they can find bread to live upon'.

Marryat died on 9 August 1848 and is buried in Langham church, where there is a tablet to him. He knew the harsh realities of maritime life: one of his sons was lost at sea in the *Avenger*.

John Fryer and the Bounty

John Fryer was born in Wells in 1753. He was sailing master on the *Bounty* in 1787, the year of the famous mutiny on the ship. Fryer, a widower, married Mary Tinkler of Wells just a few weeks before sailing and was able to persuade Captain Bligh to take her young brother Robert Tinkler as able seaman. The mutiny took place on 28 April 1789, and Fryer and Tinkler were with Bligh when he and a few supporters were put on board one of the ship's boats to fend for themselves. Fryer recalled the mutineers on the ship calling out, 'Now let the b----r see if he can live on three quarters of a pound of yams' as they parted. He shared in Bligh's epic journey to Timor in an open boat, travelling more than 3,600 miles in a voyage lasting 48 days, and made his own journal of the voyage, which has never been published in book form. Fryer returned to England and resumed his naval career. He died in 1812 at the age of 59, having amassed considerable wealth: he left each of his daughters £200 and a share of the family silver. Tinkler died in Norwich eight years later. Fryer was buried in Wells churchyard. Over time, the tombstone fell down, and the whereabouts of the grave was forgotten. It was rediscovered in May 2000 by Mike Welland, Tom Sands and Alan Leventhall, and can now be seen in the church porch.

FARMING

The light soils of north Norfolk, together with improvements in farming practices, meant that more and more barley was being produced, and much of it was shipped from the coastal ports, above all to London. The amount exported from Wells, now clearly the most important of the ports, doubled between 1727 and 1750. The link between farming and shipping is shown by the fact that farmers often owned ships or had shares in them. This was sometimes specifically to transport their own products. Arthur Young, writing in 1804, says,

> Mr Overman of Burnham has a small ship which he keeps constantly employed carrying his corn to London, in bringing rape-cake for manure from Holland, London or Hull, or wherever it is to be produced at the cheapest rate. Where his farm does not in this manner produce employment, he sends for coals, or any service which time and markets render eligible.

Another farmer, Mr Davy of Waterden, who was a tenant of the Cokes, owned a 50-ton sloop which he used to carry oak hurdles from Sussex.

However, the big farmers were also the enemies of the ports when they drained the marshes to create pasture, as this reduced the water in nearby creeks which previously helped to flush out the channels to the harbour and prevent them silting up. When Sir John Turner enclosed 66 acres of marshes east of Wells, he was taken to court three times by the Wells Harbour Commissioners – in 1779, 1781 and 1784 – in attempts to force him to remove the embankment. The jury eventually decided in favour of the Commissioners, although some of them had doubts about how great an injury the bank did to the harbour, and pointed out that the Commissioners had allowed the bank to stand for over twenty years before doing anything about the matter. The Coke family of Holkham already owned the marshes west of Wells, which they had enclosed as long ago as 1719; in 1784, they purchased the Warham estate from the Turners, so that they now owned the marshes on both sides of the harbour channel. 'Improvement' was not long in coming: in 1808, Coke proposed to the Commissioners that he be allowed to rebuild Turner's embankment. He promised them that he would build a tidal reservoir that would provide more water to scour the channel than ever came off the marshes. They agreed, specifying that the reservoir should contain at least five thousand tons of water. Coke went ahead – but he never built the promised reservoir.[14]

The technology of the age was most forcibly expressed in mills, both water and wind powered, and several are features of the north Norfolk landscape today. Eighteenth-century mills were tower mills, where a solid tower, usually of brick, stands still, while the sails and the cap move into the direction of the wind. The most well-known is that in Cley, endlessly photographed and painted by amateur artists. The mill has the date 1713 on the structure in two places, on a flint outbuilding and on a piece of timber let into the wall of a room. However, these are not part of the original structure, and in fact appear to have been added after the First World War. The mill was actually built in about 1819. The *Norfolk Chronicle* ran an advertisement in the summer of 1822 advertising for sale 'a new erected tower mill … at Cley, adjoining the Quay. A very extensive business is capable of carrying on here at a comparatively trifling expense, as the flour may be sent out to sea without any land carriage.'

67 *Cley Mill, perhaps the most photographed and painted building in Norfolk.*

Almost every village had a windmill, and many had more than one, but almost no surviving structures are earlier than the 19th century; the exception is at Blakeney, which was erected before 1769. Two windmills are shown side by side at Langham on Faden's map of 1797. The miller here, Solomon Colls, appears to have gone bankrupt in 1783, a common fate among millers as we shall see. There were three mills in late 18th-century Holt. That on Mill Street was described as 'newly erected' in 1792, and its first miller was Charles Kendle. One on the Thornage Road is shown on Faden's map; according to Mary Hardy's diary it burnt down in May 1794, another common hazard for mills. Bryant's map of 1826 shows a third mill on the Cromer Road; three millers appear to have gone bankrupt here in quick succession, William Copland in 1822, Stephen Storey, who wound up a debtor in Norwich Castle prison in 1827, and Henry Raven two years later.

Watermill technology also flourished, often in conjunction with an adjacent windmill. Two watermills on the river Burn at Burnham Overy are still attractive features in the landscape. The upper, Union Mills, has the date 1737; the windmill was added in 1814. The complex was still in daily use in the mid-20th century, grinding and crushing oats. The lower watermill was constructed in 1795 and was operated in conjunction with a windmill 200 yards away, now a private house. There was a fire at the watermill in 1959, and it has since been partly rebuilt. At Sheringham in the mid-18th century, the windmill and watermill were also being run by the same miller, Joseph Priest, followed by his son Robert. At Stiffkey, too, the watermill and windmill were a unit, sold together in 1857, 1861 and 1881. The water mill was still in use in

68   *Heacham Lavender, situated in an 18th-century watermill.*

1861, but by the 1881 sale it is described as a 'warehouse of three storeys formerly used as a Water Mill'. The 'watermill' most visited today is a building that many are not even aware is a mill – Heacham Lavender. This is an early 19th-century building of local carstone, with the L'Estrange family arms on the porch. It was very unusual in having the water wheel outside the building; the mill race can still be seen.

THE TWO COKES OF HOLKHAM

Thomas Coke inherited the Coke estates in 1707 at the age of 10; they brought in annual rents of £5,800 and casual profits of up to £1,000. His guardians took the estate in hand, re-organising it to increase profits. The farming practices introduced were not of course new, but techniques already practiced by a few local farmers which were developed on an enormous scale. The estate is particularly associated with marling, and with the use of turnips and clover. Marling involves digging up the subsoil and mingling it with the topsoil to strengthen a light topsoil and increase its fertility. Turnips were being grown experimentally in Norfolk as early as 1650; they are said to have been brought over from the Low Countries. They have many advantages, succinctly expressed by R.A.C. Parker:

> they were essential for feeding cattle and sheep in the winter. They brought direct benefit, therefore, in increasing the amount of livestock it was possible to maintain, with the consequent indirect benefit of providing more animal manure. [On light soils] sheep could be usefully fed with turnips on the land on which the turnips had been grown; the effect was to manure the soil and also to improve its texture by the trampling of the animals. Thus turnips had a valuable effect on a succeeding cereal crop. If the turnip fields were adequately hoed, weeds could be controlled as effectively as by the use of unprofitable fallows.

As Arthur Young tells us, Coke found a pleasingly natural solution to the problem of turnip fly: he sent 400 ducks into the field to feed on the caterpillars. 'In five days, they cleared the whole most completely, marching … through the fields on the hunt, eyeing the leaves on both sides with great care to devour everything they could see.' A crop worth £60 was saved.

Clover enriches the soil with nitrogen and thus provides plant food for subsequent crops. Using clover and sown grasses means that more livestock can be raised on a farm without reducing the amount of arable. Clover was in use on several estates in the region by the end of the 17th century, and was grown on the Holkham estates by 1709.

Wheat and barley were already the main crops in north-western Norfolk, but the quantities greatly increased in the 18th century. Wheat was grown on its own, or mixed with rye – this is known as maslin or mixtlyn. Barley was usually the predominant crop. A typical farm is the delightfully named Honclecronkdale Farm on the Holkham estate. In 1709, it carried 67 acres of barley, seven acres of maslin, 24 acres of clover, 11 acres of peas, 5½ acres of turnips, five acres of vetches and 1½ acres of wheat. The tenant taking on Honclecronkdale agreed to leave at the end of his tenure 15 acres ploughed and harrowed for turnips.

Coke was created Earl of Leicester in 1744. He once said, 'it is a melancholy thing to stand alone in one's own country. I look around, not a house to be seen but my own. I am Giant, of Giant Castle, and have ate up all my neighbours – my nearest neighbour is the King of Denmark.' Marxist historians take this to mean that this was a result of his enclosures, but the reverse could be argued – his work actually gave work to more farm labourers than before. He reclaimed 400 acres from the sea, planted trees as a windbreak, and grew turnips by 1723 and wheat, clover and lucerne a few years later. As early as 1752, it was said that these practices gave three times as much work for labourers in ploughing, hedging and threshing.

Apart from his farming, Coke is famous as the builder of Holkham Hall, one of the great houses of England. From 1712 to 1718, Coke travelled throughout Europe. In 1714, he met William Kent in Rome, and they went through Italy together in the next few years. Kent also bought marble and works of art in Italy for Coke.

Holkham Hall was built on the site of the old manor house of the Wheatleys. Coke decided to build the house of brick and found a brick earth of the right tint in nearby Burnham Norton; cheaper red brick is used for the less visible parts around the courtyard elevations. The great architectural writer Vitruvius stated that the

69 *Holkham Hall and the lake, formerly an inlet of the sea.*

ancient Romans thought that brick buildings were firmer and more durable than those of marble. The foundations are of great strength: there are as many bricks below the surface as above it. It is a wonderful building and packed with sensational works of art, a monument to the best tastes of the time. The house and park at Holkham cost an incredible £90,000 and took over thirty years to build. Leicester died in 1759 with his buildings incomplete; he ordered his executors to spend £2,000 a year to finish the work, which was completed in 1765.

On Coke's death, his estates passed to his son-in-law, Wenman Roberts, who naturally took on the surname Coke himself. He died in 1776 and his son Thomas Wenman Coke thus at the age of 22 inherited the Holkham estates. He held them for an incredible 66 years before he died aged 88 in 1842. Thomas Wenman was also a great agriculturalist. His great success was in publicising improvements to his Holkham estates, many of which we have seen were introduced several generations earlier. One way he did this was by holding his well-known sheep-shearing events, held every year from the 1780s until 1821. At each show, prizes were offered for best shearer, and also for the best sheep in various classes, the best boar and so on. Coke also sold sheep and cattle, making over £2,000 in 1806 for example.

Actual innovations included introducing new types of sheep to Norfolk. Coke bought Leicesters and Southdowns, finding both breeds superior to native Norfolk sheep. He kept both for 13 years, before finally deciding in favour of Southdowns. He also experimented with Merinos, and with a cross between Merinos and Southdowns. Coke also introduced a new breed of cattle, the North Devon red; 30 arrived at the Hall one day, thereby bringing what landscape historian Harold Fox has called 'the red tides of Devon' to Norfolk. In 1821, Coke wrote that 'The Devon breed of cattle are much preferable upon poor land, to either of the two most celebrated breeds – the Shorthorns and Herefords. The Norfolk cattle are mongrel-bred animals, and many of them are of the worst possible description.'

Other improvements on the estate were in the rotation of crops: the tenant's lease would instruct him what rotation he was to follow. The most famous was that known as the Norfolk four-course: turnips as a crop for feeding cows on the farm, and also sheep in the field; barley, laid down with grass seeds; grass; corn or grain. There were many variations according to the soil, of which the most common was a five-year rotation, with a second year of grass following straight on from the first year. There were also six-year rotations involving a year of peas or beans. Coke also promoted the drilling of seed, rather than spreading it broadcast. Improvements in machinery were on show at the sheep-shearings, especially improved seed drills.[15]

Each of the Cokes has a monument in Holkham Park. The obelisk to the south of the Hall was erected by Kent in 1729-30: it is 80 feet tall and stands on the highest ground in the Park. The Leicester monument was paid for by T.W. Coke's tenants as a tribute to him and was erected in 1845-8. At the corners are the symbols of Coke's success: a Devon ox, a Southdown sheep, a seed-drill and a plough.

TOURISM

In 1724, Defoe said of Cromer, 'I know nothing it is famous for except good lobsters', but towards the end of the 18th century a new phenomenon came to the town: tourism. In 1800, Edmund Bartell of Holt published his *Observations upon the Town of Cromer, considered as a Watering Place.* He wrote:

> the want of a large and well conducted In is amongst those few things which are chiefly to be regretted by those who pay a visit to Cromer … However, I think the trial of it might prove successful. Cromer would perhaps in the course of a few years stand a chance of rivalling some of the more celebrated bathing places. Lobsters, crabs, whitings, codfish and herrings are caught here in the finest perfection.

A letter in the *Monthly Register* in 1803 was generous in its praise:

> the town is built on the very extremity of the cliff, and as some of the houses even stand upon the declivity itself, it gives the town the appearance as if it was gradually sliding into the sea. The cliff itself is bold and more rough and lofty than upon any other part of the eastern coast; as it is seen from the sands below it excites in the mind of the spectator the emotion which is usually inspired by the sublime and beautiful of nature. The beach is equally deserving of remark, it has even been considered as more suited to bathers and as affording a more pleasing promenade than any other sea port or bathing place in England. In a word, if anyone seeks in a summer recess what should only be sought – a retreat from the dust, bustle and bad air of the capital, to an air freshened amidst the heat of summer by breezes from the sea, I can venture the town of Cromer as suited to his purpose. With the greater part of the annual visitants of a bathing place economy is a circumstance which is most considered. In no place in England is a temporary abode more reasonable than in Cromer. There are two good Inns, the *New Inn* opposite the church, and the *King's Arms* upon the edge of the cliff. Each of them are cheap and equally well provided with excellent wines and every other article of convenience … Fish is nowhere more plentiful, more excellent, and more cheap.

The *Bath House Hotel* at Cromer was originally built in 1814, the bath facilities being added 10 years later; the lead-lined tank into which sea water was pumped still exists inside the building. It was the first building on the Promenade rather than on the top of the cliff. It was followed by Marine View, originally built as a two-storey building in 1823.[16]

In Jane Austen's *Emma*, published in 1816, Mr Woodhouse and Mrs Knightley have a discussion about the relative merits of Southend and Cromer. Mr Woodhouse says:

> You should have gone to Cromer, my dear, if you went anywhere. Perry was a
> week at Cromer once, and he holds it to be the best of all the sea-bathing places.
> A fine open sea, he says, and very pure air. And, by what I understand, you might
> have had lodgings there quite away from the sea – a quarter of a mile off – very
> comfortable. You should have consulted Perry.

Mrs Knightley replies: 'But, my dear sir, the difference of the journey: only consider
how great it would have been. A hundred miles perhaps, instead of forty.' Her
husband later puts the same point with greater force; 'If Mr Perry can tell me how
to convey a wife and five children a distance of a hundred and thirty miles with no
greater expense or inconvenience than a distance of forty, I should be as willing to
prefer Cromer to Southend as he could himself.'

One early tourist was Mr Marten, a Free Church minister from London, who
visited Cromer with his wife and daughter in September 1826. They stayed first at
Norwich and travelled by coach, leaving the *Norfolk Hotel* at 3.40 p.m. and arriving in
Cromer over four hours later, just before 8 p.m. The coach stopped at the *New Hotel*
so they put up there for the night. On the next day they looked for 'more comfortable
lodgings' but failed to find any, and decided to remain at the *New Hotel* for the rest of
their stay. These are Marten's observations on that first September morning:

> A thick mist over the sea impenetrable by the eye at a half-mile's distance. A boat
> came in this morning with herrings, the catch of the past night. There are seven
> Bathing Machines – warm and cold baths and shower baths – a subscription room
> on the beach – a lifeboat on wheels ready for an instant start to the water – a pier
> of about 200 feet long, well floored for a promenade, and, altho' the sea may
> be said to be little more than undulating, the waves roll in with a noble break
> and the pebbles speak loudly as the water forced on shore returns to meet the
> succeeding swell.

A *Guide* published the year after Marten's visit says:

> As there are neither ball-rooms, nor card-assemblies yet established here, company
> derive their chief amusement from riding, walking and sailing; and to such as can
> find delight in such cheap and unadulterated pleasures, no bathing-place can possess
> more charms … The bathing machines are on a good plan, and are attended by
> careful persons. The shore, which is a fine firm sand, not only renders bathing
> delightful, but, when the tide retires, presents a charming level surface for several
> miles … The ocean, with its perpetual motion, presents a scene that never tires,
> and here it is generally enlivened by shipping; the passing trade from Newcastle,
> Sunderland and the Baltic, keeping up a constant change of moving objects.

The anonymous diarist who disliked Wells was in Cromer in June 1827, describing
it as 'a small fishing village much frequented by company in summer'. However, the
lodgings were 'extravagantly high in their charges', and the lobsters were 'quite as
dear as in any inland town, sometimes not so cheap as at Norwich'. He also found it
windy: 'a very keen, cold air, very bracing, but fit only for people in good health, and
would be comfortless in winter, and in summer the season is short, the place does not
fill till August and the company leaves in September'. Perhaps for that reason, progress

was slow: figures in the 1841 Census Report show that there were just 50 visitors at Cromer in June of that year.

RELIGION

Nonconformity was slow to reach north Norfolk: none of the 54 chapels registered in the early 18th century in Norfolk was in this region. Then came the growth: at Wells, for example, a Wesleyan chapel was built in 1759, the Quaker Meeting House followed in 1783 and the Congregational chapel on Chubb's Lane in 1816. A Methodist chapel was registered at Cley in 1799. The spread of Primitive Methodism (its preachers known as 'Ranters') in the 19th century eventually led to almost every community having at least one chapel. Many of these chapels now have been put to other uses: the libraries at both Wells and Cromer for example are in former chapel buildings. The former Ranters' chapel at Wells, with a datestone of 1836, is now a garage.[17]

No new Anglican churches were built in this period, and some fell into decay. At Cromer, the chancel, proudly paid for by local men three centuries earlier, was pulled down in 1681, its materials sold and the chancel arch walled up. It is said that gunpowder was used to destroy the chancel, but one large fragment remained, which can be seen in Blomefield's drawing of 1737 and on a map of Cromer made in 1747. It was suggested that the whole building should be pulled down but it was saved by the intervention of William Windham. In 1758, the building was inspected by the Norwich architect Thomas Ivory. He suggested a new roof and recommended slate. The cost of this and other much-needed repairs would be £750; almost £500 of

71   *Cromer church, showing the chancel in ruins.*

this could be raised by selling the lead of the old roof and some of the church bells. However, nothing was done for nine years, with the inevitable result that by 1767, 'the roof was chiefly fallen down, and the remainder, for preventing further damage, with great danger and expence have been taken down'. The estimate for repair had now risen to £1,000. Action was finally taken: the lead was sold along with the timber and boards from the old roof and four of the five bells, and the money used to put the church 'into such order as that (although it be not restored to its former State) Divine Service may with decency be celebrated therein'. It was another century before the church was to be restored to the glory that we see today.[18]

North Norfolk seems to have always had more than its fair share of unusual clergymen. The story of the rector of Wiveton was as well known in its time as that of the rector of Stiffkey over a century later. Arthur Mee tells it in his inimitable way:

> Something of the story of James Hackman belongs to Wiveton, for it was on 7 April 1779, five weeks after he had come to the village as rector, that he shot the lady of his affections while she was getting into her coach when leaving Covent Garden Theatre. Hackman had fallen in love with a stay-maker's daughter named Martha Ray, whom he had met at Hinchingbrooke, the ancestral home of the Cromwell's at Huntingdon. Hackman, who left the army for the church, remained in love with her in spite of her resentment of his attentions. As she fell dead outside the theatre he tried to kill himself, but was thwarted, and was hanged at Tyburn in twelve days, Johnson's Boswell riding with him to the scaffold.[19]

TOWN AND VILLAGE

The continuing prosperity of maritime trade is reflected in the many 18th-century buildings in the coastal towns. At Blakeney, for example,

> the prosperity bought by fishing and by trade with countries as far distant as Iceland continued into the post medieval period, and manifested itself in the wealth of post medieval flint buildings that still dominate the village. Quay House is an early 18th century house, which may be built around an earlier core, and the 18th century façade of the Old Rectory conceals a much older timber framed hall house. Many of the buildings in the High Street date to the 18th and 19th centuries when Blakeney was still enjoying a buoyant economic life. A number of post medieval earthwork banks on the marshes were constructed, often by local landowners such as the Calthorpe family, to turn it into more valuable land. The gradual silting up of the estuary, encouraged by reclamation schemes, led to the decline of the Glaven ports, which was hastened by the arrival of large steam ships and the railway in the mid 19th century, which allowed cheaper and faster transportation of goods. Today the most poignant reminders of Blakeney's vibrant seafaring past are the wrecks of ships that are scattered along the coastline.[20]

Improvements to the infrastructure at Cley were set down in its parish registers, such as the paving of the streets in 1738. A wooden bridge was constructed across the salt marshes to Wiveton in 1739, and this caused problems. A list of subscribers to it in 1789 survives, so it was presumably in need of repair at that date. In 1799, the two parishes were charged by Norfolk Quarter Sessions Court with failing to repair the bridge.[21]

Holt was developing all the attractions of a market town. The Shire Hall is an 18th-century rebuilding of the medieval Corn Hall. Holt also had a theatre, and other forms of entertainment. Holt Jubilee was held in the week starting 27 January 1783, with deer hunting, fox hunting and hare hunting, a Ball on Thursday evening, and on Friday 'various amusements such as Ass Racing, Sack Races, Grinning Matches etc.' The *Norfolk Guide* said of the town:

> Holt is an irregular and ill-built town, though considerably improved of late years, and, from its high situation, is remarkably clean; and its site, though certainly not, as it has been termed, the garden of Norfolk, has, on the high ground to the west, some extensive and beautiful prospects. On the small common near the town on this side, is a spring, or collection of springs, walled in; which affords, in summer and winter, in drought or in wet seasons, an equable stream of very soft and very pure water, which is greatly esteemed by many as a natural curiosity.

The antiquarian Thomas Kerrich visited Holt in 1821 and did not think much of the church, writing that, 'lowness and clumsiness form its character and that character runs through every part of it … NB – There is no one thing at Holt worth looking

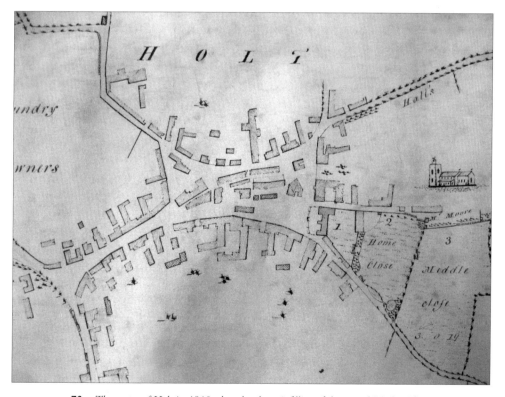

72   *The centre of Holt in 1810: there has been infilling of the central Market Place.*

at. Mem: Never to go there again.' Cobbett, visiting Holt in the same year, saw it as a farmer rather than as an antiquarian: 'Holt is a little, old-fashioned substantially-built market-town. The land just about it, or at least towards the east, is poor, and has been lately enclosed.' The anonymous diarist mentioned earlier came here after his visit to Wells and was more impressed, writing, 'Holt is most picturesquely situated, hill, dale and wood so intimately blended together, that it makes it perfectly charming', but admitted that 'the town itself has no good buildings in it'.[22]

There was more industry in these little towns than might be supposed: two bells in Langham church were cast in Blakeney in 1699 and 1702. There were brick kilns east of Old Hunstanton where an area is called Bricklin on a 1765 map and green glazed brick fragments have been found. The most important industrial building of the period only had a relatively short life, however: the largest malthouse in Britain was built at Brancaster staithe in 1747, using Roman material from the fort, but was demolished in the early 19th century. The Coal Barn at Thornham was originally a net house, later used for storing coal; it featured in BBC TV's 'Great Expectations' in 1998.

Some fine private houses survive, such as Burnham Westgate Hall, a late 18th-century house within a small park. Thornham Hall was built about 1780 for George Hogge, a rich merchant from Kings Lynn; it has a landscaped park around it, with a 19th-century brick icehouse. Cromer Hall was rebuilt in Gothic Revival style in 1829 on the site of an earlier building.

The most important house apart from Holkham Hall is Sheringham Hall, the home of the Upcher family. Abbot Upcher was originally from Yarmouth; he began buying up land in Sheringham from about 1811, and bought the Sheringham Hall estate with over 1,100 acres including farmland, heath and 'newly enclosed land'. Further purchases included the *Red Lion* on the Beckham road in 1814. When Upcher bought the estate, the principal house was the farm, and he invited William Repton from Aylsham to choose a site for the new house. Repton chose a spot sheltered by woods from the north winds and facing south to get the sun. However, the house and grounds are mainly the work of Humphry Repton, the well-known landscape gardener and the father of William; he claimed later that it was his personal favourite among all his designs, calling it his 'favourite and darling child in Norfolk'.

Humphry Repton died in 1818 and Abbot Upcher soon followed him into the grave, dying in 1819 at the age of 35, leaving a widow, Charlotte, and infant children. His tomb can be seen in the chancel of Upper Sheringham church. At Abbot's death, the house was left unfinished and unfurnished until his eldest son, Henry Ramey Upcher, and his wife Caroline completed the work in the late 1830s. They bought much of their furniture in London; it came by sea to the Old Hythe in Sheringham, where it was unloaded and brought to the house by farm wagon.[23]

Caroline Upcher was a leader in the long campaign to abolish slavery in the British Empire. The ultimate success of the campaign was celebrated with a fête at Sheringham on 1 August 1834. It began with an early meeting in the village schoolhouse, followed by breakfast on the Hall lawn. There was a mass dinner at one o'clock: 'the merry sound of three times three [cheers] sounded over hill and dale when the toasts were given, including "King William and His 800,000 Free Subjects"'. The day came to

73 *'The village shoemaker':*
Jacob Holliday of Blakeney.

a dramatic end: 'when the last rays of the setting sun had vanished, and all around was dark, again the busy feet of the multitude was heard and a shout of joy – a brilliant light was seen proceeding from a bonfire blazing from the same favoured hill'. In this way, the end of slavery was commemorated on the north Norfolk coast.

Only a few high-status houses had drains: at Blakeney, the parsonage house drainage arrangements were thought worthy of being recorded in the parish registers. In 1757, a cess-pool was made, with an arched drain running into it from the cellar window. It received waste from the pantry, powdering-room and larder, before running under the threshold of the brewhouse door. It was a clever design: 'on the outside of the threshold is a cess-pool, into which a stone hangs to hinder the return of the stink'. Ten years later, in 1767, a cess-pool eight feet deep and five feet wide was dug, into which the drains from the house and its stables emptied. The arrangements were extended when a Servants' Hall was added in 1808: a marked pavement was created, to be taken up whenever the cess-pool was cleaned.

It is hard to imagine now just how difficult fresh water was to obtain in some places. Several of the Gurney sisters were staying with their uncle Richard Gurney at Northrepps Hall in 1797. Louisa Gurney recalled that they walked to Felbrigg and were shown over the house. Then,

> we were *so* thirsty we called for some water at a poor cottage. A nice poor woman said she could not give us water [no doubt, she did not have any] but she hoped we would have a little of her beer. She got a mug and having filled it out of a pitcher that seemed the only one in her house we drank it with great pleasure, for hunger and thirst give a relish to most things. After we had offered her a shilling which with difficulty we made her accept we went away.[24]

Sheringham reservoir, still to be seen in front of Upper Sheringham church, was built in 1814 as a war memorial. The water flows into it from a spring above the church: it was originally worked by a hydraulic ram, and later by oil engines. It supplied nearly all the village and flowed away through the Meadow to the sea. It was a suggestion of William Ketton-Cremer's that the reservoir had been designed by Humphry Repton. In 1862, Sheringham vestry decided that the supply was unsatisfactory as the stream 'ran through lands on which cattle were turned so as to make it quite unfit to drink', and proposed to run it under the field through a pipe. In his diary, Sheringham farmer James Riseboro records the reservoir being repaired in 1892.

One day Marten noticed a large number of women and children at the low tide mark in Cromer and was surprised to find that they were collecting fresh water for 'washing and other domestic purposes'. 'I tasted the water and found it perfectly fresh and of delightful taste. The women were dipping basins into little pools in the sand which the sea had just left: a spring in the sand kept the pool full.' Marten gave the children a few pence and the women some religious tracts, which he commented, perhaps optimistically, 'appeared to give a general satisfaction'.

TRAVEL AND COMMUNICATIONS

Heavy goods were still generally transported by sea, as the records of the Windhams of Felbrigg illustrate. In 1749, William Windham inherited the estate on the death of his father, Ashe Windham, and he at once ordered all sorts of items to be sent to him by ship to Cley, including a large supply of wine, two dozen calico shirts worth a guinea apiece, Mrs Lukin's stay-buckles and a small fire-engine. Three years later he ordered his agent to charter a ship from Wells or Yarmouth to bring from London a cargo of items for Felbrigg Hall that included the dining room chimney piece – 'a substantial affair requiring much intricate carving of lions' masks, vine-leaves, oak leaves, grapes, and acorns' – as well as the iron-work for the new staircase and a large number of paintings. However, Windham also realised there was a risk in transporting valuables by sea, writing about one very large painting of his that 'my great Van de Velde I cannot trust to the seas, so that alone shall go by land'.[25]

There was never a turnpike road along the coast: turnpiked roads ran south from the main towns, from Hunstanton to Lynn, from Wells to Fakenham, and from Cromer to Norwich. The turnpike road from Norwich to Cromer opened in 1811; one Cromer innkeeper, George Turner, saw the opportunities opened up by improved travel and contributed £100 to the project. A milestone in Hunstanton, now beside the busy main road, records the distance to Lynn. In 1826, a turnpike trust was authorised to build a new road between Fakenham and Wells. The road was made toll free in 1881. In 1837, an advertisement in the *Norfolk Chronicle* promoted a coach between Wells and London, going via Lynn; the fare was £2 for an inside seat or £1 4s. for an outside one, which the proprietors claimed was a reduction on the previous price.[26]

A related monument at Holt is a pineapple-topped obelisk recording distances to various places. The keen-eyed observer may notice both that the distances are incorrect from where it now stands, and also that it names just as many grand houses as it does towns – Holkham, Blickling and Felbrigg among others. This is because it has been moved from Melton Constable Hall, where it originally served as a gatepost. Its companion went to East Dereham. The story is that during the last war, the people of Dereham, deciding that the information would be useful to an invading German army, threw it down a deep well, where it remains to this day. The cannier people of Holt (who are known locally as 'Owls' because of their wisdom) merely whitewashed theirs over.

Archaeology has provided some evidence of travellers from further afield. Finds at North Creake include a Swiss silver coin made in 1718 and a Netherlands 'doit' coin made in 1720. A group of silver coins including several of Charles III of Spain, Naples and Sicily, and one of Louis XIV of France, were found in Sheringham in the 1940s.

THE POOR

For centuries each parish had been regarded as having responsibility for its own poor, and might have a small parish workhouse to put them in. By the late 18th century, some parishes were banding together into groups to practice economies of scale, such as the parishes in the Sheringham/Cromer area. They built a large workhouse west of Upper Sheringham church, and the building can still be seen, now converted into houses.

Protests among the poor were common, including attacks on labour-saving equipment. In 1831, farm labourers in the Burnhams gathered together and equipped themselves with sledge-hammers. They destroyed a threshing machine in Burnham Thorpe and went on to smash one in Burnham Overy, which was on one of Coke's farms. Although he was 77 years old Coke took action, leading a group of about fifteen of his men to meet the rioters, of whom there were over one hundred. Coke spoke to the men, and read the King's proclamation for the suppression of assemblies, but they carried on their work of destruction. Coke picked out the ringleaders and dealt with them. One was released because of his previous good character but four others were seized and taken to the Bridewell at Walsingham; the remaining rioters were dispersed. In the same period, rick-burning and other forms of arson broke out in the area, and Coke bought two bloodhounds to use in tracking arsonists.

Emigration was often encouraged by parish authorities and by leading families in an area. Notes by the Upcher family record 16 emigrants from Sheringham to the New World in 1830 and 1831, the greater number being made up by the Shepherd family – John and Esther Shepherd sailed to Quebec with their nine children. Others included Alexander Pegg, James Loades and Robert Lown. Coke also encouraged emigration. He paid one third of the expense in parishes where he was the sole landowner, and a proportion where he was not. If he actually owned the farm where the potential emigrant worked, he contributed a larger share. Coke's steward, William Baker, wrote to a correspondent in Manchester:

> the greatest drawback we have is the superabundance of Agricultural labourers which press hard upon the occupiers of the Soil. I often wish we could transport a few into Your district, as we learn from report that you stand in great need of them, and are giving high wages.

In another letter, he wrote, 'we have lately sent from one Parish 26 Young Men into Northamptonshire to seek employment on the Rail Roads'.

However, the estate later changed its view, Baker writing, 'as to the consequences of emigration, I have my fears that it may be carried too far, particularly as you cannot choose your Emigrants, and it is beyond doubt that the best labourers and most Industrious persons are the people now leaving the Country'. After 1836, Coke decided not to give further help to those wanting to emigrate.

Under the New Poor Law Act of 1834, villages were grouped together into unions, each with one large workhouse – the so-called 'Pauper Palace'. For the coastal parishes in the west, as far as the Burnhams, a new workhouse to take up to 450 paupers was built at Docking. The parishes between Holkham and Wiveton were served by a new building at Great Snoring, built to take 250 people. The parishes east of Cley made use of the workhouse at Sheringham until 1848 when a new one was built at West Beckham intended to house no less than 500 paupers. Into these institutions went the unfortunates of all kinds: orphans, single mothers, the aged and infirm, and the mentally and physically handicapped. Paradoxically, the one group for whom they were really intended, the able-bodied unemployed, were not often housed in them as it was cheaper to pay them small sums while they lived in their own homes rather than institutionalise them.

These new workhouses led to protests. Several hundred labourers from villages in the Docking Union assembled at Great Bircham on 29 June 1835. They stormed the farms of the two parish overseers of the poor, turned cattle into their corn, destroyed their furniture and tried to set fire to their houses. The nearest body of armed men were the coastguards, who restored some order on the following day, and the process was completed by a troop of dragoons who arrived from Norwich on the day after that. The authorities were always anxious to identify and punish ringleaders rather than their followers, and 10 of the rioters were tried at Walsingham sessions. They were sentenced to terms of imprisonment with hard labour varying from one month to two years.

The system was intended to ensure that no-one actually died from want, so that the case of George Tallowan aroused controversy. He was a 74-year-old Snettisham man who was found lying in the road on Boxing Day 1836 and died soon after. This was reported in the *Norfolk Chronicle* in 1837, and the clerk to the Docking Union responded in the next edition of the paper. He claimed that Tallowan had been given a loaf every day up to and including Christmas Eve; he was seen that day, drunk, at Heacham. On Christmas Day he was again seen at Heacham, and was drunk by lunchtime. Later he was found lying in the road, freezing cold and unable to walk. He was taken to a nearby beer-shop run by Mr and Mrs Daw. The overseer was sent for, and Mrs Daw gave Tallowan some warm beer and some bread and meat. However, Mr Daw's Christmas spirit did not extend to putting up Tallowan for the night. He and the overseer took him to the out-house in which he was in the habit of sleeping, where they furnished him with a flannel waistcoat and laid him upon some straw. According to the clerk, Daw and the overseer left Tallowan 'much better and revived and thankful'. However, he was found in the road on Boxing Day, and, although medical aid was called for, he died later. He had been given two shillings during the week as well as the bread, but presumably spent the money on drink rather than lodging: 'his person and habits were so filthy that no person had latterly allowed him a bed, and it is supposed that he had not slept in one for more than nine months'.

WILLIAM WINDHAM AND THE SPORT OF 'CAMPING'

Perhaps the most distinguished member of the Windham family of Felbrigg Hall was William Windham, who was Secretary of War in Pitt's cabinet from 1794 and was at Felbrigg when a letter arrived from Pitt announcing Nelson's victory at the Battle of the Nile. He resigned in 1801 but served once more in the government known as the 'Ministry of All the Talents' in 1806 and 1807. Windham favoured a 19th-century equivalent to Dad's Army to defend the Norfolk coast against Napoleon:

> the greatest, possibly, of all the advantages which I should be inclined to hope from this plan is, that it will produce that most important of all preparations, the preparation of the mind. Both a sense of the danger, and a knowledge of the means necessary to be employed against it, will be carried into every farmhouse and every cottage. It will be the conversation of the village green, of the church porch, and what is not least perhaps, of the alehouse.

Windham was a believer in active and risky sports: he was one of the first men to go up in a balloon. He loved a good prize fight, and also promoted the traditional game of 'camping'. This was a primitive and violent predecessor of football, played in many villages; the name 'Camping Hill' in Stiffkey refers to this sport, not to modern holidays under canvas. An early 17th-century field book mentions another camping-land at Morston. Forby defines the game:

> the two sides, as they are called, rush forward. The sturdiest and most active of each encounter those of the other. The contest for the ball begins, and never ends without black eyes and bloody noses, broke heads or shins, and some serious mischiefs. If the ball can be carried, kicked or thrown to one of the goals, in spite of all the resistance of the other party, it is reckoned for one towards the game; which has sometimes been known to last two or three hours.

A printed notice still survives for a camping match at Felbrigg in 1789:

CAMPING

On SATURDAY the 17th of this instant <u>October</u>

A PRIZE will be given to be camped for in FELBRIGG PARK: The Prize to the Winners to be a HAT each, of the real value of <u>Ten Shillings</u>, as cost at the shop; – and to the Losers, a PAIR of STOCKINGS each, of the real value of <u>Two Shillings and Sixpence</u>. – The men who mean to camp must give in their names by <u>Half past One</u> o'clock, and the Match to begin, at latest, by <u>Three</u>. – If no Match is formed by that time, no Camp will take place.

Felbrigg, 8 Oct. 1789

Windham thought through all the details of the event. He told his agent to go to a one-armed publican in Southrepps by the name of Somers. Somers was to decide how to organise the men to make an equal match, and was to be allowed to set up a booth in the park and sell beer, but he must find the boundary ropes for the pitch. Windham thought that camping 'combined all athletic excellence; that to excel in it, a man must be a good boxer, runner and wrestler: in short a sort of *pancratiast*'. He also opposed attempts in Parliament to abolish bull-baiting. His argument was that it would be a restriction on the pleasures of the poor, whom he imagined as saying,

> Why interfere with the few sports that we have, while you leave to the rich as great a variety? You have your carriages, your town-houses, and your country-houses; your balls, your plays, your operas, your masquerades, your card-parties, your books, your dogs and your horses to amuse you. On yourselves you lay no restraint – but from us you wish to take the little we have.[27]

Coke of Holkham also liked these sports. He enjoyed the spectacle of bull-baiting, and on days when it was too wet to shoot at Holkham Hall, he and his guests would watch from the windows as cock-fights took place in the portico. Coke and Windham were friends. Windham's diary records a visit to Holkham Hall on an exceptionally cold January day in 1786: 'the pond at the back of the house was frozen for two days so as to bear, and the ice was so clear and the weather so pleasant, that all the pleasure which solitary skating can give, existed in perfection'.[28]

FIVE

The Victorian Coast

THE VICTORIAN PERIOD saw the rise of Wells to its peak as a port and also its decline. Many farmers along the coast invested in ships to carry their own produce, as we have seen, while others invested their savings in ships as a form of income, as did the Wells merchants. In 1844, there were 67 vessels registered at Wells and 115 at Cley, many built locally. The Time and Tide Museum in Yarmouth has a model depicting the launch of the *Countess of Leicester*, built by Henry J. Tyrrell and launched in Wells on 24 April 1847. The owners of the *Countess* were all local men – three merchants including Tyrrell himself and three farmers. The last ship launched in the yard was the schooner *Advance* in 1862, and the last large ship to be launched in Wells was the *Blanche*, 116 tons, completed in 1864. Tyrrell's successor, Frederick Whitaker, continued ship repair and the building of small fishing craft until his death in 1905, after which the yard was sold.

As ships got larger, a port like Wells was unable to take them. The *Countess of Leicester* was not intended to trade from Wells with barley, but between Yarmouth and the Mediterranean, exporting herrings and importing fruit. Other ships in which Wells men invested were also too big to come into Wells harbour, such as the barque *Orkney Lass*, 318 tons, which was bought in 1858 by Joseph Haycock and John Powditch. By this time, another form of investment in the infrastructure of the region was available. The railway between Wells and Fakenham was built under an Act of 1854. The major investor was the Earl of Leicester, who put in £10,000, but a further £14,000 was raised by local traders who, a few years earlier, might well have put their money into ships instead. The railway opened in 1857, and the fortnightly packet ships between Wells and London soon came to an end. Other factors in the decline of the ports included agricultural depression from the 1870s and the growth of steamships. As the locally owned ships aged in the last decades of the century, they were not replaced.[1]

Before the railway came, fuel was a growing import along the coast. Three ships landed coal at Cromer, the *Commerce*, *Wensleydale* and *Ellis*. The *Commerce* came to a sad end: she was observed one day in 1876 passing Cromer in a severe snow squall, and was never seen again. The crew of four were drowned, the body of the master, Matthew Brooks of Cromer, being picked up by a ship off the Sunk Sand. The *Wensleydale* was sold in 1879. The *Ellis* alone continued the trade, making her last voyage in March 1887. From 1881 there was also a trade into Wells of anthracite, brought from Swansea, which was used in malting as it burned with a good heat but without smoke. There were about two cargoes from Swansea a year – and the return ships sometimes took malt on to Dublin, presumably for manufacturing Guinness.[2]

The decline of Blakeney and Cley was demonstrated in 1853 when they officially ceased to be classed as a head port: the Customs House was transferred to Wells. Both customs buildings still exist and have features worth looking at. That at Cley has a panel above the door showing Cley mill in relief. The Customs House at Wells, mentioned in the diaries of Samuel Pepys but sold by the authority in 1927, has a cast-iron coat of arms on the wall.

Many families along the coast boasted several generations of mariners. The Mann family of Cley is a good example. Robert Mann was captain of a 90-ton schooner captured from the French in the Napoleonic wars and renamed *Duke of Wellington*. Mann and his son both drowned when the ship was wrecked off the African coast in 1845. A later member of the family, also Robert Mann, commanded the *Mary* of Cley, which carried coal from Newcastle to London or to France. Another, Wilson Mann, was chief engineer on the steamship *Umona*, which traded between Britain, Africa and India; the ship's name was given to the family cottage, a common practice in Blakeney and Cley.[3]

The Dix family of Salthouse followed a similar pattern. James Dix, at the age of 16, was registered as cook and cabin boy at Cley in 1848. He rose quickly, becoming a mate in 1863 and a master in 1865. In 1871, he became captain of the *Jane Pardew*, a 120ft barque registered in South Shields. He was drowned in the Black Sea in 1885, when he was mate on the steamship *Horner*. At least three of his sons went to sea, and two of them drowned. James Dix was killed in 1879, falling from the foretop of the *Agenoria* when she was in Marseilles; he was 17 years old. Samuel Dix was 30 years old when he was drowned in the *Helston* off the coast of Ushant.[4]

Norfolk coast men were involved in adventures at sea all across the world. Some lost their lives, such as Charles Wood of Morston, who was a midshipman on board HMS *Sampson*. In October 1851, he was put in charge, under Lieutenant Gilbert Elliott with 12 seamen and a carpenter, of a slave felucca captured by the *Sampson*. On 31 October the felucca left St Thomas for Badajoz, a distance of five or six days' sail, and she was never seen again. Warships looked for her in vain, and it was thought that she was lost in a tornado.

Fishing continued to employ many local men. There were 50 crab boats at Cromer and 100 at Sheringham in the 1870s, the season running from 1 April to 20 June. Fishing in general employed 450 men and 94 boys in the two towns in 1887, their activities including crab, lobster and whelk potting, drift netting for herrings, line fishing for cod, plaice and skate, and beam trawling for plaice and shrimps.

In 1875, Frank Buckland, the Inspector of Salmon Fisheries, presented a report on crab and lobster fishing in Norfolk. He blamed a recent decline in the business on new technology, and also directed attention to the cruelty in the trade. According to Buckland,

> in former times the crabs were caught by what is called the 'Hoop net'. This was sunk to the bottom of the sea and worked with the hand after the fashion of a minnow net, but about twelve years ago Crab Pots were invented. They were made of a cage of thick string netting, fastened across bows of iron or wood.

The issue, as so often, was the treatment of baby crabs: apparently many thousands of them were smashed at sea and used as bait for the small fish which were themselves used as bait in the crab pots. He noted a dispute between Cromer and Sheringham men about the issue. Cromer men returned baby crabs to the sea, but Sheringham men caught them and either used them as bait or sold them. One Sheringham fish merchant estimated that in just one day 28,800 undersized crabs were brought ashore and sold for about a farthing each. Over a month, this figure would equate to three quarters of a million crabs sold for £500. This was against the long-term interests of the fishermen themselves: if the baby crabs had been returned to the sea to grow to adulthood, they would then be worth ten times as much.

On the cruelty issue, Buckland wrote:

> It is my duty when writing about the Crab and Lobster Fisheries of Norfolk to call the public attention to the horrible cruelties practised to prepare crabs for the market. They are actually placed in cold water, a fire lighted, and gradually boiled. The reason stated is, if they were put into boiled water at once they would cast their claws. I understand from Mr Sandford of Cromer that the crabs and lobsters are all sent away live from the Norfolk coast packed in hampers. This boiling crabs alive, I understand, takes place at their several destinations or markets. Wherever it occurs it should at once be stopped.

Fishing continued to flourish in the small coastal ports, but at the western end of the coast, as Gore tells us:

74 *Maintaining the lifeboat at Blakeney.*

Hunstanton was never a commercial fishing port, and so consequently it bred no traditional fishermen; only the local long-shore rowing boats that chiefly fished for sea trout from March to September when the wind and weather were in the right direction, which they sold to the local hotels and the gentry.[5]

STORMS AND WRECKS

On 24 February 1838, the *Benwell*, 300 tons, bound from Newcastle to London with a cargo valued at £20,000, was lost on Sheringham shoals: 'the crew of eleven hands, two male and five female passengers, were landed on Burnham beach almost in a state of nudity'. On 28 May 1860, a violent gale from the north-west did extensive damage. More than 200 men and boys from Yarmouth and Lowestoft were lost and the windows of Cromer church blown in. In February 1861, eight local men drowned crossing the bar at Blakeney harbour on their way to the assistance of a wrecked ship. A great storm in October 1880 destroyed many vessels, including the *Gleaner* of Sheringham, which was driven ashore at Beeston with the loss of all 11 of her crew, including George Craske, her owner-skipper.[6]

On 21 December 1862, the sea broke over the sand-hills at Wells and flooded about 700 acres of the west marshes, which had been reclaimed from the sea by the Earl of Leicester. The damage was estimated at £10,000. In March 1883, high wind and spring tide led to a sea water surge, damaging the promenade and sea front at Hunstanton, and flooding the marshes between the town and Heacham.

There was a great storm along the coast in November 1897. At Cley, 1,000 acres of marsh were flooded by the sea. An eyewitness says:

> between eight o'clock and noon the crests of the breakers were visible to an unusual extent above the ridge of the sea-wall. Presently a rent was made, speedily to be followed by others, and mighty waves coursed inland, filling the dykes and flooding the marshes … To such a height did the water rise that the waves in some cases broke against the upper storeys of the houses, flowed out by the back doors, and destroyed the buildings and garden produce in the rear.

James Riseboro wrote in his diary for 29 November:

> Heavy gale – the hardest gale known at Sheringham in the remembrance of man. The great[est] destruction done all along the coast that ever was known, especially at Sheringham, Salthouse and Cley. It washed the gangways and sea-walls away at Sheringham and flooded the houses at Salthouse, knocked down all the front walls, smashed out doors and windows and many people had a very narrow escape from being drownded [*sic*].

On 27 February 1898 an attempt to deliver a copper lamp to the harbour master in Wells cost 11 lives. The naval cutter *Alarm* launched its boat which overturned in rough sea, drowning six men. The coastguard boat went to their rescue but capsized, resulting in five more drownings.

New lifeboats were established along the coast. In 1869, a new self-righting boat was launched at Wells, named the *Eliza Adams*. The money to pay for it had been

75   *One of the windmills of Holt.*

raised by E.B. Adams, a Bungay surgeon, from proceeds of 'penny readings' given throughout England. These raised over £500, of which Norfolk people contributed £161, almost a third of the total. The Lifeboat House on Wells Quay opened that year, designed by RNLI architect Charles Cooke. His lifeboat houses were to an almost standardised design, of which only two others survive (at Teignmouth and Walmer), but that at Wells is built in local carstone. On 29 October 1880, there was a disaster when the *Eliza Adams*, manned by 13 men, capsized while going to a distressed ship: 11 of the crew were drowned. The RNLI gave £1,000 to a fund started for the welfare of their families. It was difficult for the lifeboat to reach the sea from the harbour when fighting against contrary tides and winds, and in 1893 a new lifeboat station was built further downstream. The Old Lifeboat House, as it now became, was sold to Wells Council in 1896 for £75. It became the Jubilee Tea Rooms and continued as a café until the end of the 20th century, when it was refurbished as the Harbour Office.

Hunstanton's 19th-century lifeboats included the *Licensed Victualler* series, three successive boats paid for by the Association of that name. The first was launched in 1867: 32 feet long and with 10 oars, she cost £253. She capsized the next year while on service but no lives were lost. She had already been into action: on 18 November 1867, when the Swedish barque *Thetis* grounded on the sands in the Wash, the crew of 16 were rescued from their own ship's boat and brought to Hunstanton beach.

In 1884, the three-masted barque *Alabama* of Helsingborg with a crew of 12 was grounded on the sands off Old Hunstanton. Glimpsing lights in a thick fog, the captain, according to Gore, had thought he was off the mouth of the Humber; however, the local newspaper, the *Hunstanton Telephone*, said that he had seen the lights of Hunstanton lighthouse and thought that it was Cromer lighthouse. The ship's rudder was smashed and she drifted further inshore, coming to rest half a mile from Hunstanton Coastguard Station. The lifeboat was called out, but had great difficulty getting alongside because the ship's masts had collapsed. The crew were eventually successfully rescued.

76   *Sketch of the old school building in Holt Market Place.*

77 *Engraving showing Cromer with the old lighthouse in the distance.*

78 *Blakeney in 1769. The busy harbour, the church with two towers and the windmill are shown.*

Other incidents involved local people, such as Ted Haines who took his boat out duck shooting one evening. A thick fog came up, and eventually the vicar, Adolphus Waller, went to the old school, where choir practice was going on, and suggested the school bell be taken down to the beach and rung to guide Haines back to shore. This was done and the bell rang on the beach through the fog for several hours but Haines did not return: he and his boat were never seen again.

Sometimes the lifeboat was taken by a cart pulled by eight horses to be launched at Holme or Thornham. On one occasion, the boat rolled off the cart and the horses galloped away; eventually they were caught and the lifeboat put back on the cart to continue its journey to Thornham. This was not the end of the incidents of that night. Launched there in a storm, the lifeboat ran into an anchored yacht and sank her; the yacht belonged to Mrs Ames-Lyde, of whom more later.[7]

HOLIDAY RESORTS

The development of Hunstanton as a seaside resort was entirely the work of one man, Henry le Strange of Hunstanton Hall, the family now reverting to this spelling of their name. Born Henry Styleman on 25 January 1815, he assumed the name le Strange in 1839. He had a vision of a new watering place on his estates, appointing the architect William Butterfield and producing a draft prospectus. Butterfield planned the village in 'the old English style'. The prospectus states that the village was to have 60 to 80 detached cottages of various sizes, with a hotel, bath house, library, shops and other buildings. There was also to be a site for a chapel. The health benefits of the area were also promoted: one reason for visiting would be to take a pleasant walk to the chalybeate spring (containing mineral waters), which was less than a mile away. It was claimed the water contained more iron than that at Harrogate. With no railway line at this date, le Strange wrote a letter explaining that he was counting on people travelling from Norfolk, Cambridgeshire, Huntingdonshire, Leicestershire, Rutlandshire, and Lincolnshire by road.

The resort began with the building of the *New Inn* (now the *Golden Lion*), built in 1847. The old wayside cross, such a feature of the Green, was brought here, probably from Snettisham, although some authorities say it came from Old Hunstanton. At the time there were just two small cottages in the area – these were the only buildings between Hunstanton lighthouse and the village of Heacham. The inn was known as 'le Strange's folly', and indeed he did not live to see his dream fulfilled, dying on 27 July 1862. His funeral was attended by more than one thousand mourners.

However, he was proved right. The population of the village in 1861 was 490, the same as in 1851, almost all, of course, in Old Hunstanton. It jumped to 816 in 1871 and to 1,509 in 1881 – and all of these newcomers were living in New Hunstanton. A new Anglican church was built, designed by Frederick Preedy, a cousin of the le Stranges, and a church intended for all Nonconformist denominations, still a prominent building in the town, was also constructed. A sign of the increase in population was the opening of a new elementary school in 1874. The town hall was built in 1896, designed by Norwich architect George Skipper, and the General Post Office opened in 1899. John Storer Cobb wrote in 1868,

> When it is said that it possesses a mineral spring, that it is the only place in the Eastern Counties which is open to the sea with a westerly aspect, and that the sands cannot be excelled for bathing, or for promenading for pleasure, it is not saying a little, but it is far from saying all. Until recently, however, it was beyond reach of nineteenth century locomotion, and was therefore but little used or visited, but since the introduction of the railway it has been much sought after, insomuch, that for the accommodation of those who are annually drawn here, either for pleasure or for health, a new town, called St Edmunds, is rapidly springing up about the Terminus. Hunstanton may look forward to being considered, before it is many years older, as one of the famous watering places of England, and our children will come here and wonder how their fathers could have been so long blind to the virtues of the place.

The railway had arrived in 1862. There was a fatal accident on the line on 3 August 1863: a train hit a bull and was derailed, killing seven passengers and seriously injuring another thirty. There was another tragedy in the town on 25 August 1870 when the Hunstanton yawl *Princess of Wales* capsized on a trip across the Wash to Skegness with 16 people on board, five of whom were drowned. Despite these setbacks, trains were soon bringing holidaymakers into the town and boating trips were becoming a popular attraction. A major new element of the town, Hunstanton

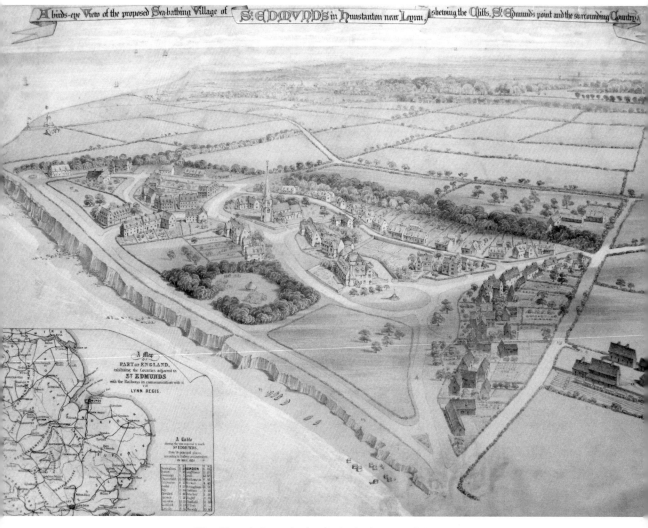

79 *Henry le Strange's plan for the development of Hunstanton.*

80 *Hunstanton Cross and Pier.*

Pier, opened in 1870. It was 830 feet long, and 30 feet above the beach; there was a stairway at the end from which to board steamers or to swim. Originally free of charge, entrance admission was soon fixed at twopence (half-price for children), rising to sixpence by the end of the century. By then, the Pier Pavilion had been added, becoming a popular tearoom as well as a place for evening entertainment. An 1873 *Town Guide* says,

> the New Town of St Edmunds is in the vicinity of the railway station, handsomely and substantially built, with the *Royal Golden Lion Hotel* forming the nucleus. The workmanship is careful and there are several classes of houses. It is a block plan with the houses placed singly or in groups, in masses of irregular form and size, interspersed with gardens and open space to avoid uniformity. There is an enforced similarity of style … and houses for all, from the Peer to the peasant. However, the supply fails to keep pace with the demand.[8]

At the other end of the coast, the expansion of Cromer as a seaside resort came rather later in the century. On 17 and 18 February 1837, there was a furious storm, and very high tides:

> The day previous had been particularly fine, and the wind was gentle; all had retired to rest in apparent security. In the middle of the night, however, an alarm was given; the tide was rising to an unprecedented height, threatening to engulf all within reach. In a few moments all was terror and confusion; the Cliff was crowded with spectators, every assistance was afforded to those immediately exposed to the fury of the mighty billows which poured in, and happily the loss of one life alone is to be deplored. This poor man was removing the furniture in Simon's Bath House, and remaining too long on the premises, was borne away by the waters, together with the house, and his body was afterwards picked up at Bacton, a distance of twelve miles.
>
> Morning presented an awful spectacle, and scarcely could the inhabitants recognise their own beach. But the alarm and the danger had not subsided: the wind continued to blow from the same quarter with equal violence throughout the day, and the tide was equally high. On the morning of the 18th the Cliff, being undermined, fell in, bringing down with it one house; at the same time two vessels were lost, the one off the Lighthouse Hills, the other on the western edge of the town. The crew of the former were saved; five of those of the latter perished in an attempt to reach the shore by means of the boat. They were both from South Shields.[9]

In 1838, it was proposed to build a sea wall at Cromer, and a rate was raised – those who had houses on the Cliff were rated at 20s. in the pound, those further away at 10s. An Act of Parliament to this effect was passed in 1845 and a wall and jetty erected that summer at a cost of £6,000. As a contemporary writer said,

> A noble esplanade now extends the whole length of the town. A Breakwater was also built, as a further security. The Jetty is the fashionable resort in the evening. No one who has not witnessed a fine sunset at Cromer can have any idea of its beauty. Cromer, indeed, possesses the double advantage that the sun both rises and sets in the sea.

Benjamin Armstrong, vicar of East Dereham, made several visits to Cromer and recorded his impressions in his diary. On 31 August 1852, he drove there with his family in a phaeton: 'as to Cromer, it is the most aristocratic place of the kind in Norfolk. The church tower is superb but the South porch and the chancel are no more … A well-ordered company promenaded the jetty in the evening to an efficient band.' They returned to Dereham the following day. Armstrong visited Cromer again at the end of September 1853, commenting 'a few stylish people are here. But the sea and the neighbouring country are the chief recommendations, the village itself being very small and behind the age.' Armstrong was back in August 1870: 'When at Cromer with my elder daughter visited the "Lion's Mouth" at Felbrigg – a deep ravine with bracken in *seas* – fallen trees and Scotch firs. It is extremely beautiful and unlike anything else in Norfolk.'[10]

There was a dramatic wreck one summer, as reported in the local press:

> On Thursday [9 August 1888], the steam tug *Victoria* of Yarmouth, struck on what is known as the 'Old Church Rock', just as she was leaving with her passengers. The weather was fine and the sea smooth, with the flood then coming. The boat being holed, she filled rapidly and settled on the rock. The boat belonging to the tug was lowered, and with several Cromer boats, assisted in landing the passengers as quickly as possible, without accident. All movable stores were saved. The master of the *Victoria* stated that there were about 100 passengers on board. At a quarter past three he weighed anchor. He steamed ahead and shortly struck the rock. All the passengers were sent home by rail. The tug was not insured and was valued at £3,000 to £4,000. She was used for towage and salvage purposes during the winter.
>
> A gentleman states that when the tug started a direction was taken which called from one of the Cromer fishermen who was standing on the beach, the remark that 'they were going towards the rock', and that he personally had lately touched the rock with his oar whilst coming in by his boat.
>
> For a day or two the fishermen did a good business by taking out many sightseers, who were able to go aboard as the decks were clear at low water. A diver was below on Saturday, and in the afternoon the tug *Meteor* arrived with a couple of lighters from Yarmouth. The vessel was holed on the port side, and during Saturday evening she changed her position. The vessel was nearly raised when the ropes parted, and she became a total wreck.

81   *A very early photograph of the beach at Cromer.*

82 *Cromer beach: fishing boats and bathing machines.*

An attempt was made to haul her ashore, using a traction engine with a winding drum in front, but the hawser kept parting, and in the end, the wreck was blown up by Trinity House as a danger to shipping.

Two 19th-century opinions of Cromer are currently picked out on the pavement not far from the Bath House. Elizabeth Gaskell wrote in 1855, 'she used to sit long hours on the beach, gazing intently on the waves as they chafed with perpetual motion against the busy shore'. The quotation is from her book *North and South* (1855), describing a visit by her heroine Margaret Hale to Cromer. The quote continues – 'or she looked out upon the more distant heave and sparkle against the sky, and heard, without being conscious of hearing, the eternal psalm, which went up continually. She was soothed, without knowing how or why.' There is also a less appreciative comment from Winston Churchill about thirty years later: 'I am not enjoying myself very much.'

The *Bath House* was rebuilt after the 1837 storm, becoming the building we see today. A wing with a verandah was added in 1872, in which year it became a hotel. Swinburne and Watts-Dunton stayed there in the 1880s, the former describing Cromer as a place 'where the small town smiles, a warm still sea-side nest'.

Several hotels were built by George Skipper, very much the architect of Cromer. They included two that have since disappeared, the *Metropole*, built in 1893, one of whose wrought-iron gates can still be seen in Tucker Street, and the *Grand*. This was built in 1891, leading to the development of the west cliffs: the White Steps were built to allow the hotel guests direct access to the beach. They were removed during the Second World War in case of invasion, but have been reinstated; however, the *Grand* itself has disappeared, replaced by the block of flats called Albany Court. Skipper also designed the grandest hotel building to be seen today, the *Hotel de Paris*, dominating the cliff above the pier. Originally a boarding house, it was a hotel by 1845. In 1894, Skipper was commissioned by the Jarvis family to redesign it on a much larger scale, incorporating Albert House and part of the *Belle Vue*; the work cost £8,000. The ground floor was devoted to lounges, dining and drawing rooms, with kitchens in the basement. There were 56 bedrooms for guests on three floors as well as some private suites – and nine rooms were set aside for the use of the guests' chauffeurs, a clear sign of changing times. The actor Stephen Fry worked as a waiter at the hotel for some time when a young man.

Other hotels included the *Royal Cromer Hotel*, which began as a private residence; guests included Tennyson, Oscar Wilde and Winston Churchill. Wilde visited Cromer several times, describing it as a good place for writing – and an even better one for golf. Oliver Locker-Lampson turned the house into a hotel in 1915, and many members of European royal families stayed there. The small hotel already existing on the cliff called the *Red Lion* was rebuilt on a much larger scale in 1887. *Tucker's Hotel* in Tucker Street was supplemented by a separate building on the Promenade itself in 1875. This building still exists although the main hotel has disappeared. The *Royal Links Hotel*, built in 1895, was destroyed by fire in the 1940s. Arthur Conan Doyle was a regular visitor and the idea for his novel *The Hound of the Baskervilles* is supposed to have been inspired by hearing stories of the Norfolk ghost-dog Old Shuck while staying at the hotel.[11]

83   *Cromer, the eastern promenade in 1875,* Bath Hotel *in foreground.*

Many smaller hotels, boarding houses and large private villas were built at Cromer in the last decades of the 19th century. Among the most pleasant of these are Kingswear and Faldonside (formerly Moriston), a pair of about 1885 set each side of the entrance to Cliff Road from Norwich Road, and the Bungalows of about 1890 on the Norwich Road. Cromer town hall, also designed by Skipper, opened in 1890, in a nice contrast of style to his Hunstanton building. The police station and adjoining court room were built in Church Street in 1897. It was replaced in 1937 by the present building in Holt Road, but the Victorian building still survives as offices. A Board School was built in Cross Street in 1896, but was converted to housing a century later.

The area around Cromer was popularised by Clement Scott under the name of Poppyland. He deplored the tendency of holidaymakers to remain in the town rather than explore the surrounding countryside:

84 *A tale of two piers: Hunstanton Pier, opened in 1870 ...*

Custom had established a certain fashion at this pretty little watering-place, and
it was religiously obeyed; it was the rule to go on the sands in the morning, to
walk on one cliff for a mile in the afternoon, to take another mile in the opposite
direction at sunset, and to crowd upon the little pier at night. But the limit was
a mile either way. No one thought of going beyond the lighthouse; that was the
boundary of all investigation. Outside that mark the country, the farms and the
villages were as lonely as in the Highlands.[12]

85 *... and Cromer Pier,*
opened in 1901.

86   *The original cover of the 1905 edition of* Poppyland, *by Clement Scott, published by Jarrold and Sons of Norwich.*

Thanks to Scott, a holiday in Cromer involved walks around the local area, so that many a happy visitor could 'recollect the poppies misty / and the footpaths climbing twisty / under cedar-shaded palings'. His description of holidaymakers at Cromer is a classic piece of writing:

Come with me, now that the luncheon-bells are ringing at all the little inns and boarding-houses, and see of what Cromer society is composed. We will stand at the head of the cliff staircase by the coastguard station, for here all Cromer must pass on the way to those lobsters awaiting them on the hospitable board. It is a very charming and select society. Boys in flannels and striped cricket-caps come with their butterfly-nets from happy hunting-grounds within a good square mile of the lighthouse hill; girls and maidens in fantastic costumes, bright-eyed, active, and full of health, troop in from the cliffs and country lanes about Overstrand with sheaves of fern and wild flowers under their arms; young fellows, very probably in the first eleven at some public school, toil across the sand and up the steps towards home burdened with lawn-tennis nets, and followed half wearily by disappointed or successful players; mermaidens with hair streaming down their backs mount to the cliff freshened from the bathe; up they come from fishing, from sailing, from exploring, from paddling, from dozing, and from dreaming, and they are followed presently by the really studious with a volume of Ruskin in the pocket or a life of Goethe under the arm, and are joined by a whole army of intelligent young ladies, who, with sketch-books and easels, turn out Cromer beeches, Cromer mornings, Cromer nooks, Cromer caves, and Cromer sunsets as rapidly as the copyists in Continental picture-galleries.[13]

In the final years of the century, the infrastructure of the resort was transformed; surviving features include the Shelter on West Promenade and the six benches in front of the *Hotel de Paris*, built by the two great Norwich engineering firms Barnards and Boulton & Paul. Cromer Pier opened in 1901, replacing a landing stage destroyed in a storm in 1895; the two rival railway companies each brought in their own guests for the occasion, from Birmingham and London respectively. The pier is 166 yards long, and so much shorter and wider than most seaside piers. The lifeboat station at the sea end was added in 1923, replaced in 1996 by the present structure, and the concrete buildings on the pier are of the 1930s.

Sheringham remained primarily a fishing settlement. The population in 1801 was about 600, equally divided between the upper and lower towns. A century later, the population of the lower town was six times that of Upper Sheringham – and in 2001 it had 20 times the number of people. The fishing industry was at its peak in the 1850s:

By 1850 over 100 fishing boats were being launched from Sheringham beach, with lobsters and crabs the main catches. During the 1880s the railway link was completed and Sheringham village began to develop as a coastal resort. In 1887 a street was constructed to link Sheringham station with the sea front. 1895 saw the construction of a sea wall and promenade and a plaque incorporated into the modern sea wall commemorates this. In 1906 the railway/sea front street was lined with poplars and the circular St Nicholas's gardens were laid out. Grand Lees and Burlington Lees gardens on the cliff top were also established.[14]

If one man made Sheringham a holiday resort, it was Robert Pegg, known as 'Gofather' (a family nickname coming from his attempts as a small child to say 'Grandfather'). Gofather went to sea in his uncle's boat when he was only nine years old, working not for wages but just for his food. In 1883, Sheringham was home to almost 300 fishermen catching crabs, lobsters, whelks and codling. A few visitors were starting to come and Pegg made the first five bathing tents on the beach that year. They were so successful that he made five more in the following year, and eventually he owned 60 bell tents on the beach. He also provided beach chairs, and was the first person to take visitors on short sea trips, buying a dinghy named the *Four Sisters* for this purpose. The holiday trade was given a great boost in 1887 when the railway arrived, leading to the development of hotels in the town.

Pegg recalled that in 1870 there were 50 or so children employed in picking stones on the beach, and that men loaded these onto ships from Boston which came ashore on the flood tide, and were floated off when they had been filled with stones. Some fishermen disapproved of this, as the stones formed a natural sea defence, but Pegg noted that the stones continued to come onto the beach, adding, 'I think they grow!'

Pegg was constantly on the beach, and as a result saved people's lives on several occasions. One of the rescued was Mr Johnson, owner of several hotels, including the *Burlington* still prominent on the sea front. He had dived into the water from a small boat and got into difficulties.

87a and b   *Holiday scenes at Cromer, from 'Poppyland'.*

88   *Sailing ships on graves in Cromer Old Cemetery.*

In about 1917, a local fisherman, Henry Scotter West, and his son were returning from a fishing trip when their boat was capsized by a freak wave. The boy scrambled onto the upturned boat, but West was trapped beneath it: Pegg was able to rescue him. On another occasion, he rescued a young woman who had rushed into the water at dawn with the intention of drowning herself: she had been disappointed in love.[15]

An early visitor recorded her impressions of Sheringham in her diary: Helen Richmond, aged 18, came on holiday with her mother, three brothers and a friend, staying for over a month. Even by train, the journey was a long one. Helen wrote on 4 August 1888:

> a bus took us to St Pancras, where the crowd was awful but luckily we had a carriage. We fed in the train which was larks. There were no knives and everybody held chicken on the end of a fork and tore it with their teeth. We had to change at Lynn and wait 40 minutes, so Lily, Chunks and I went for a walk after we'd had tea. It was an awful slow train, and we only got there at nine, in the rain as I prophesised. Our house stands on top of a little cliff, and when we arrived lots of little fisher boys were tobogganing down it. Nothing but fishermen to be seen about the village.

One evening they went to the entertainment at the *Lobster* after supper, 'quite one of the most amusing I have ever been at. The fishermen's band played to us most frightfully out of tune, a fisherman sang to us, and Mr Grimes danced a hornpipe which was quite wonderful.' She was impressed by the coast west of the town:

> 9 Sept: After tea I walked to West Runton and inspected Beeston Church on the way, which I thought distinctly ghostly, all alone, no houses near, no road leading to it and the cliffs so near that you could hear the waves, and the sky and sea black and stormy. I came back by the cliffs. There was rather a squeamish bit just before Woman's Hythe, where a good deal of cliff has crumbled away and goes down very steep to the sea, while the ground above it is very steep and the grass decidedly slippery. With very little difficulty I could have lost my head and slid down and nobody been any the wiser.

On 13 September, it was time to go home:

> up at seven, breakfast soon after, and everybody very cross. Clocks all wrong, some slow, some fast, so we tore off to the station in a desperate hurry and then had twenty minutes to wait … We cried as we passed the cliffs and thought that it was all over. We had three changes, at Melton Constable, at Lynn, and at Peterborough. The rest of the way we did not stop, and had a carriage to ourselves, a most luxurious 3rd class.[16]

Sheringham had two problems to overcome, which were recognised when the local Board of Guardians met in 1890 'to discuss the filthy condition of the beach at Sheringham'. One was sanitation: houses had earth closets but many locals preferred to defecate under the retaining wall at the top of the beach. In 1885, two visitors died during a typhoid epidemic – apparently locals did not die because they were used to the poor quality of the water. This led to the introduction of a sewage system in Lower Sheringham in 1891, designed by William Marriott, a civil engineer famous for his work on railways. The scheme cost £1,200, the untreated sewage simply being discharged into the sea below low water mark. The other problem was that, to the fishermen, the beach was a place of work. Visitors liked to see the fishermen but not the spoils of their craft: the guts and other rejected bits of fish, and the overwhelming stench. Strict regulations succeeded in cleaning up the beach, enabling a local newspaper to enthuse in 1901:

> Sheringham has ceased to be the odiferous, dirty little refuse-heap of decaying fish, which led us to satirise its 'attractions' a few years ago. It is a bright little seaside resort, striving valiantly to do justice to the perpetual delights of its unrivalled environment and its beauteous scenery.[17]

Caroline Upcher of Sheringham Hall wrote to a relative in America in 1896:

> this beautiful home in which I live is going through many changes. The air is so fine on this Northeastern coast, that doctors recommend patients to come here, and what was once a nice quiet little fishing village of two or three hundred inhabitants, is now rapidly becoming a watering place, with exceedingly ugly houses spring up in all directions, and numbers of people living here, and sometimes a thousand or two coming in the season. I allow them to drive and walk through these woods which is a great pleasure, and they behave very well on the whole, and do no harm. I am extremely interested in building a new church as we need it so badly. It has to be large to accommodate the numerous population, and it is rather difficult to scrape the money together, but we hope to have it finished by the end of June.[18]

89 *One of Cromer's biggest hotels, the* Grand, *designed by George Skipper and built in 1895-6.*

90 *The steamer* Amphion *ashore on Sheringham beach, 1866.*

The medieval church for the village was in Upper Sheringham. A fisherman's chapel had been provided by the Upcher family in 1842. The church mentioned by Caroline Upcher is St Peter's church begun in 1895, costing £8,000. It was followed by the Roman Catholic church, built in 1908-9 to a very striking design by Sir Giles Gilbert Scott.

A new promenade was opened at Wells in July 1859; running along the west bank of the channel, it was one mile 232 yards long. It was paid for by the Earl of Leicester, who gained 500 acres of pasture by building it. No embankment was ever built on the east side of the channel. Wells parish church burned down in 1879, when the tower was struck by lightning; it was replaced in 1883 at a cost of £7,000. The brass lectern and the church chest survived the fire, though scorch marks can still be seen on the chest.

As people began coming to Wells beach there were some fatalities due to the dangers of the tide. Three teenagers from Norwich were on the beach at Wells on

91 *Wells church on fire: it was struck by lightning at 5.50 a.m. on 3 August 1879.*

21 August 1895, when one, 15-year-old Frederick Bennington, was carried out to sea. A boat came on the scene and put out an oar: the boy was too exhausted to grab hold, and disappeared under the water before he could be pulled out. It was rumoured that the three had been daring each other to venture into the sea – none of them could swim – but this was denied by the two survivors. In the following summer, three sisters from South Creake, Clara, Eleanor and Ida Vipan, went for a walk from Holkham to Wells on a July afternoon: they were seen on the beach at about 3 p.m. by Thomas Cringle, a local fisherman, two hours before high tide. What exactly happened next will never be known: Eleanor's body was found in the water by another fishermen that evening and the two others on the following day, all fully clothed apart from shoes, stockings and hats.

The resorts of the coast were being recognised at last, but progress was slow. The 1871 census listed 48 seaside resorts in Britain, but none on this coast. Thirty years later, the 1901 census named 65 resorts, now including Cromer – but not Hunstanton or Sheringham. However, a more detailed listing five years earlier, 'Seaside Watering Places', does include all three towns, along with Wells and even Holkham.[19]

RAILWAYS

In the 19th century, railway mania came to north Norfolk, as to everywhere else. Investors hoped that trains would open up the coast in two ways, the trade in the ports, Wells above all, and the growing holiday industry. Some landowners encouraged the coming of railways but others opposed them.

The line northwards to Wells came first. Fakenham had been reached from Dereham in 1849. The Earl of Leicester formed the Wells and Fakenham Railway Company in 1853, supported by local landowners and a group of Norfolk Railway directors. The line opened in December 1857, and a branch to Wells harbour was added two years later. There was a fatal crash at Wells station in 1879 when the driver of the engine of a passenger train from Norwich was unable to control the brakes, and the engine crashed though the station, coming to a standstill partly in the street; a young man named John Cook was killed. At the inquest a verdict of accidental death was returned, and at the subsequent Board of Trade inquiry, the engine-driver was exonerated of blame. By 1892, there was a daily through-carriage between Wells and London. However, partly because of silting, Wells harbour failed to develop as was hoped.

The line to Hunstanton came next. The Le Stranges saw it as a key part of the development of their new resort, providing much of the land without charge and persuading their neighbours to either give their land or sell it at cheap rates. The line opened on 3 October 1862 and, because it had been built for less than £60,000, was soon returning a five per cent dividend. The line was a great success: Hunstanton soon acquired facilities such as the *Sandringham Hotel* by the station, built by the Great Eastern Railway Company, and many day-trippers came from Cambridge and the Midlands.

The line from Heacham to Burnham Market and Wells opened in 1866. Apart from enabling the Prince of Wales to travel by train from Sandringham to his friends the Leicesters at Holkham, its effects on the region were not dramatic. Gordon says that

92   *Steam train at Hunstanton, with the* Sandringham Hotel *behind.*

93   *A railway crossing keeper's cottage in the Burnhams.*

'the line rescued north-west Norfolk from isolation and saved it from the worst effects of depression, but without stimulating any economic development of note'.[20]

Cromer was an obvious target for the railway companies and eventually there were three lines into the town at two different stations. North Walsham was reached from Norwich in 1874 and Cromer itself in 1877, but because some local landowners did not want the line across their land, the station was Cromer High, inconveniently placed on the steep hill above the town. The present, much more central, station, originally known as Cromer Beach, was opened in 1887. This second line into Cromer ran through Sheringham and Holt to the junction at Melton Constable, sometimes known as 'the Crewe of Norfolk', and on to Midland towns like Leicester and Nottingham. The 1885 station building at Cromer Beach still survives, now a public house: the initials of the MGN railway company can still be seen in the spandrels of the canopy above what was originally the station entrance. The third line also ran into Cromer Beach: this was a branch from North Walsham intended to develop the coastal villages of Mundesley, Trimingham and Overstrand, opening in 1898.

94   *The railways along the coast.*

It was hoped that the railways would lead to the development of trading links. In 1881, Cromer fishermen sent one of their number, James Curtis, to London to put before Parliament the case for the second line into the town, and a station nearer the beach as he thought it would enable the men to send fresh fish to markets as far away as Birmingham and even Manchester. In 1882, the Eastern & Midlands Railway planned to purchase the Blakeney Harbour Company. The intention was to build a railway through Cley to Blakeney and on to Stiffkey. They would construct a new wharf next to the Pit, where the deep-water ships moored, and run a railway to the wharf. This attempt to revive the maritime trade came to nothing, and by 1900 *Kelly's Directory* said simply: 'This was formerly a port called Blakeney and Cley ... the coasting trade, once considerable, has rapidly declined.' The attempts to use the railway to open up the ports of north Norfolk had failed, but the new communications did open up the area for tourists.

FARMING

Farming continued to employ a large number of people. Clement Scott idealised the life of the north Norfolk farm labourer:

> The labourers, for all they may tell you to the contrary, thrive well on the fresh air and sea breezes. Their children have no ache or ailment. The youngest mother is up and about within a few days of her latest trouble. Their wages scarcely ever run to a pound a week; but the food they eat is wholesome, the air they breathe is sweet; they have kind friends at the parsonage or the big house to look after them when they are in trouble; they can raise flowers and grow vegetables; their cottages are bright in front with marigold and lavender, and well stocked behind with French beans and potatoes and vegetable marrow. Each tiny homestead is furnished with its cottage garden, and when I see these healthy labourers, their buxom wives, and strong-limbed children, I cannot find it in my utmost sympathy to pity these tillers of the soil, notwithstanding their twelve odd shillings a week wage and abated harvest money.'[21]

He spoke to an elderly labourer that he met, who 'in sixty years had only once seen Norwich, an hour's journey by rail. As for London, I might as well have spoken of Melbourne for aught he knew or cared about it.' Scott says the man was not concerned with 'politics, the imminent elections, or the overcrowding of great cities', but, in fact, many Norfolk labourers did care passionately about politics. In 1885, Joseph Arch, the founder of the Agricultural Workers' Union, was elected MP for North West Norfolk. Riseboro recorded in his diary for 1 December 1885, 'My first vote'. He names the candidates in his constituency – Cozens-Hardy for the Liberals and Samuel Hoare for the Conservatives – but does not tell us for which of them he voted! (The winner was Cozens-Hardy.)

MILLS

Many new corn windmills were erected in the Victorian period, including that at Weybourne, still a dominant landscape feature today. It is not on the village tithe map of 1840, the first known miller being Daniel Brett in 1850. In the 1860s, John

95   *Harvest in north Norfolk, from 'Poppyland'.*

Dawson was working three mills in Weybourne – this tower mill, a post mill and a watermill, but he went bankrupt in 1869. Another mill that has left a footprint is the post mill at Staithe Road in Thornham, first recorded in 1863. Milling appears to have stopped here in about 1900: it was derelict by 1926 and was demolished in 1949. The brick roundhouse survived and can still be seen. Most people passing by probably think it is the remains of a tower mill, but in fact it is too small for this, with an inside diameter of 11ft 6in. Scott had a vision of the future use of wind power that has taken a century to be fulfilled:

> Standing that sunny morning with the blue sea before me and the smiling landscape round about, with the whirling sails rushing through the air, I wondered if these old-fashioned windmills, dotted all over England, could ever be utilised for the collection and storage of one of the forces that are in time to supersede steam. It would be decidedly an original idea to collect force at a country windmill, to pack it up on the spot, and to deliver it, carriage paid, by the parcels post.[22]

The many markets that existed along the coast in the Middle Ages had dwindled to just two by the mid-19th century – Holt and Wells. The Revd Armstrong visited the former in 1852, describing it as 'the pretty clean town of Holt with its antiquated Grammar School and insufficient church'. The jubilee of Queen Victoria in 1887 saw celebrations and some permanent monuments in the towns and villages, such as the lamp at Holt. This was put up in the centre of the Market Place, but in 1920 it was decided to erect Holt's war memorial there, and the lamp was moved to its present site next to the obelisk. The lantern at the top is a replica of the original and was made in 1992 by local ironworker Tony Sizeland.[23]

These villages produced their own characters. The most famous resident of Runton since the elephant of 600,000 years earlier was probably James Leak, the local blacksmith in the early 19th century, who was also a bare-knuckle prize fighter. In 1827, he developed a gangrenous toe. Unable to afford doctor's fees, he went to his forge and removed the infected toe with a hammer and chisel, cauterising the stump with a red hot poker. He made a full recovery, continued his fighting career and lived to be 82 years old.

The census returns give snapshots of life in north Norfolk villages. A typical example is Stiffkey, which had a population of 450 in 1891. There was the usual sharp contrast between the rich and poor, marked by the former having live-in servants, usually young local girls. Stiffkey Hall itself had no rich family in residence at the time of the census, just a bailiff and his wife; the wealthy houses were the Rectory and a couple of large farmhouses. The middle class were represented by the schoolmaster and mistress, James and Emma Blake, and the post-mistress, Matilda Mann, and trades by a scattering of bakers, shopkeepers, a blacksmith and a miller who was also an innkeeper. By far the greater number of workers were the 'ag labs' (agricultural labourers) so familiar to family historians, about 65 in total. Louis Elwood aged 11, John Curson, 12, and several boys aged 13 were the youngest. The oldest were John James at 84, and Robert Lee and James Green, both 77 – there was no retiring on an old-age pension in 1891. The proximity of the sea is reflected in the presence of six fishermen, three mariners and a retired sea captain, but above all in the number of people described as 'cockle-gatherers' – 15 in total, all female and aged between 15 and 71. Indeed working women had few other occupations except as laundresses and dressmakers, although there are several female farmworkers, invariably working on family-owned farms. It would be interesting to know if the cockles were gathered entirely for family use or whether there was a surplus for sale; the latter is suggested by the presence in Stiffkey of an 'Oyster and Mussell Merchant', Nathaniel Green.

The only court was at Walsingham, where the Quarter Sessions met. The prison or bridewell there was described in 1845:

> the Bridewell erected about the year 1787, on the plan recommended by Mr Howard [John Howard, the prison reformer], has been enlarged and fitted up as a county House of Correction, since the removal of the Quarter Sessions from Aylsham. It was enlarged in 1822 and 1843, so that it has now 53 cells and several day-rooms, and airing yards, and a well ventilated infirmary. There are here four tread wheels for grinding corn etc, and the prison is now conducted on the 'silent system', which is found to be very beneficial, by preventing the prisoners from instructing each other in their nefarious arts. The number of prisoners is generally about 50.

96   *Mechanisation of the harvest, at a farm near Holt.*

Emigration was still encouraged as a way of getting rid of the unwanted poor. In 1844, the churchwardens at Holt borrowed money to pay for the passage of a young labourer and his wife to Australia and of two young women and six children to Canada. They borrowed money for similar purposes in 1846 and 1849. In 1852, the vestry approved a list of six people applying for passages to Australia, and four adults and seven children to Canada. People also emigrated from Sheringham, three men leaving in April 1888, five in 1889 and another five in March 1895; it is not said if they were single men or if they took families with them. Of the three who left in April 1888, one, Jack Shepherd, was back in Sheringham two months later, and another, Robert Pegg, returned in August 1890. Two of the 1889 emigrants also returned within a couple of years. The others presumably made a success of their new life, and may well be founders of families in the United States or Canada.[24]

For those who stayed, the final destination was often the workhouse. The *Hunstanton Telephone* described a Christmas Day in Docking Workhouse in the 1880s:

> The joys of Christmas were most heartily entered into by the inmates of the Union House on Christmas Day. The proceedings commenced at 6 am by the school children, who paraded the buildings singing joyful Christmas carols. The usual liberal Christmas fare, consisting of roast beef and plum pudding, with two pints of beer each, was produced by the Guardians, and each man had an ounce of tobacco. The majority of the inmates were assembled in the kitchen in the evening, and it was interesting to see the happy faces of those whom misfortune and fate had drawn there, as they sat round the Christmas fire and sung the song of other days to a whiff of the pipe. A good supply of fruit, sweets and nuts was handed round by the officers and friends, and the master was specially at home in his efforts to amuse and gratify his assembled guests.

A week later, on New Year's Day, an ex-inmate of the workhouse, who had been brought up there, sent a hamper of 300 oranges, while a female benefactor handed out to the inmates 'an appropriate Christian letter'.

Court records show another side of the picture, with rural protest often including damage to workhouses as well as to farmers' property, as a sample of cases in the

1880s demonstrates. In October 1885, two young men, Horace Pegg (17) and John Harmer (16), set fire to a stack of barley and wheat straw on the farm of George Hill at Little Walsingham. They were each sentenced to 18 months in prison. Seven months later, William Bone was charged with an assault on William Dawson in the same village and given a 20-month sentence. He had committed nine previous offences over

97   *Farmworkers' cottages in Burnham Overy.*

10 years including five poaching offences, an assault on a police constable and two offences of misconduct in the workhouse. In 1888, there was a much more serious case: a 55-year-old labourer named James Shepherd tried to set fire to West Beckham Workhouse. He was sentenced to 10 years in prison.

THREE THORNHAM ARTISTS

John Francis (1780-1861) was born in Lincolnshire but moved to Thornham when he married Mary Evetts, a Thornham miller's daughter. His talents as a sculptor came to the notice of Thomas Coke, and through him the royal family. His work includes a model of Eos, the favourite greyhound of Prince Albert. This was cast in bronze and a copy placed on the animal's grave at Windsor; there is another at Osborne House, Isle of Wight. He died in 1861 and is buried in Highgate Cemetery.

His daughter was Mary Francis (1809-95). She was born in Thornham but baptised at Redruth in Cornwall. She married Thomas Thornycroft in 1840. Mary is best known for busts and statues of the royal family. One of her works, 'Skipping Girl', was shown at the Paris Exhibition in 1855, and was reportedly described by the Dutch sculptor J.A. Jerichau as 'one of six of the finest statues in the world'. Mary died in 1895 and is buried at Chiswick.

The Hogge family built Thornham Hall in 1788. The last Hogge was a daughter, Edith, born in 1850, who married Lionel Ames in 1873; he added 'Lyde' to the family name at the time of their marriage. The couple attended a County Ball given by the Prince of Wales at Sandringham in 1881. Ames-Lyde died in 1883 and Edith acted as the 'lady of the manor' for the rest of her life. She was a member of the parish council, founded the local Red Cross society and was a key person in the local Horticultural Show and the Thornham Cricket Club.

In 1887 she started an iron foundry in Thornham, originally to provide an evening pastime for villagers: by 1899 there were 25 men working there, producing work that included gates for Sandringham House and decorations for Balmoral House. In 1900 they made gates for the Royal Pavilion at the Paris Exhibition. King Edward and Queen Alexandra visited the foundry in 1905, but Edith was in India at the time. Edith Ames-Lyde was

98 *Thornham post mill: compare with fig. 140.*

99 *The decay of a windmill: Blakeney tower mill.*

indeed a great traveller: she died at Shanghai in 1914, and was buried where she died at her own request. The foundry finally closed in 1920. The sign of the *King's Head* in the garden of the pub at Thornham (now called the *Lemon Tree*) is an example of its work.

VICTORIAN PHILANTHROPY

The Upchers and the Bond Cabbells

Two names that have left their mark in very many places in Sheringham and Cromer are those of Upcher and Bond Cabbell, families that have enormously benefited the two towns. These new families were quite substantial landowners, as the so-called 'Norfolk Domesday Book' of 1875 reveals. By far the largest landowners along the north coast were the Leicesters of Holkham Hall, owning 43,024 acres of land. Then came two other long-established families, the le Stranges of Hunstanton Hall with almost 8,000 acres and the Felbrigg Hall estates of just under 4,500 acres. Then came the newcomers, the Upchers, owning 1,738 acres and the Bond Cabbells 1,664 acres.

Abbot Upcher, the founder of the dynasty, was discussed in the previous chapter. His eldest son, Henry Ramey Upcher, grew up to inherit the estate and was succeeded by his son, Henry Morris Upcher, and grandson, Tom; it was Tom who gave the Gardens to the National Trust. The Upchers founded a school in Sheringham, helped pay for sea defences and paid for three successive privately owned lifeboats, which never came under the RNLI. The first was the *Upcher*, a fishing boat used as a lifeboat, followed by the *Augusta*, the first purpose-built lifeboat in Sheringham. In 1841, she rescued 17 Russian seamen who had been lost at sea for two weeks under the influence of alcohol: they were steering for Brancaster church, which they had mistaken for Dover castle. In December 1882, the *Augusta* together with the *Duncan* rescued eight Norwegian sailors from the wreck of the brig *Caroline*, and this incident gave the seafront pub its name of the *Two Lifeboats*.

The next boat, the *Henry Ramey Upcher*, was launched in 1897. Led by Tom 'Coaly' Cooper, she rescued the crew of eight from the *Ispolen* in the great storm of that year, when Cooper was 70 years old. The 'HRU', as she was known, was in use until 1935 and can still be seen in the Fisherman's Heritage Centre in Sheringham, which opened in April 2006 in fishing sheds, themselves originally provided by the

100   *Wall art at Sheringham: ship in distress in a storm.*

Upcher family. In the 1990s, these buildings were threatened with demolition, but the Sheringham Preservation Society has renovated them and converted them into a fascinating museum of fishing life.

The first two generations of the family both had daughters named Augusta who died young. The memorial to Augusta, the daughter of Abbot and Charlotte, who died in 1836 aged 20, can be seen in Upper Sheringham church near that of her father. The other memorial, in the same church, is something unique. Fifteen-year-old Augusta Louisa, the daughter of Henry and Caroline, died on 26 July 1863. Her photograph had been taken and it is incorporated into the stained-glass window dedicated to her: to see this girl from 150 years ago in the glass is a moving experience.

Benjamin Bond Cabbell was born in 1783, a lawyer by profession and a Member of Parliament between 1846 and 1857. He purchased Cromer Hall in 1852 from the Windham family, paying £65,000 for the house, with its 80 acres, two lodges (which still survive), and cottages for the gardener, the coachman and the bailiff; the estate also included many of the houses in the town centre. The Hall has another claim to fame, being the birthplace in 1841 of Evelyn Baring. He rose to become consul-general and virtual ruler of Egypt for a quarter of a century from 1893, and took the name Lord Cromer on his elevation to the peerage. He retired from Egypt in 1892, and died in 1917.

The Bond Cabbells were great benefactors to Cromer. Benjamin paid £2,000 to provide a new lifeboat, which was launched in September 1868 and named after him. He also gave land to Cromer for a new cemetery (now Cromer Old Cemetery, and containing several tombstones with images of sailing vessels), and paid for a new slipway. He died in 1875, aged 93 and unmarried. The estate passed to his nephew, John Cabbell, who changed his name to John Bond-Cabbell, but who himself died just three years later. He was succeeded by his son, Benjamin Bond-Cabbell; he died in 1892 aged only 34, leaving a widow, Evelyn, and four children. Evelyn continued the charitable work of the family. She headed a committee for funding a district nurse in Cromer. This ran from 1895, and the nurse was paying about 2,500 visits to over a hundred patients each year in the 1890s. Her salary in 1904 was £70 a year.

It is hard now to imagine a time when every visit to a doctor or stay in a hospital had to be paid for. A large number of charities helped the poor to cope. The Cromer and District Hospital was established in 1867, moving to new premises in 1932. Local benefactors came forward: the children's ward was presented by Lady Battersea, wife of Cyril Flower, daughter of a Rothschild and a resident of Overstrand, while the men's ward was erected as a memorial to Alderman D. Davison. The Fletcher Convalescent Home, which opened in 1893, was the gift of B. Edgington Fletcher of Marlingford Hall, near Norwich. It was administered by the Governors of the Norfolk and Norwich Hospital. It closed in 1996, and a centre for the rehabilitation of the elderly, Benjamin Court Hospital, opened in the grounds, the building itself is now in very poor condition.

Similar charitable institutions were established elsewhere along the coast. Hunstanton Convalescent Home was set up in 1872, moving to larger premises seven years later. The Prince Edward Home in Hunstanton opened in 1905, originally intended for children but later taking adults as well. St Christopher's Home 'for waifs and strays' was opened in 1906, run by the Church of England. In the 1960s, it was taken over by Break, supplying holidays for the physically and mentally handicapped. Addenbrooke's Hospital and Home of Convalescent Recovery opened in 1899 in Felixstowe, but moved to Hunstanton seven years later; in 1909, some 78 patients were received, for an average stay of three to four weeks. Wells Cottage Hospital opened in 1910, paid for by the Holkham tenantry as a tribute to the 2nd Earl of Leicester; it contained six beds and two cots.

Other charities helped fund hospitals. One that can still be seen is the Shell Museum at Glandford, set up in its present building in 1916 by Sir Alfred Jodrell of Bayfield Hall to display his collections; admission was twopence and the proceeds went to the Norfolk and Norwich Hospital. Jodrell also sent 40 turkeys and 40 chickens to the Hospital to provide Christmas dinners every year until his death in 1928 – and, in a touch that would be much approved of today, sent fresh vegetables there every week.

This takes us well into the 20th century, when there were greater changes to life along the coast than in the previous thousand years.[25]

SIX

The Twentieth Century and Beyond ...

THE TWO THINGS that people associate with the seaside in Edwardian England are the bathing-machine and the restrictions on mixed bathing. Verily Anderson describes how the machines worked:

> a sixpence or shilling ticket – varying with the resorts – entitled a lady bather to enter one of these high wooden wagons by steps on the beach, undress in it and hang her crinoline on a peg and then, while still struggling into her complicated bathing outfit, she would hear a rattle of trace chains, a knock on the door and a cry of 'Hold Tight!' Away she would go on a bumpy swaying ride down into the sea. In the sea the horse that drew the wagon, wet to its flanks, would be withdrawn and the steps moved from the back of the wagon to the front. Over the steps would be lowered a kind of elongated tent that hinged like a pram hood, above the door.[1]

There were separate areas on beaches for men and women to swim, but mixed bathing was beginning to be permitted. Cromer was at the forefront, allowing it in some areas as early as 1898, one of the earliest resorts in the country to do so, though two parts of the beach were reserved for separate bathing for males and females for those who preferred the older ways. Bognor Regis Council wrote a scandalised letter to their Cromer counterparts: 'Do you propose to allow males and females to occupy together same machines?' Of course they did not, and they continued to insist on the correct wear for male bathers: their costume had to fully cover the body from neck to knee.

Railways brought in more and more holidaymakers, especially to the two ends of the coast. From 1897 there were daily express trains between London and Cromer, running non-stop all the way from the capital to North Walsham. In 1907, the train was renamed the Norfolk Coast Express and included sections for Mundesley and Sheringham. By 1900 there were six trains each day between London and Hunstanton, rising to 16 in the peak period, the summer of 1939. Facilities continued to expand: a new bandstand on Hunstanton Promenade was paid for by the public to commemorate the coronation of King George V in 1911. However, cliff erosion was already a problem. At a meeting of the Coastal Erosion Commission in 1907, Hamon le Strange, son of New Hunstanton's founder, said that in the 48 years from 1858 to 1906, a total of £16,734 had been spent on sea defence works at Hunstanton, and a further £5,823 on their upkeep and maintenance. It was estimated that the town was losing its cliffs by, on average, 10 inches each year. This was especially noticeable at the path between the lighthouse and the cliff edge, which grew narrower every year, sometimes with fatal consequences: one victim was H.G. Ward, secretary of Hunstanton Golf Club, who fell to his death there in February 1910.[2]

The writer L.P. Hartley, born in Whittlesey in 1895, recalled holidays in Hunstanton with his elder sister, Enid. He put his memories into his book *The Shrimp and the Anemone*, published in 1944, giving the town the name Anchorstone:

> On his left was the sea, purposefully coming in; already in its advance ripples were within a few yards of where they stood. Ahead lay long lines of breakers, sometimes four or five deep, riding in each other's tracks towards the shore. On his right was the cliff, rust-red below, with the white band of chalk above and, just visible, the crazy band of hedgerow clinging to its edge. Eustace turned round to look at the two promenades, stretching away with their burden of shops, swing boats, and shabby buildings dedicated vaguely to amusement; next came the pier striding out into the sea, and beyond it the smoke-stained sky above the railway station.

Hartley's sharp eye noted a great deal, such as the way that children on Hunstanton Beach used jumping-poles to project themselves from one rock to another, 'the soaring water-tower, a magnificent structure of red brick which he never passed without a thrill, thinking it might burst with the weight of water imprisoned in it', and the shelters along the cliff on the walk to the lighthouse, still a prominent feature in Hunstanton:

> stretching away to the right, came the familiar vista, the First Shelter, the Second Shelter, the rise in the ground that hid all but the red roof of the Third Shelter, and then the mysterious round white summit of the lighthouse. Even at this distance you could see the sun striking the great rainbow-coloured lantern within.[3]

With the decline of maritime trade, most of the 'sea-dogs' along the coast were now retired captains. One well-known character was Captain Richard Woodget, born in Burnham Norton in 1845, who was in command of the tea clipper *Cutty Sark* between 1885 and 1895. He then retired to Burnham Overy Staithe, where, according to J. Gunston,

> the Captain was responsible for beginning the disfigurement of the sand dunes by putting the first bungalow in position. This was a railway carriage that the Captain had made watertight and floated down to the dunes at high tide. Schoolboys, of whom I was one, helped in hauling the carriage into its permanent position, each getting a penny as payment.

He built a house close to the sea, named it 'The Anchorage', and erected an old mast for use as a flagstaff. Gunston recalled, 'ships continued to use the small harbour

101   *Donkeys on the beach at Runton, from a 1930s guidebook.*

for the greater part of the Captain's retirement. Today [1947], the harbour and docks are silted up and of no use for even the smallest ship.' Woodget had a stuffed dog named Lassie. In its lifetime, Lassie, a sable collie dog, was just one of many who went with him on the *Cutty Sark*; indeed, Woodget is said to have introduced the breed to Australia. Woodget died in 1928, and his grave in Burnham Norton churchyard has the appropriate symbol of a large anchor.[4]

However, fishing was still a vital component of coastal life. Freda Starr knew the fishermen at Cley:

> on warm summer evenings, the men, mostly the Brett family, who owned boats, would gather on the beach to watch for shoals of mackerel to come along near the shore. If and when they were spotted and were near enough, the boats were rushed out and huge nets laid into which these shoals would swim and then they were drawn ashore by the boatmen and willing helpers who were watching. The result would be hundreds of fish caught and sold straightaway very cheaply (about 14 for a shilling) in the villages nearby. This was called drawing the shore and was very exciting to us children, who were allowed to pick up and have free the whitebait which came in with the mackerel.[5]

The fishing business in the early part of the 20th century was remembered in later life by James Pegg, the nephew of Gofather Pegg. He recalled the catching of oysters at Blakeney:

> Years ago there was 4 big fishing smacks going after oysters and also a few from Colchester used to fish there, they used to go oyster dredging at the dudgeon just off Blakeney and they used to get good hauls if there was enough wind so the ship could pull the dredge. The dredgers was more like a farmer's big iron harrower to stir up the sea bottom. The oysters they got was very large indeed, most was as big as saucers, and they used to put them in big tubs to send to market.

Wells was *the* place for whelks – not for nothing did the writer Henry Williamson rename it 'Whelk-on-Sea'. Pegg wrote,

> it was a little trading Place for small trading vessels as it is a dry harbour, now it is a very busy place indeed, for its a very busy place for whelks … In later years the youngest fishermen have got much bigger boats, in fact they have got 5 or 6 RN Life Boats, they bought them boats what had done their services, and they go a very long way out to sea off Wells for the Whelks in summer and many days they bring in perhaps 100 bushels and sometimes more.

The trains had special fish vans to transport the produce:

> I have seen the late Mr H Johnson send 100 bags of cooked whelks, 2 bushel in a bag, and also 100 boxes of codfish in a fish van from our station [Sheringham] many a day. He had two men boiling the whelks every day. When the boats went to sea there would be 30 crab boats and 4 or 5 big Hubblers with 4 men in each Hubbler and 2 men in each crab boat.[6]

At Blakeney and elsewhere, mussels were cultivated on lays, plots of stony ground in the harbour, marked usually by rows of large stones. Most were just above the low tide line so they could easily be worked, but some were in the main channel and always under water. These were worked from a small boat by a man with an instrument like a rake with a net attached: it could be 20 feet long. Apparently this tool had a different name in each haven – a whim at Blakeney, a lab-rake at Wells, and a dydlerake at Brancaster. One fisherman, Sammy Long, recalled that before the First World War there were about sixteen lays at Blakeney, of which four belonged to his family. Not enough mussels grew there naturally to meet demand, so they would gather up small mussels in boats from scaulps at Boston, Lynn and Hunstanton and bring them back. The mussels would be allowed to grow for two or three years. They would then be harvested and brought by boat to the Carnser, where they were thrown overboard in heaps and hand-sorted. The small ones would go back to the lays, the larger ones would be taken by horse-drawn cart to Holt and sent from there by train to Norwich. Sometimes cockles were grown on the lays, and winkles were encouraged as they ate the seaweed.[7]

There were other, more marginal, livings to be made along the shore. Pegg remembered a man called Abbs, nicknamed Old Strong Arms, who lived on the top of the cliffs at Runton:

> He used to get a living cutting big long seaweed from the rocks. He had a donkey and a mule. Every day he would be after it, that was all cut from the rocks. It was very hard work. He would be near the sea at low water, but the seaweed would grow again the next year. He either sold it to Farmers and gardeners, it was lovely stuff, and also most of the fishermen would go after it in their spare time, some could make a living at it. The rocks was all covered with it, use[d] to grow on the stones but now it's altogether different, you don't see much of it now.

The coastal towns also contained support industries such as boat repair, net-making and, at Sheringham, sail-making, as Pegg remembered:

> They was all made in Sheringham. There was 2 sailmakers, one an old fisherman, his name was Old John Tarr Bishop, and the other one (Saffron Grimes) they were all lug sails. They would measure the boat, then go to the shop and buy what calico they wanted. They used to cut it in lengths, lay it on the ground, put their lengths side by side to get the measurement, then roll it up and take it in their big sheds and sow it together. They would soon do it. They would be very nice sails indeed and they did not get much for doing it, they would charge 25 to 30 shillings a sail according to the size. And the fishermen would boil it in a big tan copper and they used to come out of the copper red as cherries.

Amenities of town and village life began to spread. As already mentioned, Sheringham had installed a sewage system but this, unfortunately, led to tragedy. On 1 May 1903, the septic tank exploded with the loss of three lives – Alfred Gaff, Herbert Rogers and John West. Gaff was a blacksmith and was inside the tank with Rogers, his 16-year-old apprentice, repairing valves. One of them struck a match which caused an instant explosion, killing Rogers at once. Gaff died from his injuries five days later. Five local fishermen outside the tank were thrown into the air. West was killed and two others fell into the sewage, from which they were only rescued by the bravery of William Dack, who had been painting railings nearby and was able dive in and save them. The inquests were held at the *Lobster Inn*, and it soon emerged that there had been a similar accident at Cromer the previous year, where two men had been injured using a naked flame in the sewage tank.[8]

In 1910, the first complete valuation of properties in England since Domesday Book was carried out. Brian Short has looked at what it shows about Cromer. The great contrast is between rich and poor. The former lived in the houses that had been going up in the last 20 years, most notably those in Cliff Road with their inside toilets, large bedrooms and rooms for servants. In contrast, the poor lived in the old fishermen's cottages in the centre of town such as those in Church Street – two-up and two-down and with one outside WC shared between two houses. Other large houses were boarding houses and small hotels; one house in Cabbell Road is described as '*not* a boarding house', implying that almost all the other houses in the street were. The town was still in its period of rapid growth – over three hundred pieces of land are described as 'building plots' in the valuation.[9]

Freda Starr worked at a general store in Cley from before the First World War:

> for many years most goods came loose, such as sugar, butter, margarine, lard, dried fruit etc, and these all had to be carefully weighed – before weighing the dried fruit, it had to be cleaned, this was done by rubbing it in a sieve, after which it was put through a brushing machine – very noisy it was too!

There was as yet no electricity in Cley, and both the shop and the house were lit with oil lamps. She also talks about local communications: 'there were no buses in those days, so unless one had a bike or owned a pony trap, travelling was an event. We usually went to Sheringham once a year, which entailed hiring a wagonette and the driver.' This was obviously uncovered as on one occasion they all got soaked in a sudden thunderstorm and had to shelter under Weybourne railway bridge.[10]

The Norfolk coast had acquired a reputation for healthy living and several institutions were established in the early years of the century so that people could benefit, some of which were mentioned at the end of the previous chapter. The most important was at Kelling. Doctor Frederick Burton-Fanning, physician to the Norfolk and Norwich Hospital, had begun to send patients suffering from consumption to the Fletcher Convalescent Home at Cromer, and he also set up accommodation for his private patients at Mundesley. In 1905, he wrote *The Open Air Treatment of Tuberculosis*. The book insisted that 'the soil be dry, the air pure and bracing, and that adjacent woods be available for the patients' exercise in bad weather, and for the partial protection of the establishment in very high winds'. An associate, the Revd Percy Lloyd, bought for his own use Kelling Farm and Lodge with 50 acres of land. He built his new house, Verwoerd, on the site (it has since been known as Home Place and as Thornfield Hall, and is perhaps the most stunning piece of 'Arts and Crafts' style architecture in north Norfolk). In 1902, he gave the lodge and 35 acres of the land to be used to set up a sanatorium for working men. The main promoters of the scheme were Burton-Fanning and Dr H.W. McConnell, who was in practice at Fakenham. Money was raised, donations including £1,000 from the Earl and Countess of Leicester and £300 from Lord Iveagh.

The new building was of wood, with large windows – there was heating in the dining room but none in the bedrooms, because 'the patient should always be lying down and in that position it is not difficult to keep warm, recourse being had if necessary to such adjuncts as caps, foot-muffs, gloves, hot-water bottles. Patients become accustomed to the outside air and forget what a warm room feels like.' By 1904, 42 patients were being treated. In addition to two fixed wards, there were a series of shelters on circular tracks that could be pushed round so that their backs were to the wind. Patients stayed about twelve weeks on average. The cost was 30 shillings a week, of which the patient would pay as much as he could afford. If he could afford nothing he was still admitted and the fees were paid from the institution's funds. A woman's ward was opened in 1906, and a new ward established in 1935, intended for more advanced long-stay patients.

Further sanatoria were established nearby – Bramblewood in Kelling and the Children's Hospital, adjacent but actually in Bodham. In January 1934, the Queen and the Duchess of York paid a visit to the children's sanatorium and to Bramblewood: 'the children were engaged in lessons and the queen expressed her pleasure at the room and at the tiny seats and desks for the smaller pupils'. After the Second World War, Kelling became a local hospital, the Kelling Chest Hospital, and the open wards were enclosed and the chalets replaced. The others closed down, the chapel at Bramblewood being purchased for use as a community place of worship. The children's sanatorium closed in 1966 and became a geriatric hospital called Pineheath Hospital, and in 1989 the Pineheath Nursing Home.[11]

Market towns had their own local doctors, such as Robert Hales, a well-known Holt personality, practising medicine in the town almost all his adult life. Known to all as 'Doctor Bob', he died in 1931. His daughter Jane, born in 1904, wrote several books on local history. She described his surgery:

it was a fair-sized room with a table near the window, a counter fitted with a bench and rows of shelves filled with bottles. The room was heated by an open fire, a couple of dogs before it, and near the corner a white cockatoo with a yellow plume perched in a cage. When the bird screamed, William Dady, the dispenser, would poke it with the wooden part of a pen.[12]

102 *A typical Board School: Langham.*

School Boards made a great difference to local life. They were set up under the 1870 Education Act, and there were soon schools in every village, with their characteristic separate entrances, classrooms and playgrounds for boys and girls. The best-known school in the area also developed: in 1903, Gresham's school moved into its new buildings on the Holt Road, with a new headmaster, George Howson. It took over a campus of some 200 acres as well as keeping the old school. A new chapel followed in 1916, and a new school library opened in 1931.

Workhouses were still the destination for many. The 1911 census shows that there were 118 people in Walsingham Workhouse, including the master and his family, live-in servants and nurses – and an industrial trainer, 21-year-old Kate Spencer from Derbyshire. The inmates were almost all either the elderly or single-parent families. The old-age pension had come into being three years earlier, but many of the elderly who were unable to look after themselves in their cottages still came into the workhouse – and several who had been inside before the introduction of pensions had become institutionalised. Some were a great age, women more than men: Frances Holmes, born in Wells, 88, and Susan Strakely from Little Snoring, 87, headed the list. Where occupations or former occupations are given, the agricultural labourer is by far the most common, with the occasional former sailor, and – a touch of the exotic – an organ grinder, John Rosai; he was born in Italy but had been in Britain for 58 years.

Of the family groups in the work-house, moralists might argue as to what extent Hester Howell had brought her fate upon herself: she was an unmarried mother of five children aged between 13 and just one year. Others were clearly unfortunate, like Elizabeth Dack, a widowed mother of two young daughters, and James Leeder, a widower with two

103 *Children at Langham in the late 19th century: the girls in the front row are wearing hob-nailed boots.*

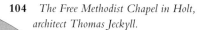

104   *The Free Methodist Chapel in Holt, architect Thomas Jeckyll.*

children. Occasionally a complete family is found, such as William and Rhoda Ransome with their three children of between three months and eight years. Unlike the elderly residents, these would not have been in the workhouse for life, leaving as and when they could find employment. The children would hopefully have been taught trades by Kate Spencer to give them a reasonable start in life.

Perhaps surprisingly, the campaign for women's suffrage played a part in the region. A by-election in North-West Norfolk in May 1912 brought suffragettes to the area from London, although some people said the ladies spent more time bathing than campaigning. One was Georgina Brackenbury, who spoke near the Jubilee Tree in Thornham to a hostile and uncomprehending audience. She was asked, 'Do you think breaking windows and doing wilful damage assists your cause?' She was sure that it did, replying, 'the public know we are in earnest'. On 3 February 1913, Mrs Pankhurst made a speech in London saying that men would give women the vote to protect their golf courses (from most of which women were excluded). This soon had local consequences, as the *Norwich Mercury* reported:

105   *High Street, Holt, a century ago.*

106   *Blakeney harbour.*

107   *Work and play at Wells: sailing ships and paddling children.*

108   *The relief of Mafeking is celebrated in Burnham Overy, in front of the* Lord Nelson.

109   *Brancaster harbour, photograph by Judith Ferrier.*

110   *Sheringham Roman Catholic church.*

On Friday night [14 February] an organised attack was made by suffragettes on over a dozen golf greens in various parts of the country. These included eight greens at Sheringham and six at Cromer, the turf being cut up by some sharp garden tool. On each was left an empty bottle that had contained acid. Around were flags with suffragette watchwords blazened forth in all colours ... It would appear that the *modus operandi* was to remove the club flags from their holes and put suffragette ones in their place ... The selected spot at Cromer was the valley side towards Overstrand. There turf-cutting was a feature. Slogans at the two courses included 'NO VOTES, NO GOLF' and 'BETTER BE HOSTILE THAN INDIFFERENT'.

Meetings in the region by suffragettes included two in March 1913, one at a crowded Concert Hall in Holt, and one at the *Sheringham Hotel*. The speaker at the latter was Dr Helen Hansen, who compared the conditions in which women and children were living in India with those in Britain – in the former's favour.

THE FIRST WORLD WAR

Many aspects of the war in north Norfolk are discussed in my *Norfolk in the First World War* (Phillimore, 2004). Here we look at one group of soldiers who paid the supreme sacrifice, and at the home front.

Gresham's suffered enormously during the war: 100 former pupils and one of the masters were killed. Many of the pupils who fought in the war wrote letters back to the school, and this enabled Sue Smart, a teacher at the school, to produce a moving book about them. The first former pupil to die, and the youngest, was John Kempson, a local boy who was born at Sheringham. He was only 17 years old when his ship the *Hawke* was torpedoed by a German submarine in 1914; fewer than fifty survived from a crew of over five hundred. Another victim was Cuthbert Hill, aged 18, killed at the Battle of Jutland on 31 May 1918. His brother Mark wrote to their mother: 'it seems incredible that so much embodied love and affection, such bright and limitless possibilities, expressions of face & speech, and marked individuality should at one blow cease to be a factor in our lives and become an intangible memory ... Brightness, uprightness, enthusiasm, love – love to give and love to inspire – these do not die but live on in all our hearts which came into contact with them.'

The teacher who died was the art master, Vivian Smith. He had come to Gresham's in 1907, and became well known in the area. He was killed in a trench by a shell while he was helping to bandage a wounded man. The editor of the school magazine wrote, 'on the marsh-swept wastes by Salthouse, in the villages that ring us, where the children loved him and many a homely cottager will mourn him, there will the past live and there we shall meet him again.'[13]

The *Cromer and North Norfolk Post* wrote on 8 January 1915:

> we hear that some residents of North Norfolk are becoming a little nervous of Zeppelins. We hasten to reassure them. The journey across the North Sea is far too perilous at this time of year for a visit. Moreover the impression is prevalent in Berlin that the Zeppelins are a failure for military purposes, practically every one used for this object having met with disaster. The Germans' tall talk of Zeppelins invading us is only for the purpose of deluding their own people, and frightening us. There is no cause for alarm.

Next day, the first air raid ever in Britain came to the coast. Two Zeppelins were seen over Cromer at about 8.30 p.m. The town's lights had already been shaded, and a few minutes before the raid there had been a warning from Yarmouth that enemy 'planes' were on the way; shopkeepers turned out their lights so that the town was in complete darkness. One of the Zeppelins passed over Sheringham at 8.45, and according to one eyewitness it was so low that it nearly touched the Roman Catholic church. One bomb fell on Windham Street, coming through the roof and the upper floor of a house and landing near the fireplace in the ground-floor room. The house

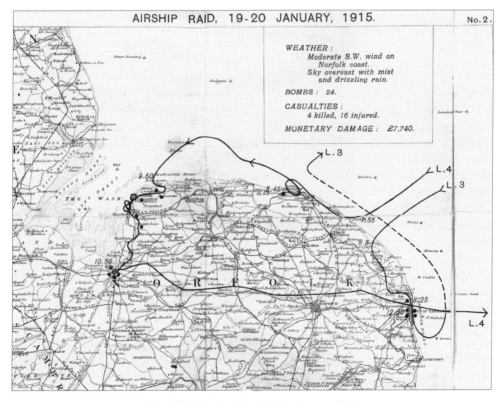

111 *The first air raid on Britain, January 1915.*

Figure II   *Hunstanton blackout poster. Source:*
L.L. Gore, History of Hunstanton *(1983)*

AIR-RAIDS

Orders for Hunstanton

1.   In the event of warning being received of the approach of hostile aircraft the Engineer at the water-works Old Hunstanton will be at once notified by the sound of the 'buzzer' three times, 30 seconds each time, with intervals of 5 seconds.

2.   On the Alarm sounding –
  (a) all gas to be turned off at once.
  (b) vehicle lights to be immediately extinguished.
  (c) Fire Brigade to get ready to turn out.
  (d) Special Constables to go to their beats, and see all lights are extinguished, and clear the streets: no one but constables and troops will be allowed in the streets.

3.   Orders for Police and troops have been communicated confidentially.

4.   House-holders are advised to have buckets of water ready for extinguishing fires.

E A Wiggin,
Brigadier General
Commanding Sub-District

Headquarters
1st Mid-Mounted Brigade
Cumberland House, Hunstanton
1st February 1915

was occupied by a family called Smith, and their child, May, was playing near the fire with a friend. May was unhurt but her companion had an injury to her wrist and her hair was singed. Another bomb fell at the back of the Avenue, made a tremendous hole and exploded; this was waste ground and no one was hurt. One Zeppelin was reported to have passed over Weybourne and skirted Holt, but dropped no bombs. The first of many spy stories surfaced: it was said that near Hunstanton the Zeppelin was guided (it was a foggy and rainy night) by a car driving along the main coast road with its lights full on.

The air raid led to the introduction of a blackout, and this led to many fines being imposed. The first cases of showing lights came up in March 1915. Olive Dent of the Bungalow, Beeston Regis, was said by the local policeman to have been showing a light at about 8.30 in the evening, which in his judgement could be seen two or three miles out to sea. Mrs Dent was the wife of a naval captain, her husband being on the *Irresistible* in the Dardanelles. She claimed she had done her best to hide the light, pulling down the blind and fixing a blanket over it. She was fined 10s., with 30s. costs – the magistrates said her naval connections should have made her especially aware of the importance of obeying the regulations. Mrs Nelson of Cabbell Road, Cromer, came before the same court: lights could be seen through the glass of the door and through several windows, which had only been covered with a very flimsy material. Mrs Nelson said that she had done all she could, but in such a bad season for tourists, she could not afford to buy big dark curtains for all the windows in her house. She was fined just five shillings, with 10s. costs.

A small number of refugees arrived in the area, such as Rachel de Keukelaire and her husband, who fled Antwerp with only the clothes they were wearing when the German army arrived. They escaped on a river steamer, but Rachel suffered badly from cold on the journey. She was cared for at Bramblewood, but died there on 2 August 1915. As a Roman Catholic, she had a funeral service at St Joseph's, Sheringham, before being interred at Kelling. She was only 35 years old.

There were real fears of a German invasion, and many rumours of spies. Freda Starr recalled that a supposed German spy lived in Priory House, Blakeney, and that it was said that flashing lights were shown out to sea. Rumours of an invasion reached a peak in Sheringham in February 1916, and Edith Upcher recorded the excitement in her diary. It was said that there were soldiers out on the Links all night, and that the lifeboat had gone out to a ship in distress off Wells and had not come back; the fear was that she had been lured out to sea and sunk by the invading German fleet. Edith went to the hospital where she worked to find the patients in a state of nerves, expecting imminent 'bombardment, invasion and all the horrors of war'. One man came to the hospital and told them that the Germans had actually landed – and that they were wearing British uniforms! Later rumours said that they were shaking hands with British troops with one hand – and knifing them with the other hand! There were more ships out to sea than usual, but the soldiers themselves were not taking the situation very seriously – Edith saw some of them making enormous snowballs on the tennis courts. At 11 in the morning the hospital was told that normal conditions had been resumed and the soldiers dispersed. Then a telephone call came from the lifeboat crew: they were fine, but were in Grimsby where they had taken a ship in distress. The panic was over.[14]

Edith was a nurse, a traditional female occupation in wartime. Other women took over jobs vacated by men who had joined up. They included two female staff members who were taken on at Cromer railway station in 1917 – Maud Watts was a clerk and Catherine Woodehouse drove a parcels cart. Inevitably they lost their jobs when the men returned in 1920.

Coastal towns experienced direct dangers in the war. On 11 September 1916, there was a resounding bang at Sheringham at five past eight in the morning – all the windows rattled. A floating mine had come ashore beside the town drain pipe. As the news got about, locals gathered to have a look. Fortunately they all got bored with looking and went home for their breakfasts. When the mine did explode, there was nobody about (it was a stormy morning) and nobody was hurt although fragments of the casing, and of the drain pipe, were scattered about the town. The luckiest escape was probably that of Mrs Craske. She was lying in bed when her husband warned her about the mine, so she got up and went downstairs; after the mine exploded, they found a large piece of metal had come in through the window and landed on the bed where she had been lying. All the windows along the sea front and many in Cliff Road were broken. Gofather Pegg told Edith Upcher that Birrell's house was 'lifted out of the ground eight inches and went back again'. He added, 'I don't think I could bear that again.' It was rumoured that, if it was an English mine, the government would have to pay damages, so people tried to gather up all the bits in order to identify it.

112   *Circular First World War pillbox at Muckleburgh.*

113   *Burnham Thorpe war memorial,*
with four men named Futter remembered.

114   *Unveiling the Holt war memorial*
in the Market Place.

Storms did not stop because of war. More than thirty men were lost at sea in one night in January 1916, when two ships foundered off Sheringham in a storm. The *Penarth* was carrying grain from the River Plate to Hull, while the *George Royle* was on her way to France from the Tyne. A few men were taken off each ship, but most were lost. On the next day the bodies of the crew of the *George Royle* were seen in the water off Weybourne; some were retrieved, but others, including that of a boy of about ten, were too far out. Six of those retrieved were buried together in Weybourne churchyard.

The local lifeboats also saw action. The last RNLI lifeboat at Blakeney was the *Caroline*, which came into service in 1908. Her finest hour was on 7/8 January 1918.

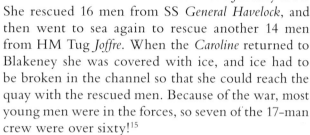

She rescued 16 men from SS *General Havelock*, and then went to sea again to rescue another 14 men from HM Tug *Joffre*. When the *Caroline* returned to Blakeney she was covered with ice, and ice had to be broken in the channel so that she could reach the quay with the rescued men. Because of the war, most young men were in the forces, so seven of the 17-man crew were over sixty![15]

The many war graves and memorials in the coastal towns remind us of the great sacrifice made. The memorial cross at Burnham Thorpe stands close to the church. It lists seven people, four of whom have the same surname – Futter. All the Futters were privates in the army. Frank was in the Coldstream Guards, and died on 11 May 1915 at the age of twenty. Walter, in the Norfolk Regiment, died four months later at the Battle of Loos. The other two died within a week of each other in March 1918: Edward was in the Bedfordshires and William in the King's Own (Royal Lancashire Regiment). The other names include two more soldiers, William Johnson of the King's Royal Rifle Corps and Edward Ward, a gunner in the Royal Field Artillery. Appropriately for Nelson's own parish, the final name is that of a sailor, William Mason, who died on HMS *Agamemnon* on 25 February 1915, at just 18 years old.

A meeting was held in Wells on 16 January 1919 to consider the question of a war memorial. Mr Loynes, the chairman, said that Wells had supplied 538 soldiers, of whom 29 had been killed, and 82 sailors, of whom 12 had died, a remarkably low level of loss as he pointed out – only nine per cent. The meeting thought that the memorial should take the form of a Working Man's Institute. Mr Peel, on behalf of the

115a and b   *Norwich children on a Sunday school outing to Cromer.*

Adult School Committee, offered billiard tables, furniture and the library from the existing institute – provided that there should be a Bible Reading Class every Sunday morning. Some people, including the rector, the Revd G. Ingle, did not want this, saying the institution should be non-sectarian and non-political. A rival proposal was for a town recreation ground, as women would be able to share in this as well as men. A memorial tablet with names was also proposed.

St Edmund's Chapel on Hunstanton cliffs was rebuilt as a garden of rest by the Revd A.A. Toms in about 1918; two of his sons had been killed in the war. It is now a garden of remembrance. On benches can be seen the names of two of the war's civilian heroes, Edith Cavell and Captain Fryatt, the latter remembered with the entire mercantile marine.

THE 1920S AND 1930S: A GOLDEN AGE

To many people, the 1920s and 1930s saw the coastal resorts at their peak. For L.P. Hartley, Hunstanton had changed for the worse since pre-war days in one respect, the lighthouse having been turned into a tea-room and painted maroon, but still had its charm. He recalled:

> And now the sun was shining on the pier-head, half a mile away. The rusty iron pillars of the pier-head had ankles bunchy with barnacles and shining, fleshy seaweed; round their feet were pools of incalculable depth, haunted by starfish; spars, black and crumbling as coal, lay about, suggesting shipwreck. It was a place of enchantment, a sudden outcropping of jungle in the well-ordered prairie of the beach.

The ultimate in new entertainment was the cinema. As might be expected, the resorts at each end of the coast led the way. The Regal in Cromer opened in 1914 as the Cromer Theatre of Varieties. In the 1930s, Victor Harrison used the Olympia, a roller-skating rink in Cromer, as a cinema; he also put on shows at the town hall after the war. Sheringham's Electric Picture Palace also opened in 1914, but it was never wired for sound so it did not long survive the arrival of the 'talkie'. The Regent opened as a concert hall in 1926, becoming a cinema in 1930. There was a second cinema, the Picture House, in Station Road, later renamed the Empire; both it and the Regent closed in 1960. Hunstanton's Capitol Cinema opened in 1928. It was bought by the council in 1981, refurbished and renamed the Princess Theatre in honour of the engagement of Prince Charles to Lady Diana Spencer. There was also the Electric, operated by Bert Wells, and occasional film shows were put on at the town hall.

Four other towns in the region had cinemas or film shows in their day. There were visiting shows in the Co-operative Hall in Holt in the 1920s, and a Picture House in the High Street, superseded by the Regal, which opened in 1937. This closed in 1960 and has since been used for bingo. Bert Wells operated the Park Cinema in Wells, later taken over by East Coast Cinemas. Meanwhile the Oddfellows Hall in the town had been showing films since before the First World War; it became the Regal in the 1920s, but closed in 1971 in favour of bingo. There was a small cinema in Burnham Market, originally the Electric, later the Cosy Cinema; it closed in the 1950s and has been demolished. Finally in Cley there were cinema shows in the town hall until the 1950s.[16]

Today, only the Regal in Cromer survives as a full-time cinema, now called the Movieplex, while the Princess in Hunstanton alternates between films and live shows. The Empire in Sheringham is now the very successful Little Theatre.

The bathing machines had gone, replaced by bathing huts and a much more relaxed attitude to swimwear, the resorts becoming places where 'the young men float on their backs, their white bellies bulge to the sun'. Hunstanton suffered several fires in the inter-war years, including the loss of the Mikado Oriental Bazaar on the front in 1923 and St Edmund's Café on North Promenade in 1938. On 12 June 1939, the Pavilion on the pier burned down. There were no casualties but two ladies were forced to dive off the end into the sea to save themselves.[17]

Hunstanton Open Air Swimming Pool opened on Whit Sunday 1928. It held half a million gallons of sea water, pumped in from the sea at 1,000 gallons a minute. In the first five weeks, almost 4,000 people used the pool, earning the Borough Council £448 – however, it had cost £20,000 to build. The Pool was formally opened by the world champion swimmer, Miss Mercedes Gleitz. A year later, on 21 June 1929, she became the first known person to swim the Wash, travelling from Boston to Heacham in 13½ hours. She was taken by boat to Hunstanton, where she stayed at the *Golden Lion*.

In 1928, there was a plan to 'HARNESS THE WASH', creating a power station with 25 miles of dams across the Wash, on which there would be a road from Skegness to Hunstanton. The scheme would cost seven million pounds and create an enormous Marina Lake of 125 square miles and 25 feet deep, but it came to nothing. Many similar suggestions have been made over the years, without effect – so far.

Cromer developed its infrastructure with more pavilions and steps, some of which still exist. Sheringham remained the quietest of the three resorts. An article on the future of the town written in 1919 said that:

116   *(Above left) The cliffs at Sheringham, with the* Burlington Hotel *in the distance.*

117   *Sheringham in the 1920s.*

118 *Blakeney harbour and the Blakeney Hotel; the latter opened in 1923.*

119 *Wells at play: the regatta.*

In the spring of 1914 the urban councillors discussed in an informal and preliminary fashion the provision of some kind of sheltered gardens, or Winter Garden – call it what you will – for the town. It was realised, at any rate, by a majority of the members, that the time had come when the visiting public would demand that Sheringham should cease to pride itself on the absence of a Pier or bandstand or a Winter gardens, and should emerge from the embryo state into an up-to-date Holiday Resort without losing its old world charm of simplicity and habit. The scheme did not get beyond the first stage because of the war, but now that is happily a thing of the past, the matter will doubtless crop up again, and an effort made to solve it.

Anyone conversant with the needs of the town will say that the most frequent query of the visitors in a spell of bad weather is, 'What shall we do, and where can we go?' and in past years that query could be tersely answered by, 'Nothing and Nowhere'. This is not right and if the town has any regard for its future the ratepayers will see to it that their governing body endeavours to settle the problem as soon as possible. Such a place would at once solve the problem of shelter and amusement on a wet or cold day, and could be made self-supporting from its inception.

Nothing was ever built.

By the 1920s, Cley and Blakeney were also holiday towns rather than ports. A 1924 newspaper says that Cley:

> Lies on the extreme north-easterly point of Norfolk, and the sea, which roars upon a shingle beach, sometimes mounts the banks, when driven by a winter storm, and pours upon Cley. Cley is prepared for such invasions: it erects tide-boards in front of its garden gates and outer doors, which secure a comparative dryness for the household. But the sea is ever threatening, and the sea will eventually triumph.
>
> Cley is for all the world like a little Dutch village carried bodily from Holland and planted down, dykes and all, in England, for the reason that Cley actually happens to be a village designed and carried out in the best days of Dutch domestic architecture by the Dutch. So, in the summer, when the wonderful flowers on its marshes have faded, Cley is invaded by an army from Chelsea, fearfully and wonderfully arrayed, which captures the main street, and entrenches itself with easel and brush on the grass-covered banks.
>
> The season of invasion is short; and for ten months in the year Cley is left to itself. Then the mystery of its salt marshes and bird-haunted, swaying reeds, becomes evident even to the least imaginative. The great water-streaked flats that once were fields become obviously sentient; the sea growls menacingly and the mysterious pool, where the river has been denied an outlet, puts off its kindliness, and seems to grab at the feet of even a strong swimmer. A few black huts remain against the sky-line, and the marshes and banks are trodden only by those who carry guns or desire to carry home driftwood.

Blakeney Hotel, still dominating the harbour, was built in 1923. It had an open-air bathing pool. In April 1934 there were complaints that bathing went on there until midnight or 1 a.m. – and started up again at 7 in the morning, resulting in an injunction forbidding use of the pool between 10 p.m. and 6 a.m.[18]

Wells was still functioning as an active port, and indeed, after declining to almost nothing in the early years of the century, had something of a revival. In 1932

120   *Wells at work: note the railway lines and trucks on the Quay.*

there was an agreement between the Port Commissioners and the Yorkshire Sugar Company which resulted in ships coming into Wells to carry Norfolk sugar beet to the Humber.[19]

Towns and villages could have housing just as bad as any in the cities, it was just that the problems were on a smaller scale. A meeting of Erpingham Rural District Council in March 1919 looked at housing in Holt, under the proposed post-war Housing Scheme. The Sanitary Committee had said in 1917 that 20 new houses should be built, but Holt parish council had thought 10 would be sufficient. There were 500 houses in the town, of which 367 were cottages. Of these, 245 had only two bedrooms – and 42 were not reasonably fit for habitation. Overcrowding was very prevalent. A Mr Benington said he had lived in many places in England, but that he had never

121   *Cromer Hospital as rebuilt in the 1930s.*

122   *Lady Noel-Buxton befriends the children of her constituency….*

seen such disgraceful cottages as in Holt. George Hewitt said there were some disgraceful houses; in one, the family lived in a cellar. However, Dr Hales said that in fact that this was not a bad house and they lived in the cellar for preference. He also said it was unnecessary to provide a garden of a quarter of an acre for each new house. Fifteen years later, Sheringham Urban District Council held a meeting concerning a slum clearance scheme, in conformity with the 1930 Housing Act. Only eight houses were involved – six in Tantivvy Yard and two in Angel Yard. They were demolished and new homes erected for the inhabitants.

Conditions for the staff working in the seaside hotels were often very poor. Speaking at an election meeting in July 1934, Lady Noel-Buxton said, 'I believe there is a great deal of child slavery today. I believe there are many page-boys in Cromer today who are really slaves. They are working in Cromer and other seaside places ten and eleven hours a day, and that seems to me to be nothing but child slavery.' Lady Noel-Buxton, who represented the Labour party, was, in fact, one of the earliest female MPs for a rural constituency anywhere in Britain, being elected for North Norfolk by just 170 votes in a by-election in July 1930 after her husband, the previous Member, had been elevated to a peerage. However, she lost the seat in the general election of the following year. Another leader in female politics was Lady Suffield of Gunton, the first woman on Norfolk County Council and the first to be a Justice of the Peace for Norfolk.[20]

Gresham's was flourishing. It was one of the first schools in England to abolish corporal punishment, the headmaster, J.R. Eccles, condemning it in a letter to *The Times* in March 1921. Famous old boys included poets Stephen Spender and W.H. Auden, composers Lennox Berkeley and Benjamin Britten, Lord Reith of the BBC, Christopher Cockerell, the inventor of the hovercraft, and Donald Maclean, diplomat and spy. Auden enjoyed some aspects of life at Gresham's: 'the first

123   *… and talks to her north Norfolk voters.*

124   *The royal family in north Norfolk: Princesses Elizabeth and Margaret buy war savings at Langham.*

125   *The royal family in north Norfolk: Prince Charles at Holkham.*

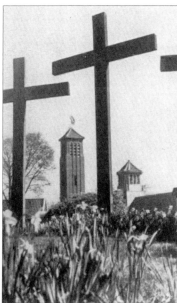

126   *Images of Walsingham in the 20th century.*

condition for a school is a beautiful situation and in that respect we were at Holt very fortunate. The school authorities, with extraordinary good sense, set virtually no bounds, a liberty I believe rarely abused. Watching a snow storm come up from the sea over the marshes at Salthouse, and walking in a June dawn (not so legally) by Hempstead Mill are only the two most vivid of a hundred such experiences.' He was, however, critical of 'the Honour system' at the school, which encouraged boys to own up to their own offences – but also to report on other boys.[21]

The 1930s saw a revival of pilgrimage to Walsingham after a lapse of 400 years. The Anglican shrine was established in the early years of the decade, led by the inspiration of the vicar, Alfred Hope Patten. The Slipper Chapel had been bought by Charlotte Boyd, a convert to Roman Catholicism, in 1896, and was finally re-opened for worship in 1934. Several new buildings have followed since, and many thousands now attend the two shrines every year.

Most of the windmills in the area ceased to function in the 1920s, and many have been destroyed, leaving no trace apart from an occasional street or field name. The name Mill Street in Holt, for example, preserves the memory of a mill whose sails were taken off in 1922; it was pulled down in 1973. Several are still prominent in the landscape, however, such as those at Cley and Weybourne. Cley Mill was bought by Mrs Wilson for £350 in 1921 and used as a house, passing through her descendants, the Blount family. At one time it was let to the Duchess of Bedford. It became a guest house in 1983. Parts of the mill machinery have been used in fitting up the interior.

Weybourne Mill also stopped working at the time of the First World War. It was restored as a private house in the 1920s, making use of the post from the old Beach Road post mill. As early as 1929, the owner, J. Sidney Brocklesby, was asking if the sails could be put back and used to generate electricity for lighting, heating and cooking. A new cap was fitted in 1968 and new sails in 1969. The mill was struck by lightning in 1978, but the only damage was a burst water pipe.

These were difficult times for agriculture. The Farm Wages Board was created in 1917 but abolished in 1924. In Norfolk, farm wages fell from 45s. a week in 1921 to 30s. by the winter of 1922. A proposed further reduction to 24s. 9d. in March 1923 led to a farm labourers' strike, which lasted a month – 7,000 men, mainly in Norfolk, were out at its height. Six hundred extra police were called into the county. At the end of the strike, 2,000 were still out – blacklisted for their solidarity. The strike led to the return of the Wages Board in 1924. Perhaps because of the strike, a tradition of rural radicalism continued, North Norfolk being one of the few rural constituencies to have a Labour MP continually between 1945 and 1970 (Edwin Gooch, followed by Bert Hazell).

At Stiffkey, the farm across the river from the Hall was farmed by Henry Williamson between 1937 and 1939. Whatever one thinks of his politics (right wing, veering towards fascism), Williamson's book of his experiences, *The Story of a Norfolk Farm*, is an evocative account of a farm in the 1930s. He describes his arrival in Norfolk:

> The country was changing, woodlands and sloping fields, and soon we came to fast level tracts of marshes stretching to the sea. They were grey, and somewhat dull. Dick said it would make all the difference if the sun came out: the air of

Norfolk was the keenest and clearest in England, and the marshes were famous for the sea-lavender and other maritime plants in summer. The road rose and fell, and passed through villages with cottages built of large pebbles or half-flints and old bricks, and roman tiles. Some were Dutch in design, and Flemish; also the Huguenots had settled here, leaving their pattern of farmhouse and cottage on the countryside. It was the least changed part of Old England, with only a few visitors in summer.[22]

FISHING

The annual report of the Eastern Sea Fisheries Inspector for 1934 sums up the state of the industry. There were 14 boats between Cromer and Caister that drifted for mackerel in May and June, but with very poor results. Sea trout were obtained in small quantities in May and June by Cromer and Blakeney boats, but fish were small until the end of the season: by the time larger fish put in an appearance it was the close season. The crab season opened in March and 639,500 crabs were landed in the region, 'below the average'. Just over 43,000 lobsters were landed, 7,000 less than the previous season. Most of the whelking was done from Sheringham, Wells and Brancaster staithe. Numbers were down on previous years; some people thought this was because of over-working the beds, others blamed the hot weather. Cockles were not plentiful in the Norfolk harbours, but those obtained were of the highest quality. Winkles were gathered only by crew from Lynn 'and females on the Norfolk coast'. Blakeney had the best trade in mussels, Brancaster not so good – 'I believe that most of the harbour men need mussels for re-stocking'. Thirteen people had been fined for breaking the laws – four for illegal trawling and nine for taking undersized mussels.

In the summer of 1934, the *Norfolk Chronicle* reported:

> Catches of mackerel without parallel in living memory have been made along the Norfolk coast this week. From Brancaster to Sheringham the shallows were teeming with the fish, and visitors and residents took them exactly as they pleased – with rod and line, net or with the hands. The swim started at Salthouse on Thursday evening, and on Friday thousands of mackerel were being hawked in the district. On Sunday the shoals were off Blakeney, and visitors were busy until midnight making 'bags' such as are usually only dreamed of.
>
> Visitors waded knee-deep into the water and snatched the fish out on to the beach, while children stood behind them to secure the mackerel that became stranded on the beach in their leaps after whitebait. Thousands of the fish were despatched to Norwich market, where the best price that could be obtained was three shillings a hundred. Coincident with the visit of the mackerel came the first of the sea trout; several nice specimens were taken at Weybourne on Wednesday.[23]

Fishing remained a dangerous profession and the sea treacherous. Two Cromer fishermen, Charles Cox and Gilbert Mayes, were drowned in July 1934 when their crab boat capsized and sank about a mile and a half to the north-east of Cromer pier. The coastguard saw their boat, the *White Heather*, capsize in heavy seas and raised the alarm. The lifeboat rushed to the rescue, watched by more than a thousand holiday-makers. They found Cox's body but no trace of the boat or of Mayes: Mayes' body was later washed up at Weybourne. Both were married men with children and themselves members of the lifeboat crew. A disaster fund was opened with immediate contributions from Lord and Lady Suffield, Lady Noel–Buxton and many others.

THREE NORTH NORFOLK 'HEROES' OF THE TWENTIES

Sidney Long

In 1918, a collection of stuffed birds that had been shot at Cley between 1887 and 1903 was sold. It included Levantine shearwater, spoonbills and stone curlew, the latter a bird of the heath rather than the marshes. However, the emphasis was moving from shooting rare birds to preserving them and their habitats, and Sidney Long led the way.

Long was born in Wells in 1870, the son of a doctor. He became a doctor himself and was a physician at the Norfolk and Norwich Hospital, living at Surrey Street in Norwich. In 1923, he played a leading role in the purchase of Scolt Head Island for the National Trust:

> the long sand spit, running for 3½ miles between Burnham Overy and Brancaster harbours, and overlooking a salt marsh beautiful in summer with sea lavender, had been dear to him since his boyhood … Scolt Head has been treasured ever since, not only as a great nesting place for terns and other sea and marshland birds, but as a classical site for the study of coastal ecology.

In 1926, he bought in his own name the 407 acres of Cley Marshes to the east of Blakeney harbour, raising the required sum of £5,160 from a dozen subscribers. The Norfolk Naturalists' Trust was formally incorporated on 5 November 1926, with Russell Colman as the first president and Long as Hon. Sec. It was the first of its kind, and no similar county trust was formed for another quarter of a century. The Trust, now called the Norfolk Wildlife Trust, has grown from this one reserve to have over 17,000 members and to own more than 2,600 hectares of Norfolk in 40 nature reserves, including six miles of coastline. It has been written of him that,

> in appearance, Sydney Long was tall and spare, with a fair drooping moustache – rather like a gentle Viking. He was reserved in speech and manner, yet had a capacity to make friends in all walks of life. The Trust, indeed, owed as much to his friendships as to his administrative ability. He also seemed to have a natural affinity with the wild creatures he loved to observe. He took it as a personal compliment when the terns, 'dive-bombing' other visitors who came too close to their nests on Scolt Head, until they drove the intruders away, contented themselves with a few thumps on his old felt hat.

Sydney Long died in 1939 at the age of 69. At his wish, his ashes were scattered on Scolt Head Island.[24]

Harold Davidson

Harold Davidson was born in 1875, the son of a clergyman. He went to Whitgift School in Croydon, where he joined a small group of actors; after leaving school in 1894, he toured with them for a time, before going to Exeter College, Oxford, to study

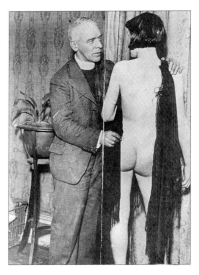

127 *Harold Davidson: one of the disputed photographs in the legal case.*

theology. While at college, he met Sir Reginald Kennedy-Cox, with whom he later founded the Docklands Settlement, a charitable organisation in East London. He also met Molly, his future wife.

He was ordained in 1903 and was briefly a curate at St Martin-in-the Fields in London. He was appointed rector of Stiffkey and Morston and served for over a quarter of a century, apart from an absence during the war when he served as a chaplain in the Royal Navy. He was affectionately known there as 'Little Jim', as he was only 5ft 3in tall; he visited all homes, whether they attended his church or not, and would help with their rents on occasion.

Davidson was involved in charity work in London, and was a frequent visitor to the city. One of these trips led to the events that caused his downfall. In November 1930, he was late returning for an Armistice Day service at Morston. His churchwarden there, Major Philip Hamond, was furious and began to investigate Davidson. His agent was Henry Dashwood, solicitor to the Church of England. Dashwood came to Stiffkey but the churchwarden there told him that no one in the village had a bad word to say about Davidson. Dashwood then hired a detective agency to follow the rector. They spoke to 40 girls but only one was critical of Davidson – and she retracted that after she had sobered up.

Davidson was eventually tried before the Consistory Court in March 1932, at Church House, Westminster. The trial lasted 26 days and was a huge sensation. Many of the charges related to inappropriate intimacy with girls employed at Lyons Tea Rooms: Davidson befriended them because they were on very low wages and liable to be easily led into prostitution. Davidson said that he had helped up to a thousand girls with advice and sometimes money, but had never had sex with them; indeed several of the girls had visited the family at Stiffkey, and met his wife and his daughter there.

The only girl who spoke against him was 'Barbara' Harris (her real name was Gwendoline), who claimed that the reason Davidson had missed his train on that fateful Remembrance Day was because he was 'trying to kiss me all the time'. More damaging were two photographs showing Davidson with a half-naked girl. Davidson always claimed that they were forged, and they do have a curious white line between the rector and the girl, either because two different photographs have been amateurishly spliced together, or because they have since been stored folded. Davidson was convicted and was formally defrocked at Norwich Cathedral.

Davidson returned to the entertainment industry, fasting in a barrel at Blackpool. His last appearance was at Skegness in July 1937, in a cage with two lions. Popular legend is that he was killed by one of the lions. In fact he had tripped on the tail of one lion, and the other had mauled him, breaking his collar bone. He was killed by an injection of insulin from a doctor who falsely diagnosed an advanced case of diabetes. He was buried at Stiffkey.

128   *Henry Blogg, lifeboatman.*

Davidson's family have fought ever since to clear his name. His granddaughter writes:

> the rector is now generally recognised as an innocent man falsely accused. Those involved in what happened are long dead and the Church has moved forward – we all have. It can afford to look into its darker corners to right the wrongs perpetrated in its name … I hope one day the church will find the wisdom to clear him, as much for his own sake as for ours, to put an end to a scandal that will continue to haunt until they do.

Davidson was a great parish clergyman. Henry Williamson wrote that sometimes, on the way to his farm, he would see sewage floating in the river Stiffkey. Then came a change: each morning a horse-drawn cart called at every house in Stiffkey and emptied the pails used as toilets by the cottagers. Before that, the waste had just been poured into a hole behind the outhouse in each cottage. Who had introduced this improvement to Stiffkey's health and hygiene? Harold Davidson – no wonder his parishioners loved him.[25]

Henry Blogg

Henry Blogg lived all his life in Cromer. Born in a cottage in New Street on 6 February 1876, he was brought up firstly by his grandmother, and later by his stepfather, John Davies, in Chapel Street. Davies had a crab boat and was also a lifeboatman. Blogg left school at the age of 11 and worked with his stepfather crab fishing. He joined the lifeboat crew when he was 18, in 1894. He took part in his first rescue on 28 December, going to the assistance of the *Fair City of Gloucester*. In 1902, Davies retired from the crew and Blogg was voted to succeed him as second coxswain. In 1909, he became coxswain.

Blogg had a unique record as a lifeboatman, being awarded three gold medals and four silver medals between 1917 and 1941. The first gold medal came in January 1917, when the lifeboat rescued 11 men from the shattered *Fernebo*. Despite having already been called out to one

129   *The Cromer lifeboat, coxswain Henry Blogg.*

launch that day, Blogg and the crew rowed to the rescue: when they finally reached the *Fernebo*, the lifeboat crew had been fighting the elements for almost 14 hours. The first motor lifeboat in Cromer came in 1923, it and its successors being named *H F Bailey* in honour of the man who had left money for them. Blogg continued as coxswain; in 1932 he and his crew saved 29 men from the Italian *Monte Nevoso*, stranded on Haisborough Sands, in a rescue that lasted over 52 hours. He also rescued the captain's dog, a Tyrolean sheepdog, which the captain gave to him in gratitude. In August 1941, the two Cromer lifeboats, along with the Sheringham and Gorleston lifeboats, were launched to rescue men from six ships of a convoy that had been wrecked in gale-force winds and heavy breaking seas. Eighty-eight men were saved and Blogg received his third gold medal. Two months later, Blogg and his crew rescued 44 men from the *English Trader*, wrecked on a sandbank outside Haisborough Sands in a full gale. Blogg finally retired at the age of 71 in 1947 after 53 years' service on the lifeboats. During his 38 years of service as coxswain, he had launched 387 times and rescued 873 people.

Blogg married Ann Brackenbury in Cromer parish church on 16 October 1901. They had two children, Henry, who was born in 1902 but died soon before his second birthday, and Annie, who died aged 28 in 1935. Ann Blogg died in 1950. Blogg himself died on 13 June 1954. An RNLI museum dedicated to Blogg was opened in 2006 by Ronnie Corbett, who had started his stage career in Cromer. There is a bronze bust of Blogg on the cliff top in North Lodge Park. On it, he is described simply as 'One of the bravest men who ever lived.'

THE SECOND WORLD WAR

In the 1930s, signs of impending war were everywhere. The rise to power of Hitler led to Jewish refugees, most notably the great scientist Albert Einstein, who was put up for a short time by Oliver Locker-Lampson at his country resort on Roughton Heath in 1933. The sculptor Jacob Epstein came to visit him and sculpted his bust. He recalled, 'Einstein appeared dressed very comfortably in a pullover with his wild hair floating in the wind. His glance contained a mixture of the humane, the humorous, and the profound.' The bust is now in the National Galleries of Scotland. Einstein continued his scientific work while he was in Roughton but moved away after a few weeks, emigrating to the United States soon after. A blue plaque on the wall of the *New Inn* in Roughton commemorates his stay in the village.

In the late 1930s, the area became full of soldiers training for war. As Henry Williamson wrote:

> Abruptly the quiet little *Turnip Arms*, where sometimes at night I had sat and listened to the talk, or watched the dart-players, had become a mass of khaki uniforms, songs and shouts. The beautiful and desolate marshes, where the sea-lavender was coming to flower, were out of bounds. Salvoes of shells from anti-aircraft gun practice made white spurts along the edge of the sea. The black hut, with its notice of FISH AND CHIPS, FRYING FRIDAYS, in the garden across the narrow road, opposite my window, became a night club for the more lively of the soldiers.

They were territorials and were there for a fortnight, so that Limehouse accents would be replaced by Yorkshire or Scottish ones.

Weybourne Camp, an anti-aircraft gunnery school, was established in 1935 – the men fired at towed gliders out to sea so often that the local fishermen complained. There were also experiments with pilotless planes. The camp and nearby village were bombed in July 1940 but there were no casualties. Winston Churchill visited the camp in June 1941. By the time the camp was closed in 1958, over 250,000 troops had fired 1,500,000 shells out to sea. In 1988, the Muckleburgh Collection of military vehicles was opened in the camp buildings; starting with about forty military vehicles, it now has over 1,500 exhibits of all kinds, ranging from the 18th century to the Iraq War.

On 2 November 1938, the Spanish Civil War came to north Norfolk: the *Cantabria* was attacked by an armed trawler of General Franco's fleet just a few miles off the coast. The conflict began at 3.45 p.m. and could be seen by crowds who gathered on Cromer cliffs. There were 45 on board, including the captain's wife and their two small children. As the crew abandoned ship, some were picked up by the trawler and others by a British steamer which landed them at Yarmouth. The captain and his family stayed on board to the last; they and a steward were finally picked up by the Cromer lifeboat, coxswain Henry Blogg, which took them into Cromer. The refugees were made welcome and put up at Locker-Lampson's *Royal Hotel*. The children were Veyona Arguelles, aged eight, and her six-year-old brother Ramon. Veyona said to the local newspaper reporter, 'I was the oldest of the children, so I just couldn't be afraid. The others all wanted to go to the [British] ship, but I wanted to stay with my mummy and daddy. I did not see any flames. I was inside all the time but there were explosions.' Honesty made her add: 'All the same I don't think I want to go to sea again.'

The story of the coast at war is told in my *Norfolk in the Second World War* (Phillimore, 2006). Two important sets of diaries are those of John Turner in Titchwell and Rhoda Dhonau in Sheringham, which give many insights into life in wartime. Turner was in the Local Defence Volunteers, later renamed the Home Guard. In June 1940, he went with two local section leaders to Hunstanton to attend a demonstration of the Molotov cocktail bomb; one of the men told Turner that he had not been as far as Hunstanton since the last war, when his wife had been a waitress at the Golf Club. Turner wrote:

it was bitterly cold on the beach, where an officer gave a number of us a lecture in the construction and use of the Molotoff [*sic*] bomb. After this he said he would show how, in action, it burst into devastating flames. So he hurled it at an iron target on the sands. Nothing happened at all. I, of course, laughed, which did not seem to strike a right note. However, the second bomb worked, and it should certainly be a pretty awful weapon landing on a tank where the flaming tar drips down on the occupants.

During the night of 3 July, a squad of regulars appeared and stood guard with the LDVs, causing the people of Brancaster to expect an imminent invasion. On the following day, the Molotov bombs were placed in position and Turner was told to carry his automatic rifle loaded wherever he went – 'Difficult to believe that this is the Norfolk we have known for so many years', he confided sadly to his diary. A squad of regular soldiers were now billeted at the *Ship* – the landlady told Turner that she felt safer with them around than with the LDV. 'Brancaster folk are delighted with their Scots troops who arrive nightly. The LDV are not so delighted. They take it as reflection on their own prowess. Little Titchwell remains, without troops, more or less pre-war as far as its mentality is concerned, except for Mrs Annis who has more or less permanent *jitters*.' There was another invasion rumour on 18 July, but Turner was unconvinced: 'the prospect of tomorrow's rumoured invasion does not seem to be affecting the Norfolk villagers over-much. Can flat-bottomed barges ride the North Sea? I doubt it. In the SE perhaps, in ideal weather. But 200 miles is a long way and the North Sea is, or can be, one of the roughest passages in the world'. The next day passed off without incident.[26]

Rachel Dhonau lived in Sheringham with her son, Timothy; her husband was away fighting. She recorded on Christmas Day 1941,

A very different Christmas from most I have spent. I missed Jakob more than I could possibly express. Our chicken arrived and we did have a Christmas pudding – but even the food doesn't taste the same without him here. We listened a lot to the wireless. I always think the king very brave to speak, but found his talk singularly uninspiring – and though I enjoyed the preceding programme, I thought war cries somehow inappropriate on a Christmas day broadcast. I went out for a walk after dinner and despite the fact that the girls in the office always say that soldiers don't like ATS girls the whole town was full of khaki pairs. I saw only one soldier with a civilian girl and it looked quite strange. I wonder what will have happened by this time next year.

131 *Cromer church and High Street after an air raid.*

Exactly a year later, on Christmas Day 1942, she wrote:

> I had a postcard from my husband … I sowed up a jersey for Timothy and then we had our dinner. Everywhere was deathly quiet – no trains, no buses, not even any soldiers in the streets. After dinner we listened to the BBC Xmas broadcast and my mother exclaimed at the improvement in the king's manner of speaking. After that we went out for a walk … We saw very few people out. After tea, I knitted and read. The unearthly and unusual quiet continued until the public houses turned out, when we heard a bit of singing.[27]

Stratford Snell, born in Burnham Sutton in 1935, recalled Burnham in the war: 'Despite the rationing we ate quite well. There was always a roast on Sunday and we had stew twice a week – it was always better on the second day – and fish and chips on Fridays from Guineys who also sold potato fritters. We would buy our sweet ration from Mrs Beaver's tiny shop at Burnham Sutton near the church.' John Utting, born in 1923, was in the LDV: 'If the invasion came during the night it was my job to cycle to the Post Office in Burnham Market to wake Frederick Stimpson, the Post Master. He would then contact the other LDV troops who had telephones and each of them would contact others who had not. Then we all turned out with 12 bore shotguns, .22 rifles and whatever came to hand.'[28]

As befits an area where water was as important as land to many people, boats from the coast were among those small craft venturing to Dunkirk to rescue British troops in 1940, including local character W.H. 'Cruso' Loose of Brancaster Staithe. Sheringham men waited on the beach until 3 a.m. in the hope that boats from Blakeney would need extra crew, but they passed by without stopping. Fifteen or sixteen crab and whelk boats from north Norfolk reached Dover, but few were allowed to cross the Channel as only boats capable of 15 knots were used, so instead they did useful work like unloading troops off the larger vessels at Dover.[29]

There were many incidents along the coast involving planes, including air raids on Cromer and Sheringham, which each involved a small loss of life, and a raid on Hunstanton which caused no casualties. On 4 May 1941 a German plane on its way home after a bombing raid on Liverpool was attacked by a British plane and came down near Breck Farm north of Sharrington. One of the crew was killed, but the other three walked northwards through Holt towards the coast. They were captured on Salthouse Heath by a policeman, PC Charles Barnard, on a bicycle. He took them to Kelling Police House, where his wife made them breakfast. They were taken back to Holt and became prisoners of war. Fifty years later the German pilot was invited over to Salthouse for a reunion with the families of his captors.

On 15 January 1945, a plane, heading for Langham after raiding Germany, tried to land at night in very poor visibility and hit a pylon at Bard Hill, Salthouse. Six of the crew of seven died instantly, and the seventh died in hospital five hours later. The remains of the pylon can still be seen on the Heath, and poppies are often placed there. A United States Army Air Force plane, 'Alfred', crashed near Sheringham on 4 January 1944, returning from a bombing mission to Kiel; five men were killed and the others looked after by locals. The names of the crew are now recorded on a plaque in Upper Sheringham churchyard.

132 (*Left*) *Spigot mortar point between Hunstanton and Holme.*
133 (*Right*) *Second World War pillbox almost hidden by the sand, Hunstanton.*

There were also prisoners of war. About 100 German POWs were held at the army camp in Salthouse from August 1946 to November 1947, made to clear mines on the beach. They gave a party for the children of Kelling School and presented them with wooden toys that the prisoners had made themselves. Some went to Christmas parties in local houses – at one of these, Kurt Dams met a local girl, Janette Cooper. The couple later married and, although some of the locals did not like the idea of a Salthouse girl marrying an 'enemy', the marriage lasted a lifetime.

There are many reminders today of the coast's part in the war, including pill-boxes, spigot mortar emplacements and gun emplacements. At Cromer, several pillboxes were disguised as ice cream stands. Anti-tank blocks can still be seen at Burnham Overy. Some buildings constructed during the war survive at Langham Airfield, including a dome trainer, one of only three surviving examples in the country. '[T]he dome was used for training anti-aircraft gunners, who fired at films of enemy planes that were projected onto the walls.' There was a signal intelligence station on Beeston Bump, and its concrete base can still be seen. The airfield at Walsingham was used by the Signal Corps to drop small pieces of metal on German cities, to confuse their radar. Defences around it include pill boxes, mortar bases, a searchlight and a Home Guard shelter. A secret auxiliary hideout nearby would have been used by the Resistance in the event of a German invasion – a very rare survival. As the years have passed, some of the pill-boxes have fallen from the cliffs or been swallowed up by the ever-shifting sands.[30]

FROM 1945 TO THE PRESENT DAY

After 1945, the war became the Cold War and this also had its consequences for north Norfolk. A Royal Observer Corps Cold War underground monitoring post, east of Snipes Marsh in Salthouse, opened in 1958 and closed in 1968. There was another at

134   *Flooding at Wells, 1949.*

Wells, now demolished. These posts were designed to monitor fallout in the event of a nuclear attack. On 19 August 1968, two RAF planes collided 14,500 feet above Holt in a thunderstorm. One witness reported seeing a fireball, and burning wreckage, including wing sections and ejector seats, rained down on roof tops and gardens. The debris spread for several miles, but Holt escaped major damage and no lives were lost on the ground. All seven members of the crew of the two planes were killed instantly; their names are now recorded on a plaque inside Holt church. The theatre/activity room at Holt Hall was turned into a mortuary and the dining room was used for labelling pieces of wreckage. Those that were too large were lined up along the drive and on the front lawn until they were identified and collected.

The weather continued to make headlines. The winter of 1946-7 was one of the coldest on record, with a tremendous quantity of snow. Redgate Hill, Hunstanton, was blocked with snow as high as the hedges – German prisoners of war were brought

135   *Maintaining the harbour channel: dredging at Wells.*

from Houghton Hall to help clear the road. The snow melted in March leading to floods. These, the first major floods of the century, led to a new Land Drainage Act and the formation of River Catchment Boards to prepare against flooding. However, nothing could prevent the dramatic events of the great floods of 1953, caused by a surge in the North Sea and affecting every community on the coast.

The story of the flood at Hunstanton will always be connected with the valiant rescue work of the men of the American Air Force from Sculthorpe, and in particular with one tall airman from Washington State, who saved 27 people by his own exertions. The American Airman 3rd Class Reis Leming, of the 67th Rescue Squadron, Sculthorpe, saved 25 women and children and assisted two airmen to escape from the stricken bungalows at South Beach, Hunstanton, by pushing a rubber dinghy for several hours before he himself collapsed in the early morning. This is his story as he told it to a reporter:

> about eight o'clock on Saturday night they came round the base and asked for volunteers to assist in rescue work. We came along directly with rescue equipment, including the aluminium boats we drop for sea rescues from B-29s. But these were of no use in the strong wind; besides the propellers got tangled up in the wires. I suppose it was about 8.45 that we launched the first of these and I know I had been in and out of the icy water many times until about midnight. I went up to the headquarters at the *Sandringham Hotel* to change my clothes. When I got back near the end of South Beach Road I put on my exposure suit (waterproof yellow rubber) and decided to try and push a six-man rubber dinghy. Boy it took some keeping into the wind, and sometimes I was right under the water in the ditches. There was no one else there who is as tall as me – I am 6 ft 3 inches – so they could not help. Once the wind and a wave carried me and the dinghy right on top of a caravan, but gradually I managed to get near the ruins of the bungalows and get the people into the dinghy. Shucks, it wasn't much.

The names of the dead are now on display in a memorial on Hunstanton sea front.

136 *Hunstanton Green: plaque to the victims of the 1953 flood.*

137   *Car abandoned at Wiveton in the 1953 floods: its American driver got out just in time.*

At Wells, high tide was due at 8 p.m., but by 5 o'clock the water was already flowing over the quay. The gale increased in velocity during the evening when the Channel bank was breached in two places. The beach road was flooded to a depth of 15 feet, becoming impassable, and about a thousand acres of cultivated marshland was turned into a roaring sea. Many families in the west end of the town were rendered homeless almost without warning by the sudden flooding. Voluntary workers of various organisations of the town and members of the Urban District Council assisted in evacuating the unfortunate families. Some were stretcher cases and rescuers had to stand waist-deep in water. They were accommodated temporarily in the primary school for the night and rehoused at various places in the town on Sunday when vehicles were obtained to remove furniture, much of which had been carried by floods into the street. In some houses the water was four feet deep.

The motor torpedo boat *Terra Nova*, weighing 160 tons, the Sea Scouts headquarters, was left high and dry on the quay having been wrenched from its moorings, as were many boats. Shop windows were smashed by the force of the water and considerable damage done to stock. The fire brigade was brought into action to pump water from houses. Not a house or shop in Freeman Street escaped, and a bakery and electrical showrooms were seriously damaged. The railway station was flooded to a depth of 12 feet. The guard arriving by the last train had to be transferred to a rowing boat. The water rushed through the van and carriages. Mr R. Tuck, signalman, was marooned in the signal box until the early hours of Sunday morning.

It was estimated that a thousand sheep grazing on the marshes were all lost, as well as many cattle, horses and pigs. However, a rescue party in search of livestock that were grazing on the marshes prior to the flood discovered several cattle, sheep and one horse alive and sheltering in the pine woods. They had fed themselves from the undergrowth.

The full force of the storm was felt at Blakeney, where a considerable amount of damage was caused. A forecast of what was likely to happen was given when the tide was seen to be lapping the sea wall fully an hour before high tide. Soon it was over the top, the bank gave way and thousands of tons of water flowed onto the fresh marshes. At the same time the bank at the Cley end was breached, bringing another inrush. Soon hundreds of acres of valuable feeding ground became a mass of turbulent waters, some six feet deep. As the water rose, boats were torn from their moorings and smashed to matchwood. Others drifted up the Glaven Valley, some reaching as far as Glandford. In the yard of the *Blakeney Hotel*, three of the larger craft were thrown together and got jammed tightly. Most of the houses in Westgate Street were flooded to a depth of several feet and the Quay Café, a wooden building, was extensively damaged. When the tide ebbed, it left behind a slimy mass of mud and weed on everything with which it had come into contact. Doors and windows had been smashed and walls had fallen down like packs of cards. Many of the people had to evacuate their homes, but fortunately there was no loss of life. There was, however, a fatality at Wiveton: Mrs Edie Dix, aged 75, was found dead in the ground floor of her house, Willow Cottage, which had been flooded.

At Cley, families were separated and the destruction of all communications, even by road, added to the sense of isolation. One typical account was given by the village shoemaker, W.D. High, who said that a warning came from the coastguard that there was danger of flooding. Cley people had had such warnings before and when the water began to seep under doors, they busied themselves trying to salvage their belongings. The water quickly mounted window-high, and doors were barricaded. It began to subside, and they thought the worst was past when suddenly, with a roar, the water rose higher than ever before and swept in. 'We had to rush upstairs and leave everything', said High. His wife had gone next door to help a neighbour, and she was unable to return. In the early hours of the morning, many of the women were rescued by soldiers through the upper windows, and taken to places of safety.

Much of Salthouse was devastated in half an hour: 30 houses were destroyed and another 20 so badly damaged as to be uninhabitable. There was only one fatality – Mrs Hannah Middleton, in her seventies. She had been placed on the kitchen table by her husband after a fall, when the sea swept through the house, carrying both of them out through the back door. Mr Middleton was rescued, but later he was to find his wife's body beside a tree in their garden. At another house, Cliff Woodhouse and his wife were trapped in an upstairs room of their house; he made a hole in the wall and they crawled through it to safety. Elsewhere in the town, Leslie Cooke waded knee-deep in swirling icy water to pass a rope to a man on the top floor of another house. A reporter visited the next day: 'all the furniture lay heaped on the floor covered in seaweed and mud. Personal belongings, house furniture, dead poultry and a dead cow lay in the fields and gardens at the back of the wrecked houses. The sea still swept through the ground floors of houses left standing.'

138   *Cley and the Glaven valley in the floods of 1953.*

There was a very cold winter in 1963. As Gore says,

> Hunstanton pier end was a picture of mosaic frozen fabric around its iron structure
> on the seaward end that local photographers flocked at low water to capture on
> film for posterity. The seawater formed a huge frozen web of intermingling icicles
> from top to bottom of the whole structure like a captured and trapped trellis of
> stalactite and stalagmite proportions.

Floods in 1978 saw the washing away of vital shingle areas, and damage to groins
and concrete walls. It also swept away Hunstanton pier and many beach huts and
coastal bungalows between Hunstanton and Heacham: 'mobile homes and caravans
in the parks were tossed around like tinder, and piled up like haycocks in heaps all
over the area on the flooded wasteland like jetsam from a holocaust aftermath of an
atomic attack'.[31]

PORTS AND FISHING

Small-scale fishing continued, and Wells remained an active port. In the 1970s,
Lambert wrote:

> a relatively important local industry, which still flourishes, is whelking. From
> Brancaster and also Wells harbour 'whelkers' regularly go out. The boats are high
> out of the water fore and aft and can be recognised for what they are a long distance
> away. Nowadays some have wheelhouses and sophisticated radar and electronic
> equipment. A day's whelking may begin in the early hours and the incoming craft
> generally reach the harbour mouth before the flood tide has risen enough to enable
> them to gain their destination without stopping. They can then be seen edging
> their way along the shingle bank which fronts the 'ternery' – the breeding place
> of probably the largest colony of sandwich terns in Britain. The fishing industry
> also includes the collection of mussels and cockles.[32]

The 1980s were good years for the port of Wells. There were a record 161 vessels in
port during 1980, with eight ships in harbour on one day, 24 September. They were
all of less than 500 tons, and brought in animal foodstuffs, soya beans and fertilisers.
However, as larger ships were introduced, they were too big to turn in the harbour
and ceased to call. In the year 2000, John Berney could write: 'today there is no
commercial traffic at all.' The last ship of any size to use the harbour was the 100ft
Dutch sailing barque *Albatross*, which regularly came from Holland loaded with soya
for Dalgety at Egmere. She berthed for the last time in 2001, and is a striking feature
of Wells harbour today.[33]

RAILWAYS

The railways had helped to kill the ports, but now they, too, fell into decline, and
the 1950s and 1960s saw the end of nearly all the railways in north Norfolk. In the
1950s there were still trains to Hunstanton from London, Peterborough, Cambridge
and Lynn, but services declined in the 1960s. In 1966, the stations became unmanned
halts and that at Hunstanton was reduced to one platform. The line closed entirely in
1969. The line between Heacham and Wells was closed to passengers in June 1952.

139   *Steam, fields and sea:*
the North Norfolk Railway.

The section between Wells and Holkham was severely damaged by the 1953 floods and abandoned, leaving a freight service between Heacham and Burnham Market only. Even this closed in December 1964.

As late as 1963, as many as 2,000 trippers came by train to Wells from Norwich on a good day, and between 1,500 and 6,000 gallons of milk were being despatched daily to London from North Elmham. The harbour branch was lifted by 1962, and the line between Wells and Fakenham closed entirely in October 1964. Many Walsingham pilgrims had come by train until the closure of the railway, and within a few years Walsingham station was converted into a Russian Orthodox chapel with an onion dome, one of the most unusual uses for a former railway station.

Cromer High station closed in September 1954, the line between Cromer and Mundesley having already closed in April 1953. The line between Sheringham, Holt and Melton Constable closed in 1964, with Sheringham, rather than Cromer, becoming the end of the line from Norwich, and this is the only railway to survive along the north Norfolk coast. The railways have left many landscape and architectural features still to be seen in the area: embankments and cuttings, the occasional re-used station building and the frequent level-crossing keepers' cottages, adapted as private homes. Nothing can now be seen at the site of Cromer High, but Station Road in Cromer leads to it and not to the present railway station. A new halt was opened not far away, at Roughton Road, in 1985.

The line between Sheringham and Holt has been lovingly restored as the Poppy Line, running steam trains in summer and at Christmas ('Santa Specials'), and is one of north Norfolk's most popular tourist attractions. They use the original station at Sheringham, which has a magnificently restored glass-roofed buffet and is set out to look like a 1950s British Railways station. The station at Holt is not original, but is the station built at Stalham in 1880, moved brick by brick by volunteers to its new setting. Beside it is the William Marriott Museum, named after the man who designed and engineered the line back in 1887.

HOLIDAYS

The state of the holiday industry in the 1960s was recorded in a draft county council report written in 1963. This divided the coast into three parts: Hunstanton/Heacham, the Cromer/Sheringham area, and the 30 miles of coast in between. They were concerned with the number of caravans, especially at the two ends of the coast – almost

140   *The remains of Thornham windmill.*

141   *Weybourne Hope: tractors and boats on
the shingle ridge.*

a thousand at Runton and Beeston Regis, and 1,840 caravans and 350 chalets in
Hunstanton and Heacham. The only major concentration in between was at Wells,
with 480 caravans. The report thought it important to keep the special character of the
central region; 'accretion has been taking place here for many years, and has resulted
in a singularly attractive landscape, low-lying, with characteristic areas of salt-marsh
or reclaimed pastureland extending behind a sand ridge'. It pointed out that the fishing
activities in the small ports and creeks – £45,000 worth of fish had been landed in
Wells alone in 1961 – were in themselves attractive to tourists. Presciently, it added,
'the area is of greatest interest to ornithologists and to those concerned with the study
of coastal change … It may well be considered an advantage – and one worthy of
protection – that access to the beaches is limited, so that peace and quiet can still be
obtained by those who make the effort to walk or boat to secluded stretches.'

The report drew attention to what it saw as the growing problem of holiday homes:
'in places like Blakeney, Cley and Burnham Overy, a small cottage consisting of two
rooms up and two down, with no bathroom or proper sanitary facilities, may cost as
much as £2,000'; this could be beyond the reach of local residents but well within
the means of city dwellers, who would then modernise the property – and leave it
empty in the winter to the detriment of the local community.[34]

At Hunstanton, many of the older attractions closed. The promenade bandstand
was demolished in 1947. The lighthouse was sold by the council in 1964 – it went
for £4,740. The swimming pool closed in 1967 and the railway station in 1969. The
most dramatic incident was when a storm swept away the pier on 11 January 1978;
what was left was beyond repair.

People were thought to want more sophisticated facilities like heated indoor pools.
In 1970, a report looked into the building of a futuristic new centre in Hunstanton,
stating that it was to provide the 'latest experience in the field of recreation and

leisure'. The main feature was to be the indoor 'lagoon', which would take more than a thousand people, and was to be of an 'adventurous/unconventional shape'. Other activities would include 'artificial sun-bathing', bingo, a beer garden, beauty contests, Punch and Judy and television (showing both children's hour and late night films). The dome structure, called the Flexihall, was to be used for archery, badminton, theatre, etc. The proposed new venture also contained a dolphinarium! This grand scheme did not come to pass, and the Oasis leisure centre, in front of where the pier used to be, is on a much more modest scale. However, the town has remained very popular as a holiday destination. In 1980, it was claimed that some 600,000 people visited Hunstanton each summer. Many activities are enjoyed on the calm waters of the Wash, such as kite surfing.

The Cromer area enjoyed a high reputation as a venue for pop music. Cromer Royal Links Pavilion ran from 1964 to 1977, groups appearing including the Tremeloes, the Who, Queen and the Sex Pistols. Nearby West Runton Pavilion hosted some of the very best bands of the '70s, including punk bands such as the Clash, heavy metal bands like Iron Maiden and also Chuck Berry and T. Rex. The Pavilion closed in 1983, and a blue plaque on the wall of the *Village Inn* recalls those days. Cromer has received a facelift at the beginning of the 21st century, with the new Henry Blogg Museum supplementing the town museum, and with many information boards describing the history of the town.

New artwork along Sheringham sea front by Colin Seal was put on display in 2008. Murals illustrate the story of Sheringham fishermen and of its lifeboats, including a dramatic depiction of a rescue by the *Augusta*. In the same year, a series of cold-cast resin sculptures by Mitchell House was put on the esplanade wall, including one showing the beach in wartime. Another shows two local fishermen, Big John Craske and James 'Red Eyes' West. They are wearing their Sheringham ganseys (jerseys), with vertical stripes and individual patterns; the caption to the piece reminds us of the ever-present danger of the fishing trade by pointing out the tradition that each man had his own gansey pattern to make it easier to identify the bodies of those lost at sea.

'Messing about in boats' has become ever more popular in the small harbours along the coast. Lambert described Brancaster in the 1970s:

142   *Official Guide to Wells, 1970.*

143   *Proposed entertainment centre at Hunstanton.*

144   *Watching the watcher:*
Hunstanton Sea Life Sanctuary.

145   *The new visitors' centre, with*
wind turbine, at Cley Bird Reserve.

there is now a flourishing Yacht Club at the head of the Staithe which, from small
beginnings in 1934, has grown a lot to cater for the ever-increasing popularity of
this sport. Its headquarters originally consisted of a houseboat moored in a creek,
but finally a more permanent structure was erected and subsequently enlarged and
improved. The Club has been responsible for yachting events but the shallow nature
of the harbour necessarily limits competitive sailing to the dinghy classes and, for
cruising, to centre boarders. Of more ancient vintage is the Regatta the origins of
which date back to the turn of the century. In those days there were swimming and
rowing races and generally much of the 'fun of the fair' augmented by the arrival
on the village green of roundabouts and side-shows. For some years the attractions
other than the yacht races lapsed, but since 1972 have been revived.[35]

The importance of the natural world as an attraction has been developed in different
ways. Hunstanton Sea Life Sanctuary began as a refuge for lost or injured seals, expanded
to house other attractions such as otters and sharks, which are fed at set times. It combines
a marine rescue centre with a visitor attraction – with Britain's first underwater tunnel.
One can also board a Second World War DUKW to see 'Seal Island', where grey and
common seals can be seen in the wild. Other trips run from Morston to see the seals
breeding on Blakeney Point: common seal pups can be seen in July and August and
grey seal pups in the winter months. Titchwell Marsh reserve was bought by the RSPB
in 1973, originally to protect the Montague's harrier – the 940 acres include freshwater
and tidal reed beds and lagoons, salt marsh and sand dunes.

Alongside tourism, small industries have been encouraged to provide year-round
employment. To take just two examples, the Norwich shoe firm of Edwards and
Holmes opened a branch of their factory in Sheringham in 1949 and later moved
to larger premises in the Cromer road. The Drayton Stone Pits were established in
Beeston Regis in 1947, and from 1950 made concrete blocks, nearly 100,000 of which
were used in the building of the Norwich Union offices in Norwich.

Facilities for education have expanded. The standard for new schools was set by the
Smithdon High School in Hunstanton, built between 1950 and 1954 and described

by Pevsner as 'the paramount example among the innumerable interesting post-war schools of England of a rigidly formal, symmetrical layout'. Holt Hall opened in December 1949 as a county council boarding school for Norfolk children, where they would spend up to a year. In 1972, it became a Residential Field Study Centre, providing short courses for the county's children, and in 2006 became part of the Children's Services Environmental and Outdoor Learning Centre, encouraging investigation of a wide range of environmental issues.

LITERARY AND ARTISTIC NORTH NORFOLK

The beauty of the area has attracted very many artists over the years. Patrick Hamilton (1904-62) had close associations with the north Norfolk coast. He wrote many novels including *Rope*, later made into a film by Alfred Hitchcock, and *Hangover Square*, which begins with the hero, George Harvey Bone, walking on Hunstanton cliffs before the scene of the story moves to London. Hamilton lived at Burnham Overy Staithe in the 1930s while working on *The Siege of Pleasure*. Later, he lived for many years in Sheringham, dying at Martincross, on the corner of the Boulevard and St Nicholas Place, aged of 58 in 1962. He had problems with alcohol, J.B. Priestley once describing him as 'an unhappy man who needed whisky as a car needs petrol'. His ashes were scattered on Blakeney Marshes.

Olive Edis was born Mary Olive Edis in London on 3 September 1876, and her family used to take holidays in Sheringham. She became a photographer with a studio in London. On 1905, she took a studio in Church Street in Sheringham with her sister Katherine. The studio was in a shed and they broke local bylaws in erecting it; one of their first portraits was of the police constable who served the writ on them. Katherine married a Cromer doctor in 1907 and moved away. Olive specialised in portraits, both of celebrities and of local fishermen. By 1912, she was one of the first women to use autochromes, inventing her own viewer. In 1918 the National War Museum commissioned her to record the work of women in the war – she was the only official female war photographer. She toured France and Flanders and the result was 171 photographs for the Museum. In 1920 she went to Canada to take publicity

146   *The 21st century: kite-surfing at Hunstanton.*

photographs for the Canadian Pacific Railway. Her portrait photographs include George Bernard Shaw, Thomas Hardy, David Lloyd George, Ramsay MacDonald and Lord Balfour.

In 1928, at the age of 52, she married Edwin Galsworthy, a cousin of the author John Galsworthy. She gave up the Church Street studio and built another studio in the garden of a house in South Street. Her collection of photographs of local fishermen included Henry Blogg. She used this collection for an exhibition in Sheringham in connection with the Festival of Britain celebrations in 1951 – the photographs were shown in the Council Chamber and on the Promenade. Edwin died in 1948, aged 86, and Olive herself died in 1955; her ashes and those of her husband are interred side by side at the Weybourne Road cemetery in Sheringham. In 2008 Cromer Museum, with the aid of various grants, was able to purchase a major archive of her work: 60 autochrome colour negatives, 1,000 glass plates and scores of prints.

Sylvia Townsend Warner (1893-1978) and her lesbian lover, Valentine Ackland, spent most of their lives in Dorset, but lived in Norfolk for a period, staying at Great Eye Folly in Salthouse, immediately beside the sea. Two of her novels relate to the county: *The Corner That Held Them* (1948) is about life in a medieval Norfolk female religious house, while *The Flint Anchor* (1954) is a family saga set in a Norfolk fishing town in the 1840s. Her published diaries record her experiences:

> 28 October 1950: An intensely stormy day – we saw the sea darken and grow sullen, and an hour later it was rent with white horses. After waiting in for a baker called Jasper who did not come, we went off to the local stores, and bought staples like potatoes and toilet paper, and then on to Holt, over a russet heath and through a violent hailstorm. Valentine bought nails at a shop resounding with anecdotes of cats, and everyone had Norfolk manners, and we much approve of Holt. In the evening, with the house practically settled, I sat writing, with the storm roaring outside, inside Niou [their Siamese cat] sitting in his child's armchair, his little bell tinkling as he stirred.

The couple left the house in March 1951. The seaward wall fell in 1953, and the whole house has since been demolished.

The poet Stephen Spender was born in London in 1909; the family moved to The Bluff in Sheringham in 1913. He later recalled seeing Zeppelins flying over the town during the war. He went to Gresham's from 1918 to 1920, when he and his family returned to London. His Sheringham days are fondly recalled in his autobiography *World With World* (1951).

P.G. Wodehouse stayed at Hunstanton Hall in the 1920s, and wrote *The Small Bachelor* while sitting in a punt on the moat. The Hall and its grounds feature in several of his books, including the short story *Jeeves and the Impending Doom*, where Bertie Wooster's cousin Thomas maroons a cabinet minister in the pouring rain on an island where a fierce swan lives: '[the lake] stood to the east of the house, beyond the rose garden, and covered several acres. In the middle was an island. In the middle of the island was a building known as the Octagon. And in the middle of the Octagon, seated on the roof and spouting water like a public fountain, was the Right Hon A B Filmer.' As ever, Jeeves proves master of the situation.

147   *Fun at 'Sunny Hunny': the carnival.*

Allan Smethurst, better known under his stage name 'the Singing Postman', was actually born at Bury, Lancashire, in 1927, but his mother was a Stiffkey girl, and the family moved to Sheringham in 1929. His songs, sung in a strong Norfolk accent with Smethurst dressed as a postman and accompanying himself on acoustic guitar, had a brief vogue in the 1960s, the best-known being 'Hev Yew Gotta Loight, Boy?' He recorded about 80 songs altogether, almost all in Norfolk dialect. Some readers will recall his song about Molly Windley, who smoked like a chimney 'down along th'Mundesley shore', thus bringing this coastal village into pop culture for the first, and probably only, time. The success was brief, however, and Smethurst, who had problems with stage fright, began drinking excessively: he died at the Salvation Army Hostel in Grimsby in December 2000.

Artists from the area currently working include Kevin Crossley-Holland, born in Buckinghamshire in 1941, who spent childhood holidays at Burnham with his grandparents. Out of these memories came the poem 'Dusk, Burnham Overy Staithe', and 'Waterslain', a sequence of 25 poems set in the marshes and evoking local characters, waterslain being an old Norfolk word meaning flooded. He is one of the founders of the annual Wells Poetry Festival. Lady Flora McDonnell, a former pupil at Gresham's, is the writer of books such as *ABC*, *I Love Animals* and *Giddy up! Let's Ride!* She is also illustrator of two children's books by poet laureate Ted Hughes, *The Mermaid's Purse* (2000) and *The Cat and the Cuckoo* (2003). Other present-day talents include Miranda Raison, born in Burnham Thorpe in 1980, the star of BBC Television drama 'Spooks', who has appeared also in 'Doctor Who', and in the films 'Match Point' and 'Land of the Blind'.

PRESENT AND FUTURE

The port of Wells has retained a small fishing fleet. In the 21st century, the port authorities have been working to secure European money to provide a facility to support and maintain the local shell fishing industry. The produce, brown crabs, velvet crabs and lobsters, have been unloaded, sorted and packed in the open air, but a new facility is envisaged with packing and loading areas, a freezer room and a cold room. As Sandra Bush of the North Norfolk District Council has written:

> A fresher, higher quality product will gain a higher price thus ensuring a more stable economic future for the fishermen, and will attract a new generation to continue this tradition in a modern world. Apart from velvet crabs that are exported live to the Continent, much of the landed catch is sold locally to restaurants, shops and for processing. Many fishing vessels along the

north Norfolk coats have now signed up to the Seafish Responsible Fishing Scheme which has been developed to raise standards in the catching sector, enabling the fishermen to demonstrated their commitment to the responsible sourcing of seafood and thereby helping to create a distinctive local brand.[36]

North Sea fishing has become regulated to preserve stocks of species like cod. As the management settles in, stocks are now recovering and the most severe restrictions are being lifted. The main difficulty for local fishermen is the way that huge fishing vessels are replacing small, independent fishermen.

Crab fishing is also regulated: the main season is between March and December. Crabs smaller than 4.5 inches cannot be landed, and in August, when hen crabs are carrying eggs, they too cannot be landed. In 2009, there were 14 boats fishing from Cromer and seven from Sheringham, landing 127,000 kilograms of crabs and 17,000 kilograms of lobsters. At Cromer, the boats are launched and retrieved by means of a tractor but at Sheringham by a winch along wooden 'skeets'.

The first wind farm in British waters was constructed in 2000. One can be seen from the cliffs at Hunstanton, that off Skegness, part of the Lynn and Inner Dowsing Offshore Wind Farm. It is three miles from shore and has 57 turbines, eventually providing enough power to meet the needs of 54,500 households; it comes ashore under Skegness golf course. It is matched by a new wind farm at the other end of the coast: Sheringham Shoal, constructed by StatoilHydro and Statkraft. It is an even larger project, with 88 turbines each 80 metres high, and will provide electricity to power 220,000 homes. The turbines are between 17 and 23 kilometres from the coast. It comes on stream in 2011. The energy comes ashore at Weybourne, from where a cable runs underground to the regional grid at Salle.

149   *Buying fresh sea food at Brancaster: this habourside shop operated for the last time in 2009.*

148   *Timeless peace: fishing vessels at high tide in Thornham.*

In 2010, the channel from the Lifeboat House to the open sea at Wells was deepened to one metre at low tide. This helps traditional users, fishing boats and yachts, who are now able to gain a safer passage into the Outer Harbour while waiting for the tide to bring them up to the Quay. It is also hoped that it will lead to a new role for Wells – use by boats servicing the rapidly growing offshore wind farm industry. The first of these is Sheringham Shoal: workboats will come into Wells but not up to the Quay – they will work from a pontoon to be built just south of the Lifeboat House.

The traditional fruits of the sea and seashore are available in shops and restaurants all along the coast; the freshest possible herring and mackerel, Cromer crabs, Stiffkey blues (cockles), Morston mussels, and samphire, freshly gathered from the marshes. As Alan Savory wrote in *Norfolk Fowler* in 1953:

> there is a place far out on the sands somewhere between High Stand Creek and Stone Meal Creek that is called Blacknock. It is a patch of mud covered with zos grass and full of blue shelled cockles known as 'Stewkey Blues'. It is a famous place for widgeon, but very dangerous to get on to and off, if one is not too certain of the way on a dark night. The women cockle gatherers from Stiffkey who have double the strength of a normal man, go right out there between the tides and get a peck of these cockles and carry them to the village, miles across the sea and saltings.

Tony Palmer describes other culinary delights:

> [Samphire] is on sale along the coast in high summer, typically from July to September … an edible seaweed that grows in mudflats just below the high tide mark, it is found anywhere along the east coast where the tidal water is calm and devoid of waves … It looks something like horsetail, that primitive weed which thrives on poor soil, or like a cluster of miniature sausages impaled on multi-pronged forks. It's a deep green, grows up to nine inches tall, and in September it comes into flower – tiny, bright-yellow things almost too small to see … That delicacy of Cromer, the crab, lives on a sea bed which locally is of chalk and sand, and so is clean, and gives the meat its distinctive but subtle sweet flavour.

There are many other high-quality food products in the area too, such as Binham Blue cheese from local cows, venison and game marketed from the Holkham estate, locally made ice cream, and ale made in Wells from locally grown barley with which to wash it all down.[37]

There is an enormous range of activities for holiday-makers along the coast. In 2007, no fewer than 88,000 people attended shows on Cromer pier, but it is a resource that takes a lot of money to maintain. In 2008, the council was faced with a £1.4 million repair bill; if nothing was done, the pier would have to be demolished in about ten years – and then the bill for demolition would be about £700,000. Other activities in the area are also flourishing: in 2008, Felbrigg Hall had 75,702 visitors in the summer season. The North Norfolk Railway attracts thousands, and the link to the mainline at Sheringham was restored in 2010 to allow through-trains to run. There are two 10¼in-gauge railways at Wells. One runs to Walsingham along the route of the old Wells to Fakenham railway, which closed in 1964. Opened in 1982, the line is four miles long, the longest in the world of this gauge. The other runs along the sea wall to the beach.

Figure III   *Weight and value of commercial landings in 1974:*

Port	Landing, in tonnes	Sale value	Main species
Brancaster	1,076	£57,867	Whelks, mussels, sea trout
Wells	1,828	£117,682	Whelks, shrimps, mussels
Blakeney	42	£2,165	Mussels, mackerel, sea trout
Cromer	195	£77,915	Crabs, lobsters, cod, whelks
Sheringham	405	£89,233	Crabs, lobsters, whelks, cod

Figure IV   *Seasonal changes in catches in Norfolk ports in 1974, in tonnes (+ indicates less than half a tonne):*

| | FISH | | | SHELLFISH | | | |
	Cod	Mackerel	Sea trout	Mussels	Whelks	Crabs	Lobsters
January	19.0	–	–	127	97	–	–
February	12.0	–	–	89	140	–	–
March	4.0	–	–	74	189	5	–
April	0.6	–	–	5	183	77	0.5
May	–	–	0.60	–	294	85	1.0
June	–	–	0.37	–	315	68	1.2
July	–	0.8	0.58	–	366	35	8.5
August	–	3.3	0.74	–	380	29	3.8
September	–	3.2	0.36	32	267	13	0.5
October	0.3	3.2	–	221	67	1	0.1
November	6.0	0.5	–	188	96	+	–
December	4.0	–	–	85	46	–	–

Source for both figures: Anon., Nature in Norfolk: a Heritage in Trust *(not dated), with permission of the publisher, Jarrold's of Norwich*

The many wildlife reserves are a great attraction in themselves. A great number of organisations now hold large areas of the region in their care, both local groups like the Norfolk Wildlife Trust and the Norfolk Ornithological Association and national bodies such as English Nature, the National Trust and the RSPB. A reserve needs careful management, of course. Looking out over the marshes from the large windows of the striking visitors' centre at Cley reserve, it is easy to imagine that the scene in front of you is simply nature in the raw, but in fact water levels are controlled to within a few centimetres by a system of pipes. Choices are constantly having to be made: if avocets' young are taken by a fox, the fox can be destroyed, but what if they are taken by herons? Should the sea be kept out by raising the shingle bank at the sea's edge, or should it simply be accepted that the marshes will flood occasionally, and efforts be concentrated on making sure the damaging saltwater is drained as quickly as possible? Traditional crafts are encouraged, for example the cutting of reeds at Cley marshes and also at Brancaster. Harvesting takes place between December and April, and the reed cut with a hook or scythe, though sometimes a machine is now used instead, adapted from one designed to cut rice.

Improvements to the infrastructure of the area may be funded by those who love the area. At Cromer, the hospital buildings of 1932 are being replaced with a new £26 million hospital, the basis of its funding being the incredible bequest of £13 million by Cromer millionairess Sagle Bernstein, and a further £1 million from Bacton holiday chalet owner Phyllis Cox in 2005.

The description of the coast by A.G.P. Powell in 1947 still applies today:

> Here, where the sun beats down beneficially, and the health-giving sea breezes blow continuously, one may lie up with a pair of glasses secure in a sand-dune or beneath a sheltering bush and ponder on the mysteries of nature, or, content and at ease, feast one's eyes on the colour of the landscape, and the views inland across the marshes to the woods and cornfields of the mainland, interspersed with red roofed villages, rising to the skyline beyond, and find that peace and refreshment which is beyond all price ... Then, caressed by the call of the curlew, the occasional whistling cry of the redshank, and the soft rhythmic wind beat of the flighting duck, we shall dream only of the joys of tomorrow, and thank God that there is at least one place left in England where one may enjoy a perfect holiday.[38]

For both visitors and residents, the north Norfolk coast is a magical place, and a rich heritage to be cared for today, to be handed on to future generations.

150 *Contemporary fishing boats in Wells harbour, 2010: small local boats and larger vessels from London.*

Notes

Chapter 1

1. Quoted in Kevin Crossley-Holland, *Eastern Light*, 1986
2. E.A.M. Powell, 'A Norfolk Bird Sanctuary', *East Anglian Magazine*, January 1947, pp.265-9
3. David Dymond, *The Norfolk Landscape*, 1985, especially chapter 1
4. E.M. Bridges, *Classic Landforms of the North Norfolk Coast*, 1998 edn, pp.28-9
5. Ashley Sampson, *Processes affecting North Norfolk's Cliffs and Coastal Defences*, 1998, *passim*
6. www.heritage.norfolk.gov.uk, reports on all parishes in the region. That on Runton is by Thomas Sunley.
7. Quoted in L.L. Gore, *The History of Hunstanton*, 1983, pp.116-17
8. Tom Williamson, *Shaping Medieval Landscapes*, 2003, pp.81-2
9. E. Ekwall, *Oxford Dictionary of English Place-Names,* 1960 edition, *passim*; Margaret Gelling, *Place-Names in the Landscape*, 2000 edition; Tom Williamson, *The Origins of Norfolk*, 1993, pp.56, 85-8
10. Robert Forby, *The Vocabulary of East Anglia*, 1830, reprinted 1970
11. www.heritage.norfolk.gov.uk, Megan Dennis on Walsingham

Chapter 2

1. Hamon le Strange, *Le Strange Records*, 1916, p.19
2. Harold Fox, *The Evolution of the Fishing Village*, 2001, pp.60-1
3. Carl Oestmann, *Lordship and Community*, 1994, pp.120-7
4. E.M. Carus-Wilson, *Medieval Merchant Venturers*, 1967 edn, pp.98-142
5. Jonathan Hooton, 'From Iceland to Crete', *Norfolk Fair*, July 1975
6. William Hassall and Jacques Beauroy, *Lordship and Landscape in Norfolk 1250-1350*, 1993, p.515; le Strange, *op. cit.* p.208
7. H.J. Hewitt, *The Organisation of War under Edward III*, 1966, pp.78, 185
8. C.L.S. Linnell, 'Seventeenth-century land reclamation', *East Anglian Magazine*, July 1937, p.437; Peter Stibbons, Katherine Lee, Martin Warren, *Crabs and Shannocks – the Longshore Fishermen of Norfolk*, 1983, *passim*; John Warrington (ed.), *The Paston Letters*, 1975 edn, part II, p.245
9. Bruce Campbell *et al.*, *A Medieval Capital and its Grain Supply*, 1993, pp.62, 120n; Warrington, *op. cit.*, part I, p.250
10. Jonathan Hooton, *Glaven Ports: Maritime History of Blakeney, Cley and Wiveton in North Norfolk*, 1996, pp.36-56; le Strange, *op. cit.*, p.270
11. Warrington, *op. cit.*, part I, pp.38, 212
12. Wilfrid Wren, *Ports of the Eastern Counties*, 1976, p.179
13. A.C. Savin, *Cromer in the County of Norfolk*, 1937, pp.1-3; Norfolk Record Office (hereafter NRO) NCC wills, Dyones Flegg, 154 Moyse als Spicer
14. NRO, NCR 13a/47; Wren, *op. cit.*, p.181
15. Le Strange, *op. cit.*, p.270
16. Quotation from Matthew Arnold, *Dover Beach*; G.F. Leake, '1381 in North Norfolk: the Rising and its Aftermath as Reflected in Manor Court Rolls', in B. Cornford (ed.), *The Rising of 1381 in Norfolk*, 1984, pp.49-58

17. H.C. Darby, *The Domesday Geography of Eastern England*, 1977, pp.367-71 for fisheries and salt pans
18. Hassall and Beauroy, *op. cit.*, pp.16-59
19. David Yaxley, *The Prior's Manor Houses*, 1988, entries for Sedgeford and Gnatingdon (an old name for a part of Sedgeford)
20. Bryan Burstall, 'A Monastic Agreement of the Fourteenth Century', *Norfolk Archaeology*, vol. xxxi, 1955, pp.211-18
21. NRO, DCN 44/73
22. www.heritage.norfolk.gov.uk, reports on all parishes in the region
23. For this section, see Frank Meeres, *Not of this World*, 2001, *passim*
24. David Knowles, *The Religious Orders in England*, vol. 1, 1979 edn, pp.196, 241
25. NRO, DCN 44/41/9
26. Samantha Letters, 'Gazetteer of Markets and Fairs in England and Wales to 1516', http://www.history. ac.uk/cmh/gaz/gazweb1.html (updated 21 January 2003)
27. NRO, DN/REG 2 book 4
28. A. Jessopp, *The Coming of the Friars and other Historic Essays*, 1889, pp.166-261
29. E. Powell, *The Rising in East Anglia in 1381*, 1896, *passim*
30. G.F. Leake, *op. cit.*, pp.49-58
31. L.L. Gore, *The History of Hunstanton*, 1983, p.71
32. Barbara Hanawalt, *Crimes in East Anglia in the 14th Century*, Norfolk Record Society, vol. 44, 1976, *passim*

Chapter 3
1. Gill Blanchard, *The Manor of Burnham Thorpe* (not dated), p.40
2. H.B. Walters, 'Inventories of Norfolk Church Goods (1552)', *Norfolk Archaeology*, vol. xxxi, 1955, pp.233-54
3. NRO, PD 2/1; *Cromer and North Norfolk Post*, 29 January 1915; NRO, BCH 47
4. Clement Tigar, *Forty Martyrs of England and Wales*, 1970 edn, pp.45-6
5. R.W. Ketton-Cremer, *Norfolk in the Civil War*, *passim*
6. R.W. Ketton-Cremer, *Forty Norfolk Essays*, 1961, pp.24-8; Lewis B. Radford, *History of Holt*, 1908, pp.54-6
7. Jonathan Hooton, three essays on the Glaven ports in *Norfolk Fair*, July, August and September 1975
8. B. Cozens-Hardy, *Maritime Trade of the Port of Blakeney*, Norfolk Record Society, 8, 1936, *passim*
9. G. Alan Metters, *The King's Lynn Port Books 1610-1614*, Norfolk Record Society, 73, 2009, pp.9-38
10. Bacon papers (see note 17), vol. 2, pp.143-50
11. R.W. Ketton-Cremer, *Felbrigg, the Story of a House*, 1962, p.32
12. Quotation from Ezra Pound, The Cantos: canto 1.
13. NRO, PD 597/1,2
14. Elizabeth Griffiths, *William Windham's Green Book*, Norfolk Record Society, 66, 2002
15. C.L.S. Linnell, 'Seventeenth-Century Land Reclamation', *East Anglian Magazine*, 1937, pp.439-41
16. A.M.W. Stirling, *Coke of Norfolk and his Friends*, p.10
17. Joan Thirsk, *The Rural Economy of England*, 1984, pp.201-2; Bacon papers (see note 18), vol. 4, pp.101-2
18. The Bacon archive has become scattered and has been recreated by A. Hassell Smith and others in four volumes published by the Norfolk Record Society: vol. 1: 1556-1577, NRS 46 (1978, 1979); vol. 2: 1578-1585, NRS 49 (1982, 1983); vol. 3: 1586-1595 NRS 53 (1987, 1988); vol. 4: 1596-1602, NRS 64 (2000)
19. The probate inventories are in the Norfolk Record Office, overall reference DN/INV: there are indexes by name, place and occupation. That of Browne is discussed in Margaret Oakden, *Blakeney in the Eighteenth Century*, for Blakeney Area Historical Society, 2002 edn
20. William Sachse, *Minutes of the Norwich Court of Mayoralty*, Norfolk Record Society, 36, 1967
21. www.heritage.norfolk.gov.uk, Piet Aldridge on Stiffkey
22. NRO, LEST P3/2, R.W. Ketton-Cremer, *Felbrigg, the Story of a House*, 1962, p.45
23. NRO, PD 2/1
24. Jonathan Hooton, *Glaven Ports: Maritime History of Blakeney, Cley and Wiveton in North Norfolk*, 1996, pp.118-22
25. Radford, *op. cit.*, pp.65-7; NRO, ACC Cozens-Hardy 11/2/76
26. Quoted at greater length in A. Savin, *Cromer in the County of Norfolk*, 1937, p.22

Chapter 4

1. Daniel Defoe, *Tour through the Eastern Counties*, 1949 edn, pp.96-9
2. NRO, MS 80
3. NRO, MC 1812/46
4. C.L.S. Linnell, 'Seventeenth-Century Land Reclamation', *East Anglian Magazine*, July 1937, p.437
5. John Barney, *The Defence of Norfolk,* 2000, pp.19-26
6. Quotation from Stephen Spender, *Seascape*; Defoe, *op. cit.*, pp.97-8
7. NRO, PD 619/3
8. B. Cozens-Hardy, *Mary Hardy's Diary*, Norfolk Record Society 36, 1968, pp.13, 32
9. NRO, MC 26/1. Marten's journal is being edited by Liz Larby for publication by Poppyland Press.
10. Douglas Hague and Rosemary Christie, *Lighthouses: their Architecture, History and Archaeology*, 1975, pp.34, 231; Neville Long, *Lights of East Anglia*, 1983, p.126; NRO, MC 26/1
11. These three stories are taken from the *Norfolk Chronicle* for the relevant dates. They are summarised in Mackie, *Norfolk Annals* (1901), under the appropriate date.
12. L.L. Gore, *The History of Hunstanton*, 1983, *passim*
13. William Dutt, *Literary Associations of East Anglia,* 1907, pp.325-31
14. M.K. Stammers, 'The Handmaiden and Victim of Agriculture: the Port of Wells-next-the Sea Norfolk in the 18th and 19th centuries', in *The Mariner's Mirror* 88, February 2000; John Barney, *The Trials of Wells Harbour*, 2000, *passim*
15. A.M.W. Stirling, *Coke of Norfolk and his Friends,* 1912, p.38; E.L. Jones (ed.), *Agriculture and Economic Growth in England 1650-1815*, 1967, p.98: Mark Overton, *Agricultural Revolution in England: the Transformation of the Agrarian Economy 1500-1850*, 1996, pp.118-19; R.A.C. Parker, *Coke of Norfolk,* 1975, *passim*; Harold Fox, *pers. comm.*
16. A.D. Boyce, *The Heritage of Cromer*, 2009, *passim*
17. N. Virgoe and T. Williamson (eds), *Religious Dissent in East Anglia*, 1993, pp.37-46
18. R.W. Ketton-Cremer, *Forty Norfolk Essays*, 1961, pp.68-9
19. Arthur Mee, *The King's England – Norfolk,* 1940, pp.451-2
20. www.heritage.norfolk.gov.uk, Sarah Spooner on Blakeney
21. NRO, PD 270/1
22. NRO, MS 80
23. NRO, UPC 61; Edward Hyams, *Capability Brown and Humphrey Repton*, 1971, pp.208-10
24. R.W. Ketton-Cremer, *Felbrigg, the Story of a House*, 1976 edn, p.107
25. R.W. Ketton-Cremer, *op. cit.*, pp.130-7
26. Valerie Belton, *The Norwich to Cromer Turnpike*, 1998, p.1
27. R.W. Ketton-Cremer, *op. cit.*, pp.208-11; NRO, WKC 7/100
28. A.M.W. Stirling, *Coke of Norfolk and his Friends,* 1912, pp.152, 204

Chapter 5

1. M.A. Stammers, 'A 19th-century shipyard model from Wells-next-the-Sea in Norfolk', *Archaeology* xlii, 1997, pp.519-26
2. M.A. Stammers, 'Anthracite for Wells-next-the-sea', *Maritime Wales*, vol. 20, 1999, pp.77-9
3. Derick Mellor, *The Glaven Valley – More Historical Jottings,* 1992, pp.31-2
4. Val Fiddian (ed.), *Salthouse, the Story of a Norfolk Village*, 2003, pp.181-4
5. L.L. Gore, *The History of Hunstanton,* 1983, pp.291-2
6. Peter Stibbons, Katherine Lee, Martin Warren, *Crabs and Shannocks – the Longshore Fishermen of Norfolk*, 1983, pp.28-9; John Wright, 'The Blakeney Disaster of 1861', *The Glaven Historian*, 3, June 2000, p.50
7. Gore, *op. cit.*
8. *Ibid.*, p.89
9. Quoted in A.C. Savin, *Cromer in the County of Norfolk,* 1937, p.30
10. Owen Chadwick (ed.), *Armstrong's Norfolk Diary*, 1963, pp.32, 44, 125
11. Elizabeth Jones, *Poppyland in Pictures*, 1983, pp.41-56; Swinburne, *A Haven*, 1884; A.D. Boyce, *The Heritage of Cromer*, 2009, *passim*
12. Clement Scott, *Poppyland*, 1905 edn, p.7
13. Quotation from John Betjeman, 'Middlesex'; Clement Scott, *op. cit.*, p.95
14. www.heritage.norfolk.gov.uk , David Robertson on Sheringham
15. Jodrell Young, 'Gofather Pegg, pioneer of Sheringham's holiday trade', *Norfolk Fair*, July 1974 pp.32-3
16. Gwenllian Meyrick, 'A Victorian Summer Holiday, Sheringham in 1888', *Norfolk Fair*, September 1975, pp.26-7

17. Quoted in Elizabeth Jones, *Poppyland in Pictures,* 1983, p.56; Peter Cox, *The Explosion at Sheringham,* 2003, *passim*
18. NRO, UPC 267
19. J.A.R. Pimlott, *The Englishman's Holiday, a Social History,* 1976 edn, pp.269-70
20. D.I. Gordon, *A Regional History of the Railways of Great Britain – the Eastern Counties,* 1977 edn, p.212
21. Clement Scott, *op. cit.,* p.44
22. *Ibid.,* p.19
23. Chadwick, *op. cit.,* p.32
24. NRO, UPC 178
25. The archives of both families are in the Norfolk Record Office: the Bond Cabbell archive has the reference MC 97, that of the Upchers has the reference UPC

Chapter 6
1. Verily Anderson, 'Bathing Machines', *Norfolk Fair,* April 1970, pp.24-6
2. L.L. Gore, *The History of Hunstanton,* 1983, p.112
3. The trilogy of novels comprises *The Shrimp and the Anenome* (1944), *The Sixth Heaven* (1946) and *Eustace and Hilda* (1952); the first and last have a great deal about Hunstanton before the First World War and in the 1920s.
4. J. Gunston, 'A Famous Norfolk Sea Captain', *East Anglian Magazine,* May 1947, pp. 461-5
5. Freda Starr, *A Village Shop,* 1979
6. NRO, MC 552
7. www.history-blakeney-area.org.uk
8. Peter Cox, *The Explosion at Sheringham,* 2003, *passim*
9. Brian Short, *Land and Society in Edwardian Britain,* 1997, pp.164-70
10. Starr, *op. cit.*
11. Dr James Slator, *Kelling Hospital Norfolk, the first sanatorium for working men,* 2000, *passim*
12. Keith Entwistle, *Holt, an Illustrated History,* 2004, p.20
13. Sue Smart, *When Heroes Die,* 2001, *passim*
14. NRO, UPC 188
15. Roger Wiltshire, *Norfolk's Lifeboats,* 1994, *passim*
16. S. Peart, *Picture Houses of East Anglia,* 1980, *passim*
17. Quotation from Walt Whitman, *Leaves of Grass*
18. There is a copy of the newspaper report in NRO, MC 579/13
19. John Barney, *The Trials of Wells Harbour,* 2000, pp.35-6
20. Pamela Brookes, *Women at Westminster,* 1967, pp 89, 93
21. Quoted in Keith Entwistle, *Holt, an Illustrated History,* 2004, p.178
22. Henry Williamson, *The Story of a Norfolk Farm*
23. *Norfolk Chronicle,* 20 July 1934
24. Anon., *Nature in Norfolk: a Heritage in Trust* (not dated), p.15, NRO, BR 122/212
25. Williamson, *op. cit.*
26. NRO, MC 2333
27. R. Malcolmson and P. Searby, *The Diary of Rachel Dhonau 1941-2,* Norfolk Record Society, 68, 2004
28. Raymond Monbiot, *The Burnhams Book of Characters and Memories,* 2002, pp.25, 66
29. R. Douglas Brown, *East Anglia 1940,* 1981, p.66
30. NRO, C/P 8; www.heritage.norfolk.gov.uk, references in almost all coastal parishes
31. Gore*, op. cit.,* pp.251-2
32. J.E.A. Lambert, 'Never the twain shall meet: portrait of Brancaster', *Norfolk Fair,* April 1975
33. Barney, *op. cit.,* p.35
34. NRO, DC 16/3/2
35. Lambert, *op. cit.*
36. Quoted in the *Norfolk Coast Guardian,* 2009
37. Alan Savory, *Norfolk Fowler,* 1973 edn, p.59; Terry Palmer, *Beautiful North Norfolk,* 2005, *passim*
38. A.G.M. Powell, 'A Norfolk Bird Sanctuary', *East Anglian Magazine,* January 1947, pp.265-9

Acknowledgements and References

Many institutions and individuals have allowed me to use their material, and I am very grateful to all of them.

A large number of images are from the collections of the Norfolk Record Office, thanks to county archivist, Dr John Alban; these are listed below with their Norfolk Record Office (NRO) reference numbers.

The lively photographs of present-day Hunstanton, images 7, 27, 144, 146, 147, are by Frank Gogerty of localimages.info.

Special thanks are due to Godfrey Sayers for allowing use of his stunning painting of Wiveton, image 24, and for image 42.

Thanks to the following for generously allowing the use of images: Gresham's school, archivist Liz Larby, for images 54, 72; The Henry Blogg Museum, Cromer, for images 128, 129; Jarrold and Sons, Norwich, for images 86, 87, 95; The North Norfolk Railway, Sheringham, for image 139; Peter Stibbons of Poppyland Publishing for images 82, 83; Roger Wiltshire for image 74; Heather Wallis for image 16.

The Muckleburgh Collection kindly allowed me access to their site to take image 112.

Norfolk Record Office images (NRO): 10: MC 365/10; 6, 19, 32: MC 578/13; 23: MC 365/26; 37; NCC wills, John Lambarde, 1539; 38: MC 2149/3; 41: ACC 2009/161; 43, 44, 52: MC 2443/3; 45; MS 17640; 47: DN/CON 207; 48a, 57: HMN 5/214; 53: ACC Cozens-Hardy 11/2/76; 60: MC 1739/10; 61. MC 26/1; 62: MC 365/27; 64: PD 523/145; 71: PD 523/147; 73: MC 2064/1; 75: C/WT 1/6/1/3; 78: BL 49/1; 79: LEST uncat; 80: MC 2194/3; 81: ACC 2005/8; 84: MC 2194/3/13; 89: ACC 2009/177; 90: PD658/80/; 91: MC 2019/59; 96: MC 2043/2/2; 98: C/WT 1/6/1/4; 99: C/WT/1/6/1/1; 102: MC 537/2; 103: MC 537/2; 104: MC 2043/2/77; 105: MC 2043/2/43; 106: BR 184/147; 107: MC 2019/48; 108: MC 2019/48/7; 109: MC 578/13; 111: MC 2321/11; 114: MC 2043/2/76; 115: FC 81/342; 116, 117: UPC 259; 118: MC 578/13; 119, 120: MC 2019/46; 121: BR 35/4/40; 122, 123: MC 2331/1; 124: MC 537/2; 125: MC 2019/53; 127: DN/ADR 15/8/9/3; 131; PD 523/156; 134: MC 2019/48/64; 135: MC 2019/48/66; 140: C/WT1/6/1/4; 142: MC 2019/60; 143: DC 16/3/7.

King's Lynn Borough Archives: 21 centre (the Lynn ship): KL/C 2/35.

Index

Please note, references in **bold** refer to illustration numbers.